Customer Connections

A little "Think" piece to go along with our Solutions

Enjoy,

Customer
Connections

NEW STRATEGIES FOR GROWTH

Robert E. Wayland
Paul M. Cole

HARVARD BUSINESS SCHOOL PRESS
BOSTON, MASSACHUSETTS

Printed in the United States of America

01 00 99 98 97 5 4 3 2 1

Library of Congress Cataloging-in-Publication Data

Wayland, Robert E. (Robert Edwin), 1946-
    Customer connections : new strategies for growth / Robert E.
Wayland, Paul M. Cole.
        p.   cm.
    Includes bibliographical references and index.
    ISBN 0-87584-799-4 (alk. paper)
    1. Customer relations.   I. Cole, Paul M. (Paul Michael), 1958-
    . II. Title.
HF5415.5.W39 1997
658.8'12--dc21   97-10783
                                                        CIP

The paper used in this publication meets the requirements of the American National Standard for
Permanence of Paper for Printed Library Materials Z39.49-1984.

To Carole, Bobby, Katie, and Mark

R.E.W.

To Lisa, Evan, and Adam

P.M.C.

Contents

Acknowledgments

In the year that this book moved from proposal to final manuscript, it has become very different and, we believe, better than what we originally planned. A part of this change resulted from the process of expressing, testing, and refining thoughts that the discipline of writing imposes. But most of the additional value was contributed by the many friends, colleagues, case study businesses, and clients who graciously collaborated with us.

A number of people helped us in researching and writing the book. John White and Andy Pierce of Marketing and Planning Systems contributed their talents to the survey research and authored the appendix. Eileen Brusger and Rick Levin examined and corrected many of the economic and financial models. Alan Thielke of Volt Management exhaustively reviewed each line and equation and found a humbling number of errors. Dave Jones of Jones Consulting introduced us to the MCI and UPS case studies and contributed his research on account management as well as reviewing the text. Cliff Moore of Moore Quality, Inc., assisted on the Delta Dental case and served as a sounding board throughout the effort. Charlie Hamlin of NFO introduced us to the *Inc.* case. Rob Duboff of

Mercer Management Consulting brought his creative flair to our thinking. Patricia Seybold of The Patricia Seybold Group helped frame the technology issues and provided access to her own research. Carole Wayland of Robert E. Wayland & Associates produced the numerous manuscript editions and kept the various parts of the project connected. Elizabeth Bishop Medina and Julie Boudreau pitched in with typing help before pressing deadlines.

We imposed on many friends to read and comment on the various drafts and acknowledge our debt to them while forgiving their candor. The following people graciously reviewed the book and unselfishly contributed ideas and suggestions to make it better: Mark Gerber of MSG, Inc.; Tom Cates of Sherbrooke and Associates; John Haigh of AT&T; Dom Geraghty of Technology Management Strategies; Bill Vinhage of New York State Electric & Gas; Dan Shaffer of S4 Consulting; Kim Heinz of Southern Energy Inc.; Minna Levine of Forbes Consulting; Randy Kreus of Scott, Madden & Associates; Larry Codey of Public Service Enterprise Group; Lawrence Baxter of Wachovia; Rod Plimpton of AEP; Mike Tennican of NERA; Dean Wise of CFGW; and Doug MacKenzie of American Express.

Many very thoughtful and creative executives took the time to work with us on the more than two dozen case studies in the book and are acknowledged individually in the notes for each chapter. Not only did they open their companies to our research but they also shared their thoughts and experience with us in ways that enriched the book beyond the specific cases. These executives and managers are the people who actually create the value for customers and shareholders that we write about. We hope our recounting of their experience does them justice.

We are grateful to senior managers of Paul's employer, Ernst & Young LLP, for providing support for the research and encouraging the effort. In particular, we thank Roger Nelson, Terry Ozan, and Chris Meyer. Terry Boyle demonstrated energy and ingenuity in serving as the research assistant on the project. Heather Miller assisted on case research and successfully kept Paul more or less on schedule throughout.

Several experienced business authors—Dwight Gertz, Stan Davis, Tom Davenport, Stephen Haekel, and Liam Fahey—reviewed early material and offered advice to us. We are also indebted to three anonymous reviewers for Harvard Business School Press who offered many helpful suggestions. Our agent, Dick Luecke, effectively guided us through the proposal and contracting phases. Sara Laschever contributed greatly to making the manuscript more readable and compact.

Our own collaboration began as partners at Temple, Barker, & Sloane (now Mercer Management Consulting), where we learned our craft and began forming many of the ideas outlined in this book. We are grateful to many former colleagues, especially Carl Sloane (now at Harvard Business School), Eric Almquist, Bob Fox, John Cripps, Phil Giudice, Pat Pollino, Jim Down, Carla Heaton, Alan Feibelman, and Mike Lovdal, who inspired us to think about these topics and supported our early efforts.

The crew at Harvard Business School Press was wonderfully supportive. The ebullient good nature of our first editor Nick Phillipson helped keep us going through the early stages. Our current editor Nikki Sabin suggested a number of important improvements and saw us through the final stages with patience and good humor. When we thought we were done, Barbara Roth found even more things to do while turning the manuscript into a book.

Our wives and children have been remarkably tolerant of yet another excuse why we couldn't do things or spend more time with them. We promise to do better and dedicate this effort to them.

Introduction

Today companies are caught in a cross fire of silver bullets: "Exceed customer expectations." "Achieve zero defections." "Isolate the segment of one." Derive "30 percent of revenues from new products." "Digitize and customize." Surely, the more thoughtful managers ask: Isn't there some point beyond which it is not worthwhile to either buyer or seller to increase quality? Isn't there some appropriate level of customer turnover above zero? Shouldn't the appropriate product introduction rate be based on something besides time and percent of revenues? Are there some situations in which customization just isn't worth it? In short, aren't there trade-offs?

BUILDING CUSTOMER *and* SHAREHOLDER VALUE

Executives who search the management literature for insights into making these trade-offs will have a hard time finding them. They seem to face a choice between the soft, intuitive perspective of the customer-driven school and the hard, shareholder or profit-driven perspective of strategic planners who seem to regard business as an abstract game of chess involving the movement of financial and physical assets into the areas promising the greatest rewards for shareholders.

Several years ago, when we first became interested in what now are called *demand-side strategies*, we noticed that those people with the most to say about creating shareholder value didn't talk much about the customer's role beyond that of a buyer, whereas those who had great insights into customer relationships tended to treat the connection with shareholder value as either self-evident or as the miraculous consequence of virtuous behavior. We believe that each view alone is too narrow and that it is possible to construct a demand-side framework that can bridge the customer and shareholder value perspectives and help managers make the trade-offs they confront.

When we speak of the gulf between the customer- and profit-driven perspectives, we are not dealing simply with seemingly contrary positions that don't matter much in the end. In a recent survey of the evolution of strategic planning, Frederick E. Webster, Jr., has shown that the debate between customer-driven and profit-driven strategies (or product-market concept) has raged for decades.[1] The customer-driven view, often called the *marketing concept*, was promulgated by Peter Drucker, Theodore Levitt, and others in the late 1950s. This view of the firm asserts that the satisfaction of customer needs is the firm's primary purpose. In this view, profits and shareholder wealth are the rewards for serving customers well, *not* the motivating purpose of the firm. Writing in 1983 to extend the tenets of the marketing concept, Theodore Levitt set out its basic premise: "The purpose of a business is to create and keep a customer." He went on, "[T]o say that profit is a purpose of business is, simply, morally shallow."[2]

Today's heirs to the customer-driven or marketing concept approach generally are found among the advocates of total quality management, customer satisfaction, and, more recently, customer loyalty perspectives. Many proponents of these concepts seem to regard profits as, at best, playing a regulating role by rewarding companies for satisfying their customers. At worst, they see profit-seeking behavior as stifling a company's true role of serving customers. Critics of the profit-driven perspective also often seem to equate profit-maximizing behavior with short-term thinking and a myopic focus on quarterly results.

Indeed, Frederick F. Reichheld, the most prominent advocate of the customer loyalty view, echoes Levitt: "The new theory sees the fundamental mission of a business not as profit but as value creation. It sees profit as a vital consequence of value creation—a means rather than an end, a result as opposed to a purpose."[3] Although Reichheld has made a major contribution by pointing managers back toward some basic values and insights about customer relationships, we disagree with this premise: Creating value for customers is a necessary but not a sufficient basis for strategy.

The pursuit of quality, customer satisfaction, core competencies, and customer loyalty per se do not constitute strategies. These approaches cannot tell a business which customers to pursue, how much and in what areas to invest to attract and retain those customers, or how to make the trade-offs inherent in all strategies. Such matters as the level of quality or customer satisfaction or degree of loyalty for which the firm should strive cannot be decided without an understanding of opportunity costs or yields. Without disparaging the value or importance of any of these factors, we contend that they are best viewed as significant variables to be managed within a broader strategy aimed at maximizing the value of the firm.

Neither of the two dominant schools of thought about what creates competitive advantage, the so-called *market-based* and *resource-based* views, addresses the customers' role in value creation. In the market-based view, most prominently articulated by Michael E. Porter, competitive advantage derives from a firm's positioning itself to capture the greatest possible value by pursuing a strategy of either cost leadership or differentiation.[4] The resource-based view, most closely identified today with Prahalad, Hamel, and Stalk,[5] approaches strategy from the internal perspective of leveraging the firm's competencies and resources either by entering markets in which those skills confer an advantage or by creating markets for products based on those competencies. In neither the market-based (despite its name) nor the resource-based view does the customer play much of a role beyond that of a buyer of the firm's output; the customer certainly is not seen as an active participant in the creation of value.

Today's emphasis on generating growth necessarily means focusing on customers. However, generating profitable growth requires focusing on the right customer relationships. In exploring customer-based strategies, we examine how a business's choice of customers affects the value of the firm, how the value proposition can be designed to enhance the value of the customer relationship, how different relationship structures affect the amount of value created, and how that value is shared by the buyer and seller. This book introduces a demand-side strategy framework that addresses these questions.

OVERVIEW *of* THIS BOOK

Central Themes

Our perspective on demand-side strategy is that it should be customer-*based*, not customer-*driven* or customer-*led*. Being obsequious to customers is not a strategy. However, recognizing that customers are ultimately the only sustainable source of shareholder value and rigorously working out the implications of this fact can provide useful strategic insights. Thus, we see the customer relationship not as an end in itself but rather as a fundamental building block of business value.

We believe that a firm's strategy can be developed as rigorously from a demand- or customer-based perspective as from the more traditional product-market or competencies perspectives. Customer relationships are assets that should be evaluated and managed as rigorously as any financial or physical assets. We stress that it is the *relationship* that is the asset, not the customer. The relationship gives rise to future cash flows that we can estimate and to which we can assign a value. The basis of that relationship value is the buyers' and sellers' knowledge about, experience with, and feelings for one another.

We also believe that the value of customer relationships can be related directly to the value of a firm and to shareholder value. In other words, the value of a firm is ultimately equal to the sum of the values of its customer relationships, and this sum can grow only through the acquisition, development, and retention of profitable customer relationships. By viewing itself as managing a portfolio of customer relationships (as opposed to managing a product or asset portfolio), a firm can take actions to maximize its value by deploying effectively its customer acquisition, development, and retention resources.

Viewing its customer relationships as its most important assets does not mean ignoring the many other relationships a company must maintain with suppliers and employees, however. As John Kay points out, "It is the totality of these relationships that defines the individual firm and creates its distinctive identity."[6] In our view, the form of these other relationships follows from the basis on which buyer and seller interact. We simply are establishing a starting point for the search for shareholder value.[7]

After reading this book, you'll see that viewing customer relationships as an asset is not a rhetorical phrase but the cornerstone of a rigorous strategic framework that will allow you to make explicit the connection between the actions you take to create value for customers and the creation of value for shareholders. In making the customer connection, you'll build your business from a new perspective; you will likely:

- Manage a portfolio of customer relationships rather than of products or physical assets.

- Achieve higher yields on investments by focusing on valuable customer relationships.

- Find new opportunities to create value for customers and capture a share of that value for shareholders.

- Leverage your knowledge of your customers to increase the value of these relationships.

- View technology as a means to deliver what customers want, when they want it, and in the way they want it.

A business cannot develop a customer-based strategy simply by bolting new customer service, satisfaction, or loyalty programs onto a vehicle propelled by product-driven thinking. A firm needs to look carefully at the total design and alignment of efforts to create value for both customers and shareholders. The next section outlines the basis for this alignment.

The Strategic Connection

A strategic framework is of little use unless it can link proposed actions with their probable consequences for firm value or shareholder wealth. The concept of *firm value*—defined in terms of net cash flows from operations—is well understood and forms the basis for capital budgeting decisions at many firms. The closely related concept of *shareholder value*, sometimes referred to as *excess returns* because it is created only when net cash flows are greater than necessary to compensate shareholders for their required return, has become something of a strategic mantra for growth-oriented firms.[8] The connection between value created for customers and the value of the firm is illustrated in Figure I-1.

We start with *customer value created*, which is what revenues really are. Revenues represent the value created for the customer, as evidenced by their willingness to pay for the output of the firm. The demand-side search for shareholder value begins by analyzing the size and distribution of revenues across individual customers or customer groups. From this demand-side perspective, the customer (rather than a project, product, or physical asset) is seen as the source of cash inflows or revenues.

Next we turn to *customer cash flow*, which represents the annual contribution to fixed costs and capital made by a customer or group of customers. Here we subtract the total cash costs of identifiable inputs associated with the customer relationship, including the cost of the product; acquisition, development, and retention costs; and taxes on operating income, to estimate customer cash flows. Obviously, if a customer does not cover the variable costs of serving her, the firm is destroying value.

Customer equity is the term used to describe the asset value of the relationship. The value of customer equity is determined by customers' volume of purchases, the margin on those purchases, and the duration of the purchase stream.

Connecting Customer and Shareholder Value

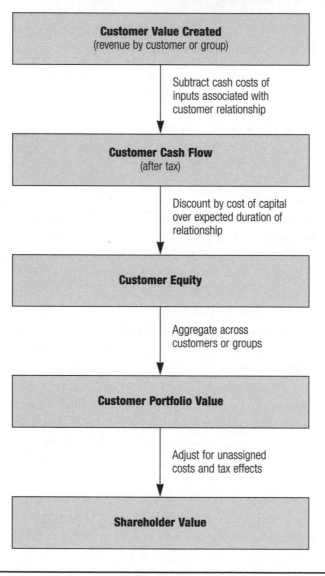

Figure I-1

To convert the cash flows from the relationship into an asset or equity figure, it is necessary to discount them by the cost of capital to the firm. The concept of customer equity is a powerful metaphor and is central to the development of demand-side strategies. We have traced the term back at least as far as 1983 in

Levitt's insightful discussion of relationship management.[9] More recently, Blattberg and Deighton have advocated the use of customer equity to guide marketing decisions and investments.[10] In this book, we expand the application of customer equity to embrace the selection of customers, the metric for evaluating changes in the nature of the value proposition, and the basis on which the rewards and risks of the relationship are shared by buyers and sellers.

Next, we introduce the notion of the *customer portfolio,* the aggregate value of all customer relationships, which is equal to the sum of customer equities for all customers or groups. The keys to customer portfolio management are understanding the expected value (mean) and variance of the distribution of relationship values and making choices about investments in the acquisition, development, and retention of customer relationships.

Finally, the *shareholder value* is equal to the aggregate value of the customer portfolio adjusted for joint or unassigned costs and tax effects that cannot be attributed to particular customers or groups and, if appropriate, other income-producing assets. Just as the traditional project or product view seeks to maximize firm or shareholder value by selecting an investment portfolio based on positive net cash flows, the customer portfolio manager maximizes shareholder value by choosing customer relationships with expected net values at least equal to the cost of acquiring and serving them.

Achieving alignment between efforts to create value for customers and shareholders (see Figure I-1) is the essence of demand-side strategies. To help achieve this alignment, we have developed a customer-based strategic framework. Although it will not fit all businesses under all circumstances, it is especially effective in service industries, in business-to-business settings, and in high-involvement consumer goods businesses. Many companies in these sectors will find it useful to begin their strategic thinking with a consideration of the existing and potential value of their customer relationships rather than from the more traditional starting points of industry selection or competencies. For many firms, it will be easier to define their "customer space" than to identify the precise boundaries of the industry in which they participate. Defining an industry often is difficult and, with modern advances, it is becoming even harder. For instance, what is the telecommunications industry— infrastructure, hardware, software...?

Though it is important to keep in mind the possibility of industry entrance or exit, such moves are infrequent. Most strategic exercises are aimed at doing better in the firm's existing business, and this necessarily involves consideration of existing and potential customers. Most firms have an installed base of customers and likely prospects that will account for the vast proportion of the value created over the planning horizon.

Moreover, some research suggests that industry choice explains a relatively small percentage of the difference in profits across firms. For example, Rumelt found that less than 10 percent of the difference in firm profitability was attributable to industry-specific factors; business unit factors explained nearly half of the variance, whereas approximately 37 percent was due to "unexplained factors."[11] In their examination of the differences between high- and low-growth firms, Gertz and Baptista also found relatively weak correlations between industries and the growth rate of firms.[12]

In asking you to buy this book and invest time in reading it, we think we owe you some explanation of why we believe the concepts and principles are valid. The basic concepts reflect many years of consulting, during which we were privileged to learn from many talented executives and colleagues. Our thinking also was formed and extended by the published works of others, many of whom are cited throughout the book.

The resulting ideas and concepts then were refined and tested in a number of ways. We developed an integrating framework and a supporting set of algorithms and models for estimating the key elements of the framework, because we believe it's important for readers to appreciate the structure and dynamics of the arguments and to assess their applicability to their own situations. We also tested the explanatory power of our framework by applying it to nearly two dozen case studies of companies that we sought out because they had a record of customer-based growth. These cases enable the reader to appreciate the growth issues faced by individual firms and to understand how these companies dealt with these issues.

Finally, with the help of the research firm Marketing and Planning Systems (MaPS), we conducted a survey of 200 executives of Fortune 1000 companies and followed up with in-depth interviews to explore the relationship between growth and the issues addressed in our model. Our hypotheses were that firms with exceptional knowledge of their customer portfolios would be able to focus more effectively on the most valuable customer relationships, would be able to leverage technology more effectively to connect with customers, and would enjoy a growth advantage over their peers. Though not dispositive, the results shown in Figure I-2 suggest that there is a measurable connection between growth and understanding customer relationship value, focusing on valuable relationships, and using technology to forge stronger customer relationships.

The Growth Connection

Indicator	High-Growth Companies	Low-Growth Companies
Percentage with "extremely clear view" of the most valuable customers	38%	22%
Percentage of revenue from top 10 percent of customers	46%	32%
Index of performance on using technologies to better connect with customers (1–10 point scale)	7.0	5.7

Figure I-2

Guide to Topics

The rest of this book is structured to help you discover new ways to think about value creation. The next chapter develops a four-part model of customer relationship value and illustrates the concepts by tracking the evolution of MCI in terms of its continued development of customer relationship value. The subsequent three chapters outline the foundations of customer knowledge, connecting technology, and customer economics that together enable you to navigate around our framework. With these foundations in place, we then turn to a more detailed examination of each of the four sources of customer and firm value, illustrating the representative positions with in-depth case studies. Finally, in the last chapter we step back and synthesize the implications of our approach for business strategy. With a good guide, a working model, and a plan for getting where you want to be, we believe you can maximize the customer connection.

The value compass

FINDING UNTAPPED SOURCES OF VALUE

In Lewis Carroll's *Through the Looking Glass*, Alice found herself in a land where, as the Red Queen says, "It takes all the running you can do to keep in the same place. If you want to get somewhere else, you must run twice as fast as that."[1] As managers try to keep pace with today's changing business landscape, many find themselves running in place with poor Alice.

Running faster by downsizing, reengineering, reducing product cycle time, and applying vigorous supply-chain management has left many firms leaner and meaner but little improved in terms of growth and profitability. This has prompted many to shift from supply-side strategies that emphasize cost reduction to demand-side strategies that search for new ways to build revenues, add value, and connect better with customers.

Although there is no such thing as a pure demand-side strategy any more than there are pure supply-side strategies, the notion expressed by the term *demand-side strategy* focuses on a critical need felt by many companies today: to pay more attention to increasing revenues as well as managing costs. Most businesses today are trying to foster stronger customer relationships, are building or planning a customer database, and are measuring customer satisfaction. Are these initiatives working?

The facts suggest that just running faster on the demand side won't necessarily break the Red Queen's grip. Despite annual spending of more than $4.5 billion on primary market research, most firms are dissatisfied with their understanding of their customers.[2] Despite billions spent trying to understand customer needs, the cost of an industrial sales call has increased nearly 50 percent, while sales productivity has declined.[3] In addition, all proclamations of getting closer to customers notwithstanding, the Product Development Managers Association reports that new product failure rates remain at 41 percent.[4]

SPEED VERSUS DIRECTION

We think it might be time to look at the problem of growth from a different perspective. Perhaps running faster and doing more cannot provide the entire answer; perhaps sometimes they are even part of the problem. Business people typically look at the gap between where they are and where they'd like to be and conclude that they simply have not run fast enough. But how much of the gap is due to lack of speed, and how much is due to running in the wrong direction? How often does a business spend aggressively to capture new accounts one year, only to see most of those accounts leave a few years later? How many product-line extensions bloom briefly and then wither, leaving total sales at approximately the same level but costs a little higher? How often do costly programs to increase customer satisfaction earn unchanged rates of defection?

For many companies, the difficulty of achieving profitable growth is not a matter of running too slowly but of chasing after the wrong customers—customers who are either unprofitable to serve or who are unlikely to form profitable relationships, and customers who drain resources and effort away from the pursuit and development of more valuable relationships. In many cases, the problem originates not in a lack of customer information but in too much attention paid to database building and not enough paid to developing and sharing useful knowledge. Equally often, businesses suffer not from a lack of product innovation but from a glut of products that blurs the company's focus and builds costs faster than revenues.

RUNNING TOGETHER

Concern about the pace of change and the rate at which technology is shaping the future accounts for much of the emphasis on seeking ways to run faster. However, we believe that you can't get to the future on time by running after your customers; you get there by running *with* your customers and understanding their destination and the role you can play in helping them arrive there. This means connecting with your customers. The metaphor of *connec-tions* is used both literally and figuratively throughout this book. We want you to think about the creation and exchange of value as a dynamic and interactive process that takes place among buyers and sellers, and so we refer not only to electronic connections such as electronic data interchange or the Internet but also to personal interactions and exchanges of information as well as intangibles such as brand equity. We also use the term connections more colloquially to suggest alignment of buyers and sellers, the point at which these parties make the "right" connection and act almost as one to create mutually the greatest pos-sible exchange of value through their relationship.

Among the firms that have been most successful in connecting with their customers, we have not seen a mood of panic over the rate of change or a sense of dread about the cataclysmic implications of technology. We do not believe that we're observing misplaced complacency, as will be shown by our research results (reported later). Instead, we see excitement and enthusiasm about the potential for creating more value and opening more avenues of contact with customers. These firms are aware of areas in which they can perform better and are moving in those directions. Nor do we believe our observations are biased toward companies that already have achieved the ultimate level of technologi-cal sophistication. Although many of these firms have been learning how to use technology strategically on the demand side of their growth equation, in most cases they have done so with adequate but hardly state-of-the-art technology. For the most part, these companies have taken a fairly balanced and evolution-ary approach to incorporating new technologies and new customer relationship strategies into their businesses, and they have learned along the way.

Don't get us wrong: We are not denying that this is an era of rapid change. We live in an increasingly connected economy in which the possibility of being able to connect with anyone, anywhere, anytime is becoming a reality. One of the hall-marks of this age is the almost limitless range of business strategies and designs now possible as technology allows us to break from old constraints of time and place. We believe business is entering an era of unprecedented creativity as peo-ple rethink the ways that they can create value and conduct business. At the same time, this freedom to create new forms of business requires a disciplined approach to identifying the best opportunities and deploying resources wisely.

To see new opportunities, we ask: What factors determine the potential value of customer relationships? What forces operate for and against achieving that value? How does the form of the customer relationship influence the business design? We have found that there are four major factors that determine the value of customer relationships, and, hence, of the firm.

- *Customer portfolio management*: refers to the selection and management of customer relationships. Creating a valuable customer portfolio requires understanding the distribution of customer relationship values and investing in acquisition, development, and retention accordingly. The levels at which businesses manage their customer portfolios may be represented by three points on this dimension: market (or index), group, and individual.

- *Value proposition design*: refers to the business's contribution to its customers' value chain or total experience. Achieving the optimal position involves understanding the total value represented on the value chain, the relative competencies of rivals for a share of that value, and customers' confidence in the business's ability to extend the range of its offer. Movement along this dimension may be described as core product, extended offer, and total solution positions.

- *Value-added role*: relates to the position of the firm within the industry value-added chain or sequence of value-adding activities. This involves finding the position relative to customer and supplier value chains that provides the greatest return to the business's competencies. Representative positions include the product manager, process manager, and network manager roles.

- *Reward and risk sharing*: refers to the basis on which customers and suppliers interact to create and share value. Movement along this dimension depends on the market structure, incentives to collaborate, and the relative risk-bearing capabilities of buyers and sellers. Representative positions range from neutral (taking what the market gives you) to performance-based sharing to sharing in the outcome of collaboration.

In short, a business can increase the value it creates for customers and shareholders by strategically deploying its customer acquisition, development, and retention efforts; optimizing its presence on the customer value chain; positioning itself to gain the greatest leverage within the industry value-added chain; and structuring its relationships to achieve the most valuable degree of collaboration or interdependence. Taken together, a firm's positions along each of these dimensions represent its demand-side strategy. In too many cases, however, these positions are chosen because they are currently fashionable. The result is a set of individual programs, not a cohesive strategy. To

Dimensions of Relationship Value

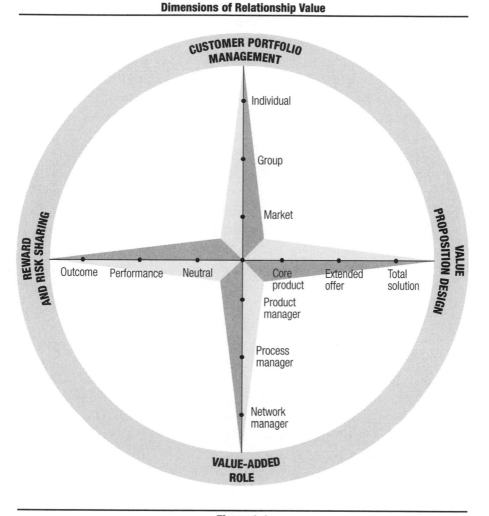

Figure 1-1

develop a sustainable plan, each company must find the combination of positions that works best for its own market.

To visualize the integration of these four dimensions, we find it useful to display them in the form of a compass to help guide the search for value, as illustrated in Figure 1-1. Movement out from the origin indicates changes in the *potential* profitability of customer relationships. Whether the potential value can be achieved depends importantly on the quality of customer knowledge and the means or technology of connecting with customers.

The value compass framework abstracts from the detail of particular situations and concentrates on the key factors that explain behavior or predict outcomes.

This framework provides a basis for thinking about the key elements of strategy from a demand-side perspective. Each element of the framework employs a set of analytic techniques and models that enables the strategist to grapple with the complexity of a wide range of factors and to assess the possibilities of alternative actions. These underlying models will be familiar to most readers as they are borrowed from economics, finance, and the business strategy literature.

Each axis of the value compass can be thought of as a terrain defined by one or more of these underlying models. Determination of the right customer portfolio is driven by statistical analysis of the distribution of relationship values, which draws on financial asset valuation theory. The range of value proposition is defined in terms of the customer value chain. The role dimension considers the potential positions on the larger venue of the industry value-added chain, and reward and risk sharing draws on the concepts of game theory, risk management, and information and search costs.

We will illustrate the dimensions of relationship value by traveling around the four axes of the framework and describing representative positions that firms might take along each dimension. Keep in mind that the positions are representative and that each dimension is a continuous spectrum.

BUILDING *the* RIGHT CUSTOMER PORTFOLIO

As Rogers Hornsby advised the young Ted Williams, the first rule of hitting is, "First get a good pitch."[5] All other aspects of strategy are for naught if you don't target the right customers. All customers are not created equal. They vary according to the amount they buy, the frequency of their purchases, their sensitivity to price and other product attributes, and the costs of acquiring, developing, and retaining them. A company that pursues unprofitable or unresponsive customers wastes resources that could have been devoted to building valuable relationships.

Choosing the right customers is equivalent to determining the right level at which to manage your customer portfolio. We can represent the level at which a business manages its customer portfolio by three points on a continuum—market, group, and individual—as illustrated in Figure 1-2. A company can choose to include every customer in the market in its portfolio, it might choose to specialize in creating relationships with customers belonging to certain groups, or it might focus on relationships with particular individual customers. It is important to note that we are referring here to the level at which relationship strategies are *planned* and *executed*. A firm may have individual accounts, but this does not mean that the company is managing its relationship strategy on an individual cus-

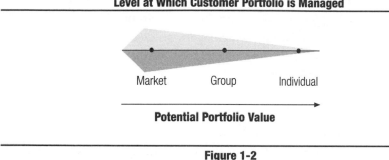

Level at Which Customer Portfolio is Managed

Market   Group   Individual

Potential Portfolio Value

Figure 1-2

tomer basis. For example, banks and magazines have individual accounts but often plan their customer portfolios on a market or group basis.

The *potential* value of a portfolio is tied directly to the level of knowledge about existing customers and prospects. With better customer knowledge, a firm can improve the value of its portfolio by accurately targeting the most promising customers and avoiding or disengaging from the unprofitable ones. If no costs were involved in acquiring knowledge and acting on the basis of that knowledge, all firms would manage their portfolios at the individual customer level and would maximize profitability by targeting only customers whose relationship value was greater than the cost of acquiring and serving them. Unfortunately, acquiring knowledge and acting on it is not free. Therefore, the *achievable* portfolio value depends on the costs of acquiring and using customer knowledge.

The right level at which to manage your customer portfolio is that point at which the value of making better decisions about investing in customer relationships is equal to the cost of acquiring and using the necessary knowledge. Even if the cost of knowledge itself is modest, making effective use of it may be too costly relative to the gains, which explains why prescriptions to employ "segment-of-one" or "one-to-one" marketing across the board will not maximize the value of all firms and might inhibit their growth. Over time, however, the economics of a business may change, new knowledge may become available, or customer-connecting technologies may become more effective. Businesses that do not periodically review and renew their portfolio management strategy risk being detached from their customer base.

Our research indicates that fewer than one-third (30%) of the Fortune 1000 companies we surveyed have a clear view of exactly what their most valuable customer relationships are. Not surprisingly, the manufacturers of consumer packaged goods have the lowest level of customer-specific knowledge, although many have extensive statistical representations of typical customers. Companies that serve as intermediaries reported the highest level of customer-specific knowledge. Many firms find it valuable to know a small part of their total customer portfolio very well and to manage all other relationships on an aggregated or undifferentiated basis. In the following sections, we outline three representative portfolio management strategies and the conditions under which they are most appropriate.

Managing the Portfolio at the Market Level

Under certain circumstances, a firm may elect, reasonably, to stock its customer portfolio with the same mix of customers as compose the market as a whole. This strategy, like an "indexed" mutual fund, creates a portfolio of customers whose intrinsic value, on average, is equal to that of the entire market. The portfolio manager acts as if all customers are created equal, or what is the same thing operationally, that differences among the customers are too costly to determine or act on. This index strategy can generate superior results only if the firm has a supply-side advantage in the form of lower production costs or better customer acquisition, development, and retention skills. In an index strategy, growth is largely a matter of increasing the number of customers and, hence, volume and share.

If the customer population is relatively homogeneous, in the sense that all customer relationships have roughly comparable values, the firm is fairly indifferent as to which customers it attracts or holds. The "trading rules" for this sort of customer portfolio are fairly simple—buy more as resources permit. However, if its customer population displays a wide diversity of customer relationship values, the firm that manages relationships at the market level is vulnerable to competitors who focus on taking away the firm's most valuable customer relationships.

In a market-level portfolio, the relationship between buyer and seller often is vicarious and is based on brand identity and self-selection. This applies to most so-called mass market goods, but it also characterizes relationships in more narrowly defined markets such as heavy-weight motorcycles, as we will discuss later in the Harley-Davidson case in Chapters 2 and 5.

Managing the Portfolio at the Group Level

Alternatively, the customer portfolio manager might focus on a particular segment or type of customer that promises a greater overall return. Doing so requires deeper customer knowledge than is needed for a market-level portfolio and sacrifices some of the benefits of diversification. This strategy ties the customer portfolio manager's fate more closely to that of a particular group of customers and pushes him to specialize in meeting that group's specific needs. Because in many cases these customers also are identifiable and desirable to rivals, the business must continually seek advantage in a distinctive position or build barriers around its customer base.

Of course, firms can elect to serve several groups within a market. The ability to do so successfully, however, depends on the firm's ability to create products that appeal to other groups without diluting or eroding their products' appeal to their best customers. For example, USAA, an insurance company, built its exceptionally valuable customer portfolio by targeting military officers and their special needs. With cutbacks in the size of defense forces, the company has widened its target base. Whether this tactic will succeed depends on how similar these new groups are and on whether accommodating any differences will dilute USAA's distinctive position. Staples, as we discuss in Chapter 5, found that meeting the distinct needs of different groups within its portfolio called for creating separate value propositions and assuming a different role in the customer-supply chain.

Managing the Portfolio at the Individual Level

At the finest level of granularity, a firm can manage its portfolio at the individual customer level. This entails an even deeper knowledge of customers than do the other strategies and, depending on the number of customers and the nature of the value exchange, also requires more sophisticated connecting technologies. In the past, only very valuable customer relationships, such as those with wealthy investors or high-stakes gamblers, warranted individualized treatment. New technologies, however, make it possible to manage even moderately valuable relationships on an individual basis.

Investing in customer-specific knowledge is profitable when the expected yield from better relationship management decisions outweighs the cost of acquiring and maintaining the information and knowledge. For improving these decisions, some variance in the distribution of customer relationship value or of customer responsiveness to initiatives must exist to make it worthwhile to understand the customer's position relative to others. Therefore, customer portfolios tend to be managed at the individual customer level when customers display a wide variance in relationship values, preferences, or needs.

Active management of individual relationships involves regularly reviewing and deciding about the level and type of investment to make in each relationship. In the past, this meant limiting the number of individually managed relationships, but improvements in information technology and customer modeling are making possible the management of very large numbers of customers on an individual basis. Wachovia Bank (discussed in Chapter 5) is developing the capacity to proactively manage each of its relationships, for example.

SELECTING *the* RIGHT RANGE *of the* VALUE PROPOSITION

The *range* of the value proposition describes the extent of the value exchange between buyer and seller. For convenience, we can portray movement along this dimension in terms of three progressively more comprehensive value propositions: *core product, extended offer,* and *total solution.* (Throughout this book we will use the term *product* in its generic sense to mean not only tangible goods but also services.)

Sellers are continually under pressure to increase the value that they deliver to their customers. The seller's opportunity to increase the range of his value proposition stems from the fact that customers generally purchase goods and services not as ends in themselves but as components in a process to meet some larger need or purpose. Customers assemble these components to produce what economists call *utility.* To meet the need for transportation, a car buyer must assemble additional factors such as financing, insurance, maintenance, and fuel. Customers incur substantial search, information, and transaction costs both in selecting individual components and in assembling them to achieve their ultimate goals. The sum of the customer's expenditures over all of these factors is the aggregate value of what we call the *total experience.* The customer's total experience may be represented either as a set of closely related products used by the customer to satisfy some common need, such as the different types of insurance purchased to meet the need for risk management, or it may be thought of as a value chain composed of processes undertaken to produce an output.

A firm can increase the value of its relationships by successfully serving a larger portion of the customers' value chain or experience. This can be accomplished by enhancing the characteristics of the product to reduce other ownership costs, by bundling or combining elements of the ownership experience at a cost below what the customer would incur, by reducing the transaction costs across all or part of the total experience, or by providing a total solution to the customer's need.

The attraction of extended value propositions is exemplified by Boeing's recent decision to provide a wide range of services to airlines from maintenance to pilot training. "Building airplanes is a $40 billion-a-year business," says Ronald Woodard, president of Boeing's airplane group and an architect of its expansion strategy. But "operating airplanes is a $400 billion-a-year busi-

Selecting the Range of Value Proposition

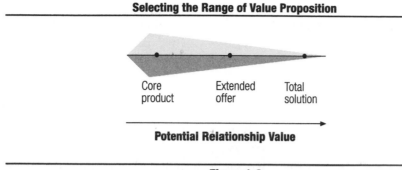

Core   Extended   Total
product   offer   solution

Potential Relationship Value

Figure 1-3

ness. We're going to look at where we can bring value to our customers and move that [corporate] boundary."[6]

Extending the value proposition is the most widely pursued strategy for building relationship value. Companies tend to get into business because they have something to sell that they believe people will buy, and they continue to push on this dimension as the business matures or until opportunities are exhausted. Most of the companies in our survey indicated that they are attempting to deliver a broad value proposition—45 percent are pushing to deliver a total solution and 44 percent an extended offer, whereas only 11 percent are emphasizing a core product. Figure 1-3 illustrates these three representative points and the potential increase in relationship value associated with each.

Core Product

A core product is a clearly defined package of attributes that addresses a specific part of the customer's value chain or element of the total experience. A core product can be consumed or used *as is* either by itself or in combination with other products. Most consumer packaged goods are core products. The concept of core product should not be confused with the popular use of the term *commodity* to denote an undifferentiated product.

Suppliers can increase their share of total value by offering core products or services that reduce the customers' total cost of achieving their objective. For example, a car manufacturer may offer an improved core product with better mileage, lower maintenance requirements, and sturdier bumpers that reduces fuel expenditures, maintenance costs, and insurance rates, thereby capturing a greater portion of its customers' total transportation expenditures in the price of its product. In some cases, a firm can enhance the value of its core product by combining it with information. By customizing information delivery regarding its product value and performance, Pioneer Hi-Bred International, which we discuss in Chapters 2 and 6, has increased the value of its relationships even though it has not ventured beyond its core product, seed.

Extended Offer

At the next level, the seller may extend his presence on the buyer's value chain by offering more of the inputs used by the customer to meet her objectives. This extended offer may be combined with the core product, as when an automobile maker offers attractive financing or insurance at a bundled cost below that which the customer can achieve on her own. Alternatively, the seller might offer a wider range of closely related products that share certain characteristics, such as different forms of insurance.

In some cases, the seller might assume responsibility for a large part of the ownership experience. Lexus, for example, has created an exceptional automobile ownership experience. It manages the maintenance process by notifying owners of the time for scheduled maintenance and then picks up and returns the car, thus saving the owner precious time. Lexus provides 24-hour-road service and even goes so far as to keep a "medical history" of the car, which can be used as proof of the vehicle's "health" when it is sold.

As the range of the value proposition migrates from the core product to more extensive coverage of the value chain or total experience, the supplier not only is capturing a greater share of the customers' total relationship value but is increasing the complexity of the offer and expanding the set of competitors. Sellers of the various components of the customer's value chain (or experience) are competing with other providers of those components and with the customers' entire supplier base, vying with one another for shares of the customers' total expenditures on their underlying needs. For example, offering roadside assistance calls for developing or contracting for a network of emergency response capabilities and puts the car company into competition with outfits such as the American Automobile Association. Therefore, decisions about the range of the value proposition must be weighed in terms of the expected change in customer relationship value, with consideration given to changes in both revenues and costs and the probable actions of competitors.

Total Solution

The total solution position involves the seller in all or nearly all of the buyer's activities related to the satisfaction of a need or achievement of a goal. It often involves a mix of channels and multiple points of interaction between the buyer and seller.

Inc., most famous for its magazine that provides information for growing businesses, also provides a full range of management education and development materials, conducts conferences, offers on-line service and advice, and provides consulting to its customers. An entrepreneur can find information, review the experience of other businesses, or gain access to an expert for advice about almost every problem he encounters. *Inc.* also has extended its value proposition to the small-business community by tracking the performance of firms, recognizing achievements, and acting as an advocate for small-business interests. The transition of *Inc.* from its core product to a comprehensive value proposition is described in Chapter 6.

PLAYING *the* RIGHT VALUE-ADDED ROLE

The role dimension refers to how the seller creates added value and how he delivers it to the buyer. In assessing its role, the firm must consider its position in the total *value-added chain* for the market in which it operates. The value-added chain represents the series of steps performed in a market from raw materials production to final consumption. The role played by a firm is defined by which steps it performs and how it engages with other players (the points of connection across their respective value chains).

The roles played by sellers in their relationships with buyers typically fall into three categories: product managers, process managers, and network managers. The product manager may be thought of as operating in a one-to-many mode. A process manager assumes or shares some responsibility with a customer on a one-to-one basis. The network manager occupies a central position between buyers and sellers, a many-to-many role.

Playing the right role is often difficult to put into operation, as it may require restructuring of the business model and might involve developing new competencies. We found that most (63 percent) companies still are operating in the traditional product manager role. A significant percentage (30 percent) have assumed the role of a process manager. The technology-enabled role of network manager is evolving rapidly but currently represents only 10 percent of the market.

In each of these three forms of value-added positioning, the intersection of the buyer and seller value chains, the nature of two-way information flows, the information content of the exchange, and the types of connecting technology used varies. Figure 1-4 depicts the general ways in which connections and roles may be configured.

Representative Roles

A. Product Manager: "One to Many"

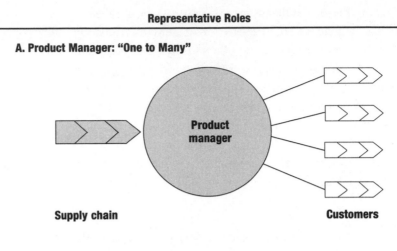

Supply chain   Customers

B. Process Manager: "One to One"

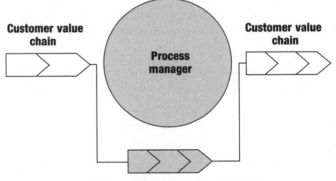

Process manager value chain

C. Network Manager: "Many to Many"

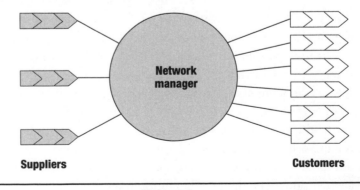

Suppliers   Customers

Figure 1-4

The Product Manager Role

The product manager creates added value by combining inputs into a product for the buyer. The product manager usually delivers the product to the buyer in a series of discrete interactions or transactions. The value exchange is discrete in the sense that there is a clear handoff or transfer of a product or service from the buyer to the seller in exchange for payment. Each party's responsibilities are defined by the transaction and are governed by relatively standard rules. In the product manager role, the seller adds value by combining inputs along his value chain. The seller transfers the output of his value chain to the buyer, where it becomes an input to her value chain. Product manager relationships are found across the full range of value propositions, from core to total solution. The important factor is that the value chains of the buyer and seller are not overlapping or interdependent beyond the specific exchange.

Use of the term *product* is not meant to imply that all transactions take place at spot terms or to exclude formal contracts that provide for a series of transactions over time. Product manager relationships may be of any duration, ranging from one-off exchanges to long-term, repeated interactions. Despite their discrete nature, product manager relationships may be very strong and long-lived. For example, you may be very loyal to Coke or Pepsi and display this loyalty over a long period of time.

The Process Manager Role

Process management relationships involve an ongoing, multipoint set of connections among customers and vendors. In this mode, the supplier undertakes to supply a portion of the customer's value chain on an ongoing or as-needed basis. For example, United Parcel Service (UPS) will manage a retailer's complete outbound logistics process. The increasing practice of outsourcing is a major source of these relationships, but not all outsourcing involves process management; it might consist simply of buying a product previously produced in-house. Clearly, the degree of interdependence and collaboration between the customer and supplier in this model is much closer than in the product manager model and requires more frequent and comprehensive information exchanges.

The process management role often is applied to a complex but noncore activity that is costly and subject to economics of scale not easily achieved by an individual customer. Companies might even decide that managing all or part of the customer relationship is not a core competency for them. Third-party customer service providers, the people who actually answer the phone when you call a manufacturer's 800 number, are one of the fastest-growing businesses in the United States.

A leading semiconductor firm described the process manager relationship to us this way:

> In the industry overall, more of the system is becoming integrated onto the silicon and more intelligence is being placed on the chip. Equipment manufacturers can't afford to have all of the semi-conductor capability in-house. As a result, they want to work in partnership with semiconductor manufacturers. The field sales reps just don't go in there with an order book anymore. The sales engineer manages the overall relationship, while the technical design people work directly with the customer to design the actual product. We're becoming a virtual partner with the customer.

Process management relationships may span the full scope of value propositions but tend to be found together with broader exchanges of value. Firms may shift from a product manager to a process manager role to capture the added value opportunities over a greater part of their customers' value chain, as when UPS moved from providing a core product (package delivery) to assuming responsibility for the outbound logistics and distribution functions for a large customer.

The Network Manager Role

The network manager role involves taking a central position and conducting multipoint and multiparty connections among buyers and sellers. In this role, the firm acts as an intermediary, actively managing or conducting the flow and matching of buyers and sellers to achieve some objective. The network manager may or may not actually provide any final product or service; the manager's role often is simply to bring the parties together. For example, health maintenance organizations (HMOs) manage networks of patients and physicians but frequently do not provide health care services directly. In fact, some HMOs that once maintained in-house clinics are considering spinning them off. Other network managers include America Online (AOL) and similar on-line providers who undertake to reduce the transaction and search costs for subscribers and provide access for those subscribers to on-line service providers.

Many companies invested in proprietary electronic links with their customers and suppliers with the intent of forging stronger bonds, only to find that their system was eclipsed by or vulnerable to broader, freely accessible networks that offer customers connections with many vendors. The network manager role has been greatly stimulated by the Internet, where a host of new markets has been created, several of which are discussed in Chapter 3.

The network manager strategic position usually involves bringing together relatively large but unorganized groups of customers and suppliers who would, by themselves, have to incur heavy search and transaction costs. It also involves controlling the means of access or exchange by building customer bases and leveraging access to these bases. For example, Delta Dental Plan of Massachusetts, a dental preferred provider organization, has achieved exceptional growth by building a strong patient base and using this to secure enrollment of dentists and favored pricing and treatment protocols.

SELECTING *the* RIGHT BALANCE *of* REWARD *and* RISK SHARING

The reward- and risk-sharing dimension of the framework addresses the ways that buyers and sellers interact in a relationship to create and share value. We define that relationship broadly to encompass not only the exchange of product for payment but all of the interactions and flows of information between the buyer and seller. We believe it is very important to think of the buyer-seller relationship as a dynamic and *mutual* value-creating process that can take many forms and evolve over time as circumstances change. As value-creating processes, relationships can be evaluated in terms of the economic value they create relative to the effort invested by the parties.

Until fairly recently, the way customers and suppliers interact was not of particular interest to strategists. Value creation was seen as a function of the proper selection of industry, market, and product; leveraging an internal competency; or satisfying a customer need. Most discussions of reward and risk sharing focus on pricing and contracting and usually emphasize strategies for *extracting* value. The idea that the form of relationship was itself a major source of value creation was not prominent until game theory highlighted the interactive process of mutual value creation through trade and exchange. Game theory brought to the fore the role that exchanges of information (signaling) and knowledge play in determining the outcome of games, particularly those that are played repeatedly over time. Our interest here is in the ways that different forms of interaction affect the total value and the division of that value. Are buyer and seller locked into a rational but suboptimal position, or could they do better by communicating, collaborating, or changing the rules of the game?

All trade or exchange is undertaken with the expectation that value will be created. If this were not so, people wouldn't engage in such activities. Both parties to an exchange have an interest in the trade taking place and naturally seek the greatest possible share of the value created. A relationship therefore involves both collaboration and competition—what game theorists call *interdependent* behavior.

The "best" relationship is the one in which neither the buyer nor seller sees any more value to be gained by greater collaboration or interdependency. The parties need not act altruistically or subordinate their interests to one another; their informed self-interest is enough to seek greater collaboration when the potential gains are large enough to warrant the costs. The search for more valuable relationships is, in many respects, an effort to increase the size of the pie through increased collaboration or interdependency.

The total value of an exchange always is set by the buyer's (usually subjective) evaluation of how much better off she will be with the product. Unfortunately, this total value is almost always invisible to the seller. The seller only can try to infer the value by observing the buyer's responses to changes in price and her behavior during negotiations or through research. Both buyer and seller want to maximize their share of the total value and will take actions, such as shopping, negotiating, and collaborating, to obtain the most favorable exchange. As a general rule, buyers and sellers will engage in these activities up to the point at which the cost of additional effort is just equal to the expected gain.

The shared incentive for innovation is one of the most important bases for collaboration between buyer and seller. MIT's Eric von Hippel was a pioneer in identifying and documenting the active role that customers play in value creation beyond simply buying the output of sellers. Von Hippel challenged the orthodox view that producers generally were exclusively responsible for innovation.[3] He showed that, in many cases, by modifying and enhancing products to meet their real needs, customers were responsible for a large number of innovations previously attributed to manufacturers. Often, manufacturers did not welcome their customers' creativity and even warned the customers that they were violating the product warranties. Von Hippel's research led him to formulate a theory: Innovation is most likely to be produced by the party with the greatest economic incentive for its creation. Like all good insights, this seems obvious after being expressed, but it allows us to predict with reasonable accuracy whether users or manufacturers will produce innovations based on an understanding of their ability to capture the benefits.[7]

Closer or more "intimate" relationships are not necessarily better than distant or remote relationships; the quality depends on how much the parties are willing to invest in specific relationships. Many companies have very effective

Reward and Risk Sharing

Neutral   Performance   Outcome

Potential Relationship Value

Figure 1-5

relationships, based on a strong reputation or brand identity, with thousands or even millions of anonymous customers. The manufacturers of Coke learned this when they tried to change the formula of the company's flagship product. Thousands of customers protested, in effect making a property rights claim to the product as they wanted it to be. Coke did the only sensible thing it could do; it backed down and restored the old formula.

The level of interdependence or pressure to collaborate depends on the significance of the series of exchanges to the buyer and seller and the competitive intensity of the market. The buyer's pressure to collaborate with a particular seller is related positively to the significance of the exchange and inversely to the availability of close substitutes. Buyers of jelly beans have little incentive to convey their desired jelly bean configuration to confectioners; it's easier to select from the available array. Buyers of machine tools, on the other hand, are willing to provide extensive information on their needs and applications to the relatively fewer, more specialized manufacturers.

The share of total value received by each party depends on a number of factors, such as their relative bargaining power, the amount of information they have, and their contribution to the total value. The three representative positions along this dimension are neutral or market-based, performance-based, and outcomes-based. The potential value of the relationship increases directly with the degree of interdependency, as shown in Figure 1-5.

It appears that businesses have ample opportunities to think more creatively about the way they share rewards and risks with their customers. Our research shows that more than three-fourths (77 percent) of firms focus on market-based reward and risk sharing. Approximately one in five (19 percent) have adopted some type of performance-based approach, whereas only 4 percent have created reward structures tied to the outcome or results that are achieved. A number of companies pursue hybrid strategies, considering both the value to the customer and market factors.

Neutral or Market-Based Rewards Sharing

The most basic terms for sharing the rewards and risks of a relationship are simply to take what the market gives you. This position is neutral because it exposes each party to no more or less risk than that of any other parties in the market at the same time. The vast majority of exchanges and relationships, by number, are conducted at prices and terms established by the market. This does not imply that there will be one price for all or that the division of value will be roughly equal for the buyer and seller. If either buyer or seller has market or bargaining power relative to the other, he will receive a proportionately larger share of the value. Extended relationships such as long-term contracts often occur in the neutral position but largely under terms shaped by the parties' relative market power.

Performance-Based Sharing

In many cases, spot markets do not exist for the product or service, or they may be volatile and subject to uncertainty. In other cases, the buyer may want to purchase what is promised but be unable to establish in advance whether the product will perform as advertised. A range of risk- and reward-sharing arrangements has evolved to meet these circumstances. Performance-based risk-reward arrangements generally involve a negotiated range of rewards that depend on one party (usually, but not always, the supplier) meeting some target set through negotiation with the other party. To secure commitments from enough airlines to warrant the development of the 777, Boeing invited several major airlines to collaborate on setting the design targets. This collaboration increased the value of the plane by making it better fit customer needs. Because the value of the plane to the airlines depends on its weight and fuel consumption, which determine range, payload, and operating costs, Boeing committed to a performance-based schedule of bonuses and penalties for various weight and fuel consumption levels.[8] Performance terms expose the supplier to some of the hazards of the customers' operation as well as its own design and support capabilities and therefore require a higher degree of trust and commitment.

In some cases, sellers can create incentives for buyer performance. In target-pricing schemes, the buyer gets a lower price on all purchases after buying a preset minimum. Target pricing increases the buyer's switching costs by introducing a high negative "scrap" cost to the relationship. Indirect pricing incentives, such as frequent-flyer programs, operate on much the same principle. Until the award levels are reached, the program member perceives that the opportunity cost of switching to another carrier includes the foregone value of accumulated points. This "negative" incentive can be extremely powerful, especially if the flyer is approaching an award level.

Warranties and guarantees are a common form of performance-based risk sharing. Self-imposed guarantees or exceptional warranties often are intended to assure buyers of the seller's commitment to the market. For example, one of the first challenges faced by Delta Dental Plan of Massachusetts was to establish its credibility with buyers who might be wary of dealing with the new company spun off from Blue Cross/Blue Shield and with rivals who might try to capitalize on these fears. Delta signaled its commitment by changing the rules of the game with a unique self-imposed set of performance guarantees that required Delta to pay the customer for every service failure and to make up the difference if the employer's administrative costs did not decrease each policy year.

Outcomes-Based Sharing

Outcomes-based sharing arrangements come closest to what many people mean by *partnering*. In these arrangements, each party assumes part of the risk that the total enterprise or a particular project will succeed, and its reward is based, to some extent, on the degree of success. Outcomes-based risk-reward arrangements are fairly common in large development projects, where it often is difficult to draw the line between a supplier and an investor. The outcomes-based arrangement frequently is coupled with a process management structure as, for example, when an energy service company undertakes to manage a customer's total energy usage and is compensated by receiving a share of the savings achieved.

FOUNDATIONS *of* CUSTOMER CONNECTION STRATEGY

In researching companies for this book, we observed that companies that were exceptionally good at managing customer relationships shared certain characteristics: They were very good at generating, managing, and making use of customer knowledge. They made effective use of what we call *customer-connecting technologies* in building their customer relationships. They understood the economics of their customer portfolios, and they acted on that understanding. In other words, these companies were well past the stage of *talking* about being "customer-oriented." They had the tools and the know-how to connect with their customers as a matter of strategy.

Customer knowledge, customer-connecting technology, and customer economics are the foundations of customer-connected strategy (Figure 1-6). They

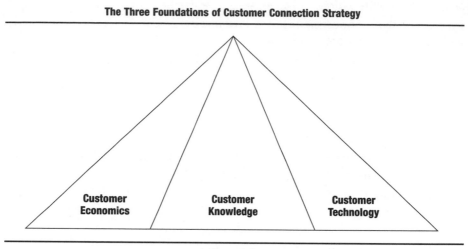

The Three Foundations of Customer Connection Strategy

Customer Economics | Customer Knowledge | Customer Technology

Figure 1-6

make it possible to determine where a business can position itself along each of the four dimensions described earlier. Each is examined in detail in the next three chapters, but we introduce them here to illustrate their importance as the foundations of a customer-connected strategy.

Customer Knowledge

We define *customer knowledge management* as the effective leverage of information and experience in the acquisition, development, and retention of a profitable customer portfolio. Each of the three words—*customer, knowledge,* and *management*—is central to the definition and highly interdependent. Many companies possess plenty of customer-related information, but more often than not it is scattered across various databases or resides in the heads of employees who do not interact. As a result, these companies fail systematically to create and apply the knowledge that would strengthen their customer relationships. On this point, our survey revealed that it is not the lack of information about the customer per se that stands in the way of building better customer connections but rather the lack of a disciplined process for managing that knowledge.

Customer-Connecting Technologies

Connecting technologies create either a direct interface with the customer or a channel for exchanging information. These connections may be used to foster conversation with customers, stimulate collaboration, or execute commerce and customer care. Connecting technologies include on-line systems (the Internet and the World Wide Web), self-service systems, opportunity management (e.g., sales force automation) systems, and customer care systems (e.g., call centers). These connecting technologies can reduce the search time and costs necessary to bring buyer and seller together. Technology then can be used to involve the customer in the specification, acquisition, or production of the good or service she desires, as in mass customization. Once an individual becomes a customer, these systems can be employed to deliver and exchange information and to provide ongoing support. Although most current applications of these technologies are tactical in nature and directed toward performing existing functions more efficiently, the technologies are increasingly capable of supporting strategic change by expanding the potential customer base, altering the value proposition, defining new roles in the value-added chain, and promoting collaboration and interdependency among buyers and sellers.

Customer Economics

Customer economics provides the tool kit by which to evaluate investments in customer knowledge and connecting technologies to achieve profitable customer portfolios and growth in firm or shareholder value. All customers are not created equal. An understanding of individual relationship value enables a firm to appreciate the distribution of relationship value and customer responsiveness and to deploy its customer acquisition, development, and retention resources effectively.

The tools of customer economics allow you to navigate around the points of the value compass: to determine the right level at which to manage your customer portfolio, the most profitable range of value proposition, the appropriate role to play in the overall value-added chain, and the balance of reward and risk sharing.

EVOLUTION *of* RELATIONSHIP STRATEGIES

The value compass is not intended to be prescriptive but is a guide in the search for untapped value. There is no single "right" position along each of the dimensions. Each business must determine what set of positions is both desirable and attainable. The solution for your firm will be determined by a combination of customer economics, customer knowledge, and connecting technologies. The appropriate position will change as these underlying factors evolve. It is important that the position represent alignment with the economic value of customer relationships. Taken together, the choices that a firm makes about its position on each of the relationship value axes constitute its customer-connection strategy.

Most firms start out fairly close to the center of the compass, the point at which the origins of the four relationship value dimensions come together. At first they define their target customers very broadly to include almost anyone in the market, in part because they are grateful to attract any customers at all. The initial value proposition usually is a well-defined core product, reflecting the insight or big idea of the founders. Businesses usually start by assuming the product manager role with respect to their customers and suppliers. Prices are market-based and neutral with respect to reward and risk sharing.

Nearly all firms start out in this sort of product-driven, broadly targeted style. In some cases, a firm can maintain this position profitably for a long time. Some of the most successful businesses in the world (e.g., Coke, Phillip Morris) occupy this position. However, in other cases, a business will exhaust the potential of its original product, competitors will erode its initial advantage, structural shifts in its market will undermine the original strategy, or all of these factors will bring pressure to change.

In response to these factors, the firm must either search for new sources of value or accommodate itself to diminished growth prospects. The framework can facilitate organization of the search for new sources of added value: changing the customer portfolio, the range of value proposition, the role in the value-added chain, or the reward- and risk-sharing arrangement.

To illustrate the application of the value compass framework, we will trace the evolution of MCI from essentially a one-product company to a provider of integrated communications solutions. In making this evolution, MCI moved out on each axis as the foundations of its relationships, customer knowledge, connecting technology, and customer economics changed.

MCI
Moving from a Single-Product to a Customer-Based Strategy

MCI's evolution illustrates how external factors lead to a significantly different relationship model, especially with its business communications customers.[9] MCI's initial outbound long-distance service, Execunet, was offered to business customers in 1975 and later expanded to residential consumers in 1979.[10] It was marketed as a low-cost replacement product to consumers and businesses alike who were customers of established carriers (overwhelmingly AT&T). Although telephone ser-

MCI's Original Relationship Strategy

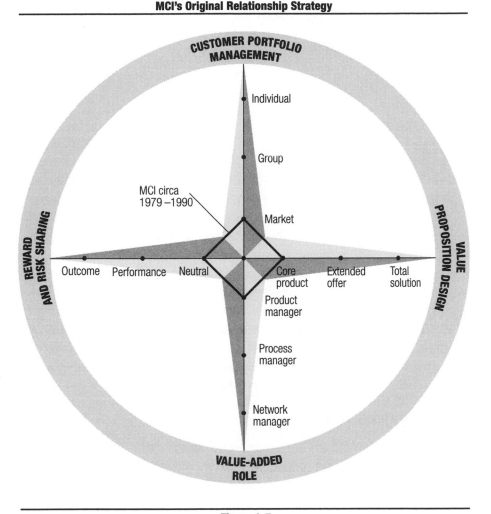

Figure 1-7

vice necessarily involves individual accounts, MCI originally made no significant distinctions among customers beyond the residential and business categories traditionally used in telephone tariffs. In Figure 1-7, the original MCI strategy is illustrated
(using our terms) by the diamond-shaped figure that connects the four points representing the company's position along each of the relationship value dimensions.

Leaving Logan Airport and heading into Boston via the Sumner Tunnel, you used to
pass (usually excruciatingly slowly) a billboard with constantly changing numbers
showing the cumulative long-distance savings realized by MCI customers.
Aggressively marketed, MCI's original single-product value proposition of lower-cost

long-distance service than was available from AT&T has earned it approximately 20 percent of the total long-distance market and a somewhat higher share of the more price-sensitive business sector since its founding less than 30 years ago. However, recent years saw the numbers on the billboard changing more slowly than they once had: Competition has driven down the price of a long-distance call by almost 60 percent in the last 10 years, and competitors, especially AT&T, have driven their cost structures down closer to MCI's. Yet MCI has continued to be a growth company. Although AT&T remains much larger, MCI captured approximately 40 percent of the total growth in telecommunications markets during the 1990s.

How has MCI managed to maintain growth in the face of a nearly 60 percent drop in prices for its core product during a period that saw AT&T, its chief rival, take enormous write-offs? MCI's success is explained in part by the fact that minutes increased by a 23 percent compound annual growth rate and billable calls increased by a 31 percent annual compound rate from 1984 to 1995, offsetting, to some extent, the decrease in prices.[11] Volumes were driven by the growth in fax traffic, data transmission, and Internet and intranet usage (nearly 40 percent of Internet traffic passes over the MCI network). However, an increasingly important reason for MCI's continued growth has been its strategy of building customer relationship value by moving deeper into its customers' value chain and across more of its customers' total communications needs. In line with this new emphasis on value rather than price alone, the billboard has been retired.

Customer Portfolio Management

From its inception, MCI targeted customers according to revenue potential. Because the marginal costs of long-distance calls are very low, revenue served as a reasonable proxy for profitability and customer relationship value. As a result, two-thirds of MCI's revenues come from business customers. MCI's limited product offerings were delivered through a marketing and sales organization organized geographically around the territories of the seven regional Bell operating companies.

By the mid-1980s, MCI began introducing a more finely segmented account management process for its largest business customers. By then, the "commoditization" of long-distance service was under way, and MCI recognized that it needed to deepen its customer relationships. This effort was facilitated, to some extent, by the large customer management expertise acquired with Satellite Business Systems. MCI manages its relationships at three levels. Federal and state governments and corporate national accounts, which are the largest and most complex, require large dedicated teams of as many as 30 to 40 people and are handled on a centralized basis. The midmarket customers (roughly

$10,000 or more per month in calls) are assigned customer account management specialists (CAMS) at the field level. The smaller business customers now are managed by tele-sales and -service.

Managing the transition from a single-product company to an integrated services provider has required a number of changes in the sales and service organization. The type of customer knowledge required has changed. To deal with the growing complexity of MCI's product line and relate it to customers' needs, the company has had to overlay groups of product experts and industry specialists onto the midmarket field sales force. Utilization of the product experts is stimulated not only by setting goals for aggregate sales for the area but also by setting specific product goals.

MCI is unusual in that it uses a "hunter-and-farmer" model in the midmarket to pursue customer acquisition, apart from the customer development and retention function. Account development manager teams (the "hunters") are charged with acquiring new customers and managing the transition for nearly 60 days before turning the relationship over to the CAMS (the "farmers"), who are responsible for increasing the number of products per account and for maintaining the relationship.

Because extended products are sold to people within the customer's organization different from the previous point of contact, the telecoms manager, MCI has had to connect to more parts of the customer organization. This has changed the nature of MCI's sales force and has led to the hiring of more people with relationship management skills, many of them from the computer industry. Compensation, too, has changed from 100 percent revenue-based to a gradual incorporation of profitability, especially at senior levels.

Extending the Value Proposition

In the 1980s, AT&T and MCI had slightly different visions of the shape of telecommunications markets in the 1990s. AT&T saw a future marked by the convergence of communications and computing and prepared to offer an integrated set of solutions. To AT&T, hardware was a major ingredient in this equation, and so it made a number of acquisitions, most notably NCR, to enable it to provide a complete line of communications and computing products. Although the basic premise of convergence may have been sound, it was never clear that customers saw any particular advantage in acquiring both components from the same provider.

MCI also saw the growing confluence of computing and communications as calling for an expanded range of communications products and creating a need for systems integration services, but largely eschewed hardware. Most significantly, MCI acquired a global network architecture and $4 billion in exchange for selling a 20 percent stake to British Telecom. BT and MCI have since created the Concert alliance. Other MCI acquisitions strengthened the firm's capabilities in software and systems integration.

As recently as 1990, more than 90 percent of MCI's revenues were generated by long-distance (both outbound and inbound) service. Softness in the outbound long-distance market in the late 1980s prompted MCI to launch a new series of products that positioned the company as a provider of communications solutions rather than merely low-cost long-distance service. MCI executives realized that the company could no longer grow solely as a low-cost replacement for AT&T.

The first of the new business products, Proof Positive, which was launched in 1993, provided customers with bottom-line confirmation of the value of their relationship with MCI and supported the transition of the customer service consultants to deliverers of product instead of sellers of long-distance services. As a diagnostic tool, Proof Positive enabled salespeople to engage in discussions with customers about what was driving the customers' usage and to uncover opportunities for extended-value services. The billing software necessary to support Proof Positive, analogously to that for Friends and Family (an earlier program), provided MCI with the flexibility to offer customized bills and to create a single, unified view of the customer across all services.

To reduce its reliance on outbound long-distance revenues, MCI expanded its range of communications products aimed at broadening its coverage of business customers' communications needs. To accomplish this, MCI had to develop a deeper understanding of its customers. MCI's own marketing programs often were seen by its customers as evidence of a capability or competency to which they wanted access. According to Marc Schaub, an MCI vice president responsible for business customer relationships, the famous Friends and Family program, originally intended as a short-term promotion, not only endured as an exceptionally successful product but made evident MCI's ability to develop and implement information-based products. Moreover, it was easier to develop new products once the billing system necessary to support Friends and Family was devised.

Aggressive efforts were made to increase inbound long-distance revenues, exemplified by the innovative "1-800-FLOWERS" system, which enabled Flowers Direct to coordinate the services of a nationwide network of florists with

MCI's Customer Communications Needs

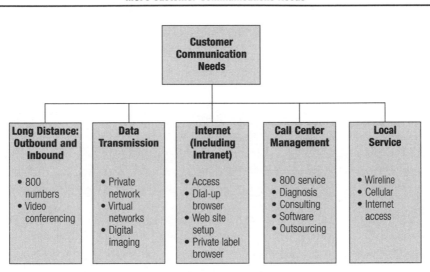

Figure 1-8

the look and feel of dealing with local merchants. Growth of the inbound long-distance market was facilitated by the Federal Communications Commission's approval of 800-number portability, which allowed MCI to convert customers' services in a way that avoided the customer's having to incur expensive switching costs or to publicize a new number.

The evolution of MCI's extended-value services generally has moved first horizontally across the customers' communications needs and then vertically or deeper into the customers' value chain. As shown in Figure 1-8, almost all of MCI's products begin with a network access product and comprise a set of extended-value services, including, in some cases, outsourcing.

Role in the Value-Added Chain

MCI has moved beyond providing a core product—long distance links—to operating communications systems for customers. MCI's outsourcing business is a case in point. Approximately 80 percent of 800 numbers terminate in a call center. MCI's efforts to sell inbound long-distance made the firm aware of the rapid growth of call centers, and its own experience running one of the United States' largest call centers provided a valuable competency much sought after by customers. MCI now offers a comprehensive suite of call-center services, including diagnosing the customers' needs, advising about system configuration and, in some cases, managing the call-center process. Similarly, for Internet services, MCI not only will hook you up but also will provide you with a dial-up browser, help you set up a Web site, host your Web site, and even build and maintain a private label browser for you.

Addressing its customers' full range of communications needs increases the value of MCI's customer relationships in three ways. First, MCI captures the minutes generated by the product. Second, the product itself produces fee revenues. Finally, the greater the number of products purchased by a customer, the lower is the probability that that customer will defect from MCI.

During the late 1980s, MCI and its rivals engaged in a continual price war that led to the 60 percent price drop mentioned earlier and resulted in significant levels of customer churn and turnover. In some cases, companies would experience turnover rates approaching 50 percent. By extending its products across all of a customer's communication needs, MCI has dramatically reduced customer turnover. Customers who purchase three or more services from MCI are very unlikely to defect.

By the year 2000, MCI plans to generate 30 to 50 percent of its revenues and profits from non–minute-based products. Ultimately, MCI sees itself managing the customer relationship all the way to the desktop. This requires taking a more customer-based approach to the market. The way that MCI structures its reward- and risk- sharing arrangements with customers is discussed next.

Reward and Risk Sharing

MCI's initial pricing strategy was simple: a little lower than AT&T. AT&T was inhibited from meeting or beating MCI's prices for a number of reasons. Regulatory constraints on its tariffs, intended to ensure that AT&T's small retail and residential customers did not subsidize larger customers, were a factor. AT&T's sheer size and inability to target prices precisely also worked against it. In confronting MCI price reductions, AT&T had to weigh the loss of margin across a large part of its revenue base against losing a fraction of those customers entirely. AT&T counterattacked as best it could by emphasizing its long history of service and suggesting that its rivals inflated their savings projections.

Proof Positive was introduced in part to respond to AT&T's charges of inflated benefits and that firm's "Get It in Writing" campaign. The unintended consequence of AT&T's challenge was that MCI did put it in writing and, in doing so, developed the customer billing capability that would later support extended and integrated communications products.

Proof Positive demonstrated the power of explicitly reinforcing the benefits of the relationship with customers and also made more visible the cost of switching to other providers. This is a double-edged sword: While it strengthens the relationship by confirming the benefit, it also provides even lower-cost providers such as resellers with a target price and savings figure and perpetuates price-driven competition.

The MCI Fund is an ingenious solution to the problem of sharing the rewards of the relationship with customers while reducing the incentive to shop. The MCI Fund allows a customer to "time-shift" forward a portion of the anticipated savings from the relationship. In return for certain customer commitments related to the volume and duration of the relationship, MCI places a portion of the projected savings into a third-party–administered fund that the customer can use to purchase ancillary equipment such as personal computers and switches. Customers, particularly those with tight capital budgets, appreciate the ability immediately to capitalize and use their savings. MCI, of course, is financially indifferent as to whether a front-loaded or pay-as-you-go discount is in force, as long as the net present values remain comparable, but the company is much better off as a result of the stronger customer relationship.

The Future

As of this writing (in mid-1996), MCI has, in selected markets, greatly expanded the boundaries of its relationship strategy. Large national accounts and many midmarket accounts are managed at the individual level. The range of MCI's value proposition has stretched from a single core product to the capacity to address total, integrated solutions. MCI's role has expanded in some areas to include managing key processes such as call centers for customers. Pricing no longer is based solely on minutes and, through programs such as the MCI Fund, customers can share in the rewards of the relationship in a number of ways. This expanded relationship model is illustrated in Figure 1-9.

MCI envisions a future in which one hand-held unit with a single address will connect with voice and data networks over wireline, wireless, or fiberoptic systems, and all services will be charged on a single, customer-designed bill. The greatest future opportunities to increase customer relationship value lie in integrating local and long-distance service and offering even more value-added products tailored

The Expansion of MCI's Customer Relationships

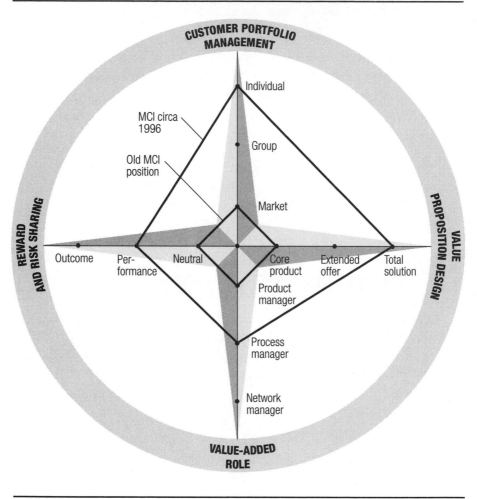

Figure 1-9

to individual customer needs. In the meantime, MCI is positioning itself to consolidate all of a business's communications services on a single, customized bill that will provide huge administrative and economic advantages to customers.

The local services market is approximately $94 billion, as compared to nearly $75 billion for long distance. Hence, the local market is about 26 percent larger. By 2002, the local market is projected to reach at least $128 billion. To prepare for this future, MCI is moving quickly toward building local networks and integrating them with its long-distance network. MCI already offers local services in 12 markets and plans to be in 24 by the end of 1996 and 50 by 1997.

MCI's organization, built and tested over 10 years, has a formidable competitive advantage over the regional Bell operating companies, which, like AT&T in the 1980s, are not accustomed to fighting for customers. "Detariffing," expected to be enacted by 1998, also will permit greater pricing flexibility and will enable MCI to offer customer-specific pricing based on the value of the relationship.

This chapter has introduced the notion of the customer relationship as a mutual value-creating process; outlined a framework for thinking about the dimensions of relationship value; discussed the foundations of knowledge, technology, and economics that determine movement along those dimensions; and illustrated the application of the framework in understanding the evolution of MCI's business strategy. With this general perspective in place, we turn, in the next three chapters, to a more detailed exploration of the foundations.

All ye need to know

CUSTOMER KNOWLEDGE MANAGEMENT

If they truly want to get to know their customers, executives need to do more than gather and analyze quantitative information, as most are accustomed to doing. Many companies go to great lengths to accumulate information about their customers, but what do they really know about their customers, and how effectively are they managing that knowledge? Unfortunately, accumulating information is only a first step in creating the knowledge that these companies need to pursue a customer-connected strategy successfully. Information is the raw material that is transformed into knowledge through its organization, analysis, and understanding. This knowledge must then be applied and managed in ways that best support investment decisions and resource deployment.

We define *customer knowledge management* as the effective leverage of information *and* experience in the acquisition, development, and retention of a profitable customer portfolio. The words *customer*, *knowledge*, and *management* are highly interdependent. To attain full value, all three elements must come together in a closed-loop environment—one that focuses on acquiring the right knowledge of the right customer and that puts that knowledge into action in ways that maximize the value of the customer relationship.

In this chapter, we discuss how companies can execute an effective closed-loop process by using knowledge effectively in planning strategy; focusing their

Customer Knowledge Management: A Closed-Loop Process

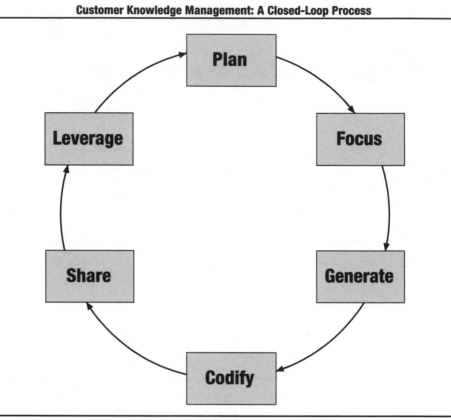

Figure 2-1

effort on the right customers and depth of knowledge; using the most appropriate approach to generating knowledge; and, finally, understanding how to codify, share, and leverage that knowledge (Figure 2-1).

Trying to manage customer relationships without an adequate knowledge base limits the amount of value that you can deliver to the customer. Possessing superior customer knowledge without putting in place the means for codifying and leveraging it across your organization will result in missed opportunities. Investing in knowledge infrastructure and processes but not incorporating them effectively into the customer-relationship management process is a waste of resources.

The simple acquisition of knowledge serves little purpose if that knowledge is not used productively, and productive use requires closing the loop by putting insight into action. Unfortunately, the closed-loop process is difficult to orchestrate in highly functionalized enterprises. Too often the knowledge manage-

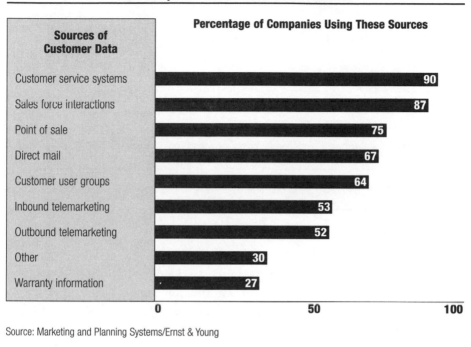

How Companies Gather Data About Customers

Sources of Customer Data	Percentage of Companies Using These Sources
Customer service systems	90
Sales force interactions	87
Point of sale	75
Direct mail	67
Customer user groups	64
Inbound telemarketing	53
Outbound telemarketing	52
Other	30
Warranty information	27

Source: Marketing and Planning Systems/Ernst & Young

Figure 2-2

ment process is fragmented. Learning about customers and knowing what they want and need is the responsibility of the market research department. Creating what they want and need is a job assigned to R&D and product management. Attracting customers is the province of the marketing department, and making the transaction falls to the sales organization. Keeping customers happy is the job of customer service personnel.

Because there are so many points of functional connection—and, therefore, points of potential failure—it is not surprising that our survey revealed that executives are less concerned with capturing customer input and feedback than they are with ways to manage the process and to make use of the knowledge they obtain. The survey research revealed that many companies collect information on customers at multiple points, as shown in Figure 2-2.

Getting information isn't usually the problem. When asked to rank their priorities for improvement, companies emphasized internal factors—namely, getting information to the right people and using that information, as shown in Figure 2-3.

Priorities for Customer Information Management

	Percentage Rated Critical by Respondents
Internal flow of customer information across the organization	61
Internal processes to leverage customer information	51
Capture of more customer feedback in the market	44
Improvement or development of models for customer acquisition and retention	42

Source: Marketing and Planning Systems/Ernst & Young

Figure 2-3

Another precondition for managing in a closed loop is to provide the appropriate access to all of your customer information and a system and set of processes for collating such information. As evidenced by our research (Figure 2-4), many Fortune 1000 companies still struggle with this. The great majority either have only a partial understanding of their customers or lack a unified system for bringing together customer knowledge from multiple sources.

It may not be necessary or even appropriate for all companies to build an integrated, single profile of their customers. However, executives in companies whose interests would clearly be served by an integrated system indicate that creating such a system poses a major challenge. The encouraging news is that the information technology vendor community and professional service firms recognize the pent-up demand for these systems and are responding with customer asset management software and systems that link the various domains of customer information: call centers, sales systems, service databases, and Web site information. This integration yields major benefits to both the company and its customers by allowing the entire set of interactions to be viewed and knowledgeable decisions to be made in the context of the total relationship.

FROM INFORMATION *to* KNOWLEDGE

The terms *information* and *knowledge* generally are used loosely and, often, interchangeably. "We know our customers and our markets," executives often

Most Fortune 1000 Companies Lack a Unified Customer Knowledge System

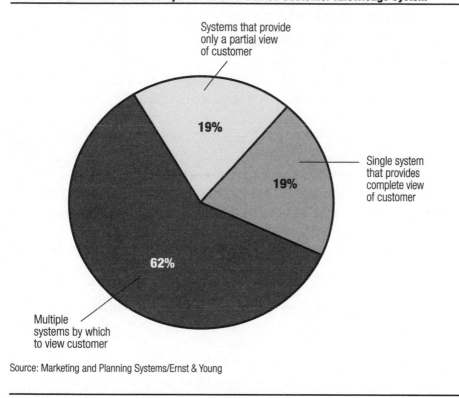

Systems that provide
only a partial view
of customer

19%

Single system
that provides
complete view
of customer

19%

62%

Multiple
systems by which
to view customer

Source: Marketing and Planning Systems/Ernst & Young

Figure 2-4

say. "We have plenty of information." However, information is only the raw material of knowledge. Possession of information tells us very little. Like pieces of a jigsaw puzzle, pieces of information become knowledge only when they are brought together in meaningful ways. Whereas information is discrete and perfectly transferable, knowledge is partly tacit and highly contextual and, therefore, only partially transferable, as described by Nonaka and Takeuchi:

> Explicit knowledge can be expressed in words and numbers, and easily communicated and shared in the form of hard data, scientific formulae, codified procedures or universal principles....Tacit knowledge is highly personal and hard to formalize, making it difficult to communicate or share with others....In our theory of organizational knowledge creation, we adopt the traditional definition of knowledge as "justified true belief."...While traditional epistemology emphasizes the absolute, static and nonhuman nature of knowledge, typically expressed in propositions

and formal logic, we consider knowledge as a *dynamic human process of justifying personal belief toward the truth* [emphasis in original].[1]

Effective customer knowledge management puts to work both the surface-level, explicit knowledge resulting from direct exchanges with customers, and the deeply embedded knowledge of the customer that resides tacitly in the heads of a company's customer-serving personnel and the customers themselves. Henry Mintzberg has observed that this informal knowledge based on conversation and interaction among managers and with customers and suppliers is a firm's most important knowledge.[2]

The idea that information about customers and markets must be integrated and imbued with insight before it has value should be fairly obvious. Still, businesses fail to accomplish this more often than we'd care to recount—and it costs them dearly. Consider most automobile manufacturers and their network of dealers. Both have substantial information in their databases about individual customers and their service experience, but most are unable to use that information either to identify potential "at-risk" customers or to provide customers with compelling reasons for remaining loyal to a particular brand. The question is: Are the manufacturers and dealers using their judgment to apply that information to benefit their customer relationships?

Many companies are very good at managing information, which is an essential first step toward the creation of knowledge. However, information management involves structure, standards, storage, and processing, whereas knowledge management involves human intervention and judgment. Knowledge management is concerned with context, socialization, interpretation, and action. The GE Answer Center illustrates a closed-loop knowledge management system that captures information, creates knowledge, and shares and leverages that knowledge across a number of functions including design, marketing, and field operations.

GE Answer Center
Closing the Loop

In 1981, General Electric's Appliance Division did what was then an unusual thing: It gave its phone number to customers.[3] As Merrill Grant, now manager of the GE Answer Center, recalls, "The original idea was to personalize GE to the consumer and to personalize the consumer to GE." As one of the first 800-number call centers in the United States, GE had few data for gauging its customers' desire to talk directly to the company rather than to the dealer from whom they had purchased an appliance. GE also didn't know what customers would want to talk about or how to measure the value of the service center. Some wondered whether many customers would call and, if they did, whether direct access would justify the cost—but call they did. Thousands of customers took advantage of the free call to air their grievances, to ask questions and, in a few cases, to praise the company or its products. Pent-up demand to reach out and touch someone at GE was so great that almost 50 percent of the early calls were for units of GE other than the appliance division.

The original Answer Center has evolved into a network of five call centers. Located in Louisville, Kentucky, the Answer Center handles several million calls per year and provides callers with general information on the use and care of appliances, diagnoses their problems, offers technical assistance, and fields prepurchase calls. Three regional local centers, located in Norfolk, Virginia, Memphis, Tennessee, and Phoenix, Arizona, schedule service calls, manage service contracts, and act as customer relations posts. The fifth call center, the Forum Center, is dedicated to retailers and builders, who account for 20 percent of appliance sales, and focuses on managing these large-account relationships.

The Answer Center, originally designed as a "back-end" or reactive tool, has developed over a decade and a half into an important relationship management capability. GE discovered that opening another communications channel to its customers not only helped the company resolve problems more quickly and efficiently but also created a flow of valuable data and information that could be converted into customer knowledge. This knowledge has enabled GE to increase the value of its customer relationships by strengthening brand loyalty, focusing product development on key areas of customer satisfaction, and identifying new sales opportunities. This expanded role in increasing the value of customer relationships is captured in the Answer Center's current mission: The Answer Center is "dedicated to achieving the highest level of consumer satisfaction, gaining incremental revenue and market share, increasing long-term brand loyalty and reducing in-warranty costs." To achieve these goals, the center has evolved from a single customer connection point into the gateway of an integrated customer knowledge and customer management process.

The competitive value of the Answer Center and the knowledge process it drives reflect the nature of the U.S. appliance market. Although very large, encompassing $14 billion in annual sales, the U.S. appliance market grows relatively slowly, at only 1 to 3 percent per year. Most major appliances have achieved or are nearing market saturation; consequently, 75 percent of sales are in the replacement market, and the remaining 25 percent are driven by housing starts. Long product lives, ranging from 10 years for a microwave oven to 18 years for a gas range, make it difficult to stay connected with customers. Given such long product lives and the comparability of products, the average same-brand repurchase rate, not surprisingly, is only 30 percent.

Increasing the value of a GE appliance customer depends largely on increasing the proportion of GE brand products in the typical customer's inventory of six to eight major appliances. This calls for building the repurchase rate of currently held GE products and increasing the cross-sell rate across all major appliances offered. Because most purchases are made to replace appliances, a practice that can be predicted fairly easily from life expectancy data and that is heavily influenced by satisfaction, building customer relationship value depends critically on knowing the customer's current appliance inventory, level of satisfaction, and repurchase intentions. With such knowledge, GE can develop interventions to increase the likelihood of purchase or repurchase. Knowing that a customer has a 13-year-old refrigerator enables the company to target a promotion to that customer and thereby to increase the likelihood of a GE purchase, for example.

The connection begins with a call from a consumer, retailer, or builder to the Answer Center. This call can cover any type of customer issue. Approximately 80 percent of the 3.1 million calls annually pertain to GE appliances; of these, nearly 80 percent originate with consumers and 20 percent originate with retailers or builders. As expected, most calls are postpurchase inquiries about service problems or questions about use and care, but a significant number of calls are prepurchase calls made by people seeking information.

During the relatively brief customer encounter on the phone (call length averages less than 4 minutes), representatives have an opportunity to increase customer relationship value in three ways: by responding effectively to the customer's inquiry, by increasing the amount of customer-specific information relating to future purchases, and by developing information to improve future products and services. By solving a customer's problem, the representative can change immediately that customer's state of satisfaction or repurchase rate. By learning more about the customer's current appliance inventory and needs, GE can better target future promotional efforts and raise awareness or consideration of its products. By accumulating customer reactions, the company can design and deliver future products that result in fewer problems, greater satisfaction, and more repurchases. Thus, the representative is operating at three levels of the relationship process, involving three levels of organizational knowledge building.

At the immediate problem-solving level, the representative relies largely on existing knowledge to diagnose and remedy the problem or provide the requested information. In performing this function, the representative uses both explicit and tacit information. Explicit knowledge in this case consists of specific data about appliances that are used to diagnose the customer's problem and to suggest a course of action. Tacit knowledge can be illustrated by the representative's ability to relate his experience base to the customer's current problem. Consider, for example, a customer who is experiencing a problem with a specific oven model but who has difficulty pinpointing the exact nature of the problem. An experienced company representative can rely on his accumulated knowledge of and experience with similar service encounters to assist the customer in ascertaining what type of repair needs to be done and whether it would be more cost-effective to buy a new model instead.

At the next level, increasing the longer-term value of the relationship, the representative is acting as the point person for an interdepartmental process. By soliciting additional information about the customer's appliance stock and repurchase intentions, the representative may increase customer awareness or consideration directly or might provide the marketing and sales department with an opportunity to do so. Other people interacting with customers, such as field technicians, have a similar opportunity.

At the third level, the interface role involves even greater interdepartmental coordination and leverage. GE's IMPACT (Important Actionable Consumer Thought) System captures and organizes customer problems or comments by category (e.g., design) and by specific model. This enables GE to spot emerging problems for immediate action and to address issues in future designs and to entertain options. Capturing this information electronically enables people throughout the organization to share it and participate in the learning experience. In addition, representatives are assigned to product categories and are asked to speak for the consumer (on the basis of the knowledge they have accumulated) in marketing and product engineering roundtable discussions.

This multifaceted customer connection is possible because GE maintains a staggeringly large database containing more than 35 million names that covers roughly one-third of all U.S. households. This database is fed by information from all of GE's customer connection points, including phone centers, the sales force, field repair personnel and technicians, dealers, and market researchers. Each of these groups not only provides data to the database but can access it for information to support marketing programs, new product development, sales lead qualification, and the like.

Complementing the customer records database is a *solutions database*, which captures expert knowledge from throughout the firm and helps representatives diagnose and solve most problems (first-pass success of more than 75 percent) while the customer is on the phone. Problems that cannot be solved by customer representatives are referred to product specialists who, after meeting the customer's need, add the solution to the database for future reference.

In recent years, by closing the loop with product design, GE has taken the system well beyond a mere means for providing quick problem resolution. As Mark Larson, manager of engineering support, points out,

> Good designers use the Answer Center every step of the process. They listen to calls several times a year, have representatives comment on the design from the level of concept through the level of prototype, and benefit from the knowledge stored in the database and in the representatives' heads.

How well has GE's Answer Center contributed to increased customer relationship value? Although all the direct and indirect effects are difficult to quantify, GE has documented several key payoffs. First, resolving immediate problems results in a probability-of-repurchase rate of 80 percent for the previously dissatisfied customer, as compared to 10 percent for the dissatisfied but uncomplaining customer and 27 percent for an average customer. In other words, by making it easier to reach the company and by responding effectively, GE gets more opportunities to convert dissatisfied customers and to strengthen relationships. Second, contact with the center significantly increases customers' awareness of the GE appliance line and their consideration level. Finally, the knowledge that is generated through customer interactions provides valuable input to the sales, marketing, and new product development processes.

As the GE case illustrates, corporations can gain tremendous "lift and loyalty" by learning to manage actively the process of knowing the customer. Back in the days when proprietors and customers knew one another by name, this was not a major problem, but the scale of modern business has made acquiring this knowledge more difficult. Today, the proprietor is often a multinational organization, and the job of knowing the customer is parsed out to employees in many functional units. A closed-loop knowledge system can help to create a unified view of the customer and to provide the customer with easy access to the company's knowledge.

In the next several sections, we discuss the types of knowledge that can be applied across the loop, moving in turn through planning, focusing, generating, and leveraging.

PLANNING: BUILDING YOUR STOCK *of* KNOWLEDGE

As we think about how we can apply our knowledge effectively to the customer relationship, it is useful to look at the relationship between knowledge and planning. As such, it is important both to identify what we already know about our markets and customers that can be used to support day-to-day planning and operations, and to build *speculative* knowledge to support longer-range planning.

What We Already Know

Francis Bacon told us centuries ago that knowledge is power,[4] but it is clear from our experience that many companies never draw on the power of the knowledge they already have. In our view, if companies only knew what they already know, could know it faster, and could share it more effectively, they could accelerate their rate of growth.

Knowing what you know is a helpful first step in speculating about how things might change, regardless of the pace of change and the degree of uncertainty within your markets. For example, in working on a client-server marketing strategy for a global information technology firm, we thought it would be a good idea to begin with an understanding of the state of the market. However, we ran into numerous roadblocks in trying to determine who knew what about the market and where supporting data and information could be found. The process of identifying useful sources consumed several weeks but eventually yielded some 90 reports related to the topic. Plenty of information about the market and customers existed, but it was not being interpreted effectively or acted on in ways that would help grow the business.

Having observed this same condition in numerous enterprises, we have come to appreciate the benefits of creating a "knowledge book." Although Bacon took all knowledge as his province and sought to organize it in his work, *Novum Organum*, our more modest goal is to create a single source catalog of what already is known about customers within the organization. A valuable by-product of assembling a knowledge book is the dialogue that ensues after everyone in the organization has been given access to the same set of facts. Once everyone has digested and agreed to these facts, a more robust and productive discussion tends to occur around how to take advantage of what is known. In the client-server example, this process helped to forge internal consensus on which customer segments to target and the investment strategy for building solutions to attract and satisfy these customers.

Although organizing a firm's customer knowledge might appear to be the natural province of market research or planning departments, it is critically important that this exercise actively involve those responsible for setting strategy within any given P&L unit. Moreover, updating the knowledge book on a periodic basis enables a firm to monitor and quickly respond to changes in market and customer circumstances. With today's technology, electronic knowledge books can be "pushed" to the desktop, making market and customer knowledge accessible throughout an organization, thereby promoting dialogue.

As Yogi Berra put it, "Prediction is very hard, especially when it is about the future." Lacking a crystal ball, how do we develop market knowledge that helps us anticipate and respond rapidly to changing conditions? Can we foresee, or at least more accurately sense, the market discontinuities that will influence materially our connection to our customers? How do we create a depth of market and customer understanding that will enable us to lead rather than merely to respond to change?

After a firm has achieved a clear understanding of what the organization already knows, its next step is to develop what we call *speculative knowledge*. Speculative knowledge combines an understanding of existing facts—current market conditions, customer requirements, competitive threats—with one's beliefs about the future of the business, in an effort to recognize patterns that suggest opportunities for creating and delivering new value.

Plenty of techniques for developing speculative knowledge are in widespread use, including scenario planning, Delphi research, development of analogs (e.g., the telecommunications market as analog for the ways in which deregulation could affect the electric utility business), and old-fashioned brainstorming. However, organizations no longer have the luxury of spending months performing situation analyses, environmental scanning, and scenario development as a prelude to decision making. Many growth-oriented managers are increasingly impatient with the time their internal staff and outside consultants take to formulate key strategic moves.

One response to this pressure for speedier strategy development was devised by Ernst and Young's management consulting organization and is a good example of new approaches to creating and applying speculative knowledge. The Accelerated Solutions Environment (ASE) combines a special work space with a process within which teams can deliver more rapid decisions. During an ASE, large groups of managers (up to 100) come together for several days of intensive sessions to move from brainstorming to action plans. The process is accelerated by a physical space conducive to creating thinking (configurable furniture, brainstorming tools, etc.), access to specialized staff (e.g., spreadsheet builders who can run scenarios, artists who can create visual expressions of ideas), and the availability of electronic knowledge bases containing business, process, and financial models. Facilitators move the group through a three-step, outside-in approach: scan, focus, act. Interestingly, the Accelerated Solutions Environment is increasingly being used to bring together members of an entire industry value web, including suppliers, intermediaries, and customers. Bringing together both the supply and demand sides of a market allows for a more comprehensive perspective on strategic possibilities and a degree of collaboration that can identify entirely new value creation opportunities.

FOCUSING: GENERATING KNOWLEDGE *at the* RIGHT LEVEL *and* DEPTH

Everyone agrees that customer knowledge is important, but *whom* do you need to know and *how much* must you know? If you design jet aircraft, a high-involvement product, you probably need to know precisely your individual customer's requirements. If bottled water is your product, it's important that you know the customers at the aggregate or market level rather than at an individual level. We call this establishing the correct knowledge *focus*. The first step is identifying the *level* at which you must generate knowledge. The second step is deciding the *depth* of knowledge you need.

When people pontificate about the need to know the customer, they often forget that customer knowledge has a price. The secret is to invest in knowledge acquisition only to the point at which the benefits of customer knowledge are equal to or greater than the cost of creating and managing such knowledge. The value compass presented in the previous chapter showed that in connecting to the "right" customers, we need also to consider the level at which we make this connection, from the most aggregated, or market, level down to the most granular, or individual customer, level. Figure 2-5 identifies the levels of knowledge aggregation, moving down from the total market to the individual.

The first step toward effective knowledge management must be determining which level of knowledge aggregation is most appropriate and most cost-effective for your business. Five factors help to determine the level at which you should know your customers.

Levels of Knowledge Aggregation

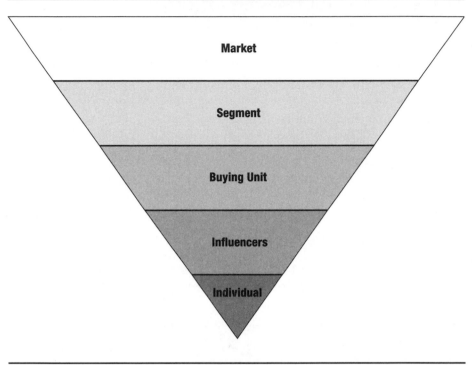

Figure 2-5

- *Level of customer involvement*: Does your offering play an important role in the customer's life?

- *Need for support or information:* Is there the need or opportunity for substantial interaction and information exchange with the customer across the product life cycle (presale, usage, service/support)?

- *Distance from the customer:* Does an existing customer connection provide a cost-effective opportunity to build a knowledge base?

- *Scope of opportunity:* Is there an opportunity to expand the value of the customer connection through a broader value proposition?

- *Economics:* Will the margin or contribution associated with the goods and services support the cost of building a customer knowledge base?

If your answers to these questions are mostly yes, then the individual customer may be the appropriate level at which to build knowledge. To illustrate how the level of knowledge building and management varies with respect to market and customer-related factors, we'll describe three companies operating across the spectrum: Pioneer Hi-Bred at the individual level, Staples at the group level, and Tyson Foods at the market level.

Pioneer Hi-Bred
Harvesting Customer Knowledge

Few people would expect a seed company to be at the forefront of customer knowledge management or to develop customer knowledge below the most aggregated, market level. However, Pioneer Hi-Bred, which provides seed to a half million corn farmers, has developed a systematic approach to capturing and managing its customer knowledge both at the individual level, where it is applied at the interface between sales rep and farmer, and at the segment and market level, where it supports broader management decision making.[5]

Pioneer believes that it can capture a premium price for its hybrid seed only if it understands and manages customer relationships at the individual level. Jerry Armstrong, director of the North American sales operation, points out that Pioneer runs a very "localized" business and that the agricultural business still is very much driven by person-to-person connections. Accordingly, Pioneer puts a tremendous amount of effort and expense into building individual customer profiles.

Helping in that effort is the company's customer and prospect system (CAPS) database, which captures and records all transactional information and allows Pioneer sales reps and managers to keep a collective finger on the pulse of the overall market. Information captured by CAPS is aggregated and analyzed in terms of the requirements of each managerial level. Interestingly, contextual and tacit knowledge about the farmer's business objectives, challenges, and relationship requirements is maintained and updated at the point of customer connection—that is, between the local sales rep and his customer. However, as each layer of management becomes further removed from the customer, the knowledge requirements shift and higher levels of aggregation are more appropriate. Whereas the sales rep can put to good use knowledge about a particular farmer's crop plan, corporate executives need aggregate data only by region to plan seed production and distribution.

Pioneer's definition of "whom we need to know" is evolving with its changing business. Not satisfied with current knowledge of its farmer customers, it is seeking to understand better the third-party "influencers" of those customers—

independent farm managers, crop consultants, and so forth—individuals who are playing an increasing role in the farm management process. We will illustrate how Pioneer has gained competitive advantage from its customer knowledge when we return to its case in Chapter 6.

Not all companies need to know customers as intimately as does Pioneer. Does the corn flakes producer truly need to "connect" to customers at the individual level? Should it attempt to build a relationship with each customer, become a bigger part of the total breakfast experience, and bundle its corn flakes into a broader breakfast solution, or should it focus on maximizing the value and appeal of its core product? In certain markets, the customer either does not want a relationship or the economics of the situation are unfavorable for a segment-of-one approach. In these cases, investing in knowing the customer by name should take a back seat to building customer knowledge at a higher level of aggregation. Having knowledge is only half of the equation. Being able to act on that knowledge cost-efficiently and in a way that provides a direct return is the other half.

Staples
Going Direct to Small Business

Staples, the originator of the office products superstore, is a company that does a superior job of gathering the information and creating the knowledge needed to execute strategy based on the different values of its customer relationships.[6] Founder Thomas Stemberg, a former grocery store executive, brought the superstore model to retailing office supplies, office electronics, and office furniture. Initially, the retail target segment was the small business, but Staples gradually refined that target to include businesses with 10 or fewer employees and the growing ranks of self-employed home office workers.

Stemberg's innovation succeeded. From the opening of its first outlet in 1986, Staples Retail expanded to 443 stores and $3.1 billion in revenue by 1995. Yet another very large segment—small- to medium-sized enterprises of 5 to 50 employees—had not been tapped. Every week, these businesses consume reams of paper, copier toner and printer cartridges, pens, pencils, and, of course, staples. Such businesses are too small to maintain central purchasing departments, and they cannot spare the time for employees to shop for materials every week. Hence, Staples offered them a simple solution in Staples Direct.

Staples Direct was launched in 1991 as a way to penetrate further the small-business customer base and to provide an efficient channel for consumables. Now the fastest-growing division within the Staples portfolio (55 percent growth in 1995), this business produces annual revenues of $350 million by knowing better than others the requirements of the segment it serves. Jim Forbush, senior vice president of marketing for Staples Direct, explains that although the company's private-label credit card and call center make it possible to know the customer at the individual level, at this point managing the customers one at a time is not economical. Instead, Staples Direct builds knowledge to support the planning and operations of the business at the segment level. As Forbush explains, "Our average account is $2,000 to $3,000 per year, with 30 percent gross margins and 15 percent variable costs. That leaves us with $300 per year per account. You don't personalize service for that."[6]

To operate this business effectively, Staples Direct managers need to know how to acquire, develop, and retain the types of customers that populate each segment. As detailed in Chapter 5, the managers apply customer economics at the segment level to determine their investment thresholds for each type of customer. Using this analysis, they determined that the 5- to 50-employee-firm segment should be sold and serviced differently from others. This segment responds most favorably to a personalized sales approach, supported by a direct-marketing (800-number) fulfillment center.

Forbush and his team understood this segment's economic drivers. They realized that the higher cost of acquiring these customers through an expensive direct-sales force would reduce profits during the first 2 years. However, over time, these customers increase in value as they tend to demonstrate above-average loyalty. By knowing the behavior patterns of these customers, overall and over time, Staples Direct was able to align its business model with its customer requirements, delivering high levels of both customer satisfaction and profitability.

At the other end of the spectrum we find Staples National, a separate division established to serve corporate procurement departments that order office supplies in every quantity from the case to the truckload. With average account revenues in excess of $1 million, Staples National can afford both to know and to manage the customer at the individual level. Hence, for each of its divisions, Staples' relationship structures are aligned with different levels of customers according to what the company needs to know to grow profitably and to manage the business and customer relationships.

Tyson Foods
Parts Is Parts

There is a good chance that chicken will be part of your dinner tonight. A combination of health concerns, changing tastes, and attractive value explains the growing popularity of chicken. In the United States, consumption of chicken has increased nearly 175 percent over the past 35 years, as compared to single-digit increases for beef and pork.

Tyson Foods, the world's largest fully integrated producer, processor, and marketer of poultry-based food products, has been a beneficiary of this trend.[7] Over the past decade, Tyson has enjoyed a compound annual growth rate of 17 percent. In 1995, it racked up $5.5 billion in revenue on sales of more than 4 billion pounds of chicken.

Operationally, Tyson focuses on maintaining a low-cost position in every major product line while developing a customer-responsive (which, in this case, is equivalent to a retailer-responsive) organization. The company invests substantial resources for marketing initiatives aimed at strengthening its brand names and relationships with distributors and supermarkets. Nonetheless, as stated in the company's corporate fact book, "Tyson's focus is on the ultimate consumer. Tyson sells *through* its distribution channels."

What is the knowledge focus here? The individual consumer? The supermarket retailer? The bulk food distributor? It is none of these; rather, Tyson builds customer knowledge at the total market level.

Fresh retail chicken is a net-weight business operating under a single universal product code (UPC). Product managers are unable to analyze sales based on price, weight, or parts description. The company claims that it knows its consumers extraordinarily well, though not by name. The typical Tyson consumer is a middle-class, 22- to 55-year-old woman with children who is responsible for preparing her family's meals. She also is likely to live in a rural area, be family-oriented, and be active in the community.

Tyson management estimates that a major percentage of the company's retail chicken sales is made to those who fit this profile. The company invests heavily in market research in an attempt to anticipate and track the changing tastes and needs of such consumers. Tyson product and marketing managers certainly would like to have more individualized information and customer knowledge, but they recognize the negative cost-benefit ratio of creating this information base. Bob Howard, Tyson's director of retail marketing, summed up the dilemma when he said, "[W]e have a limited number of marketing dollars, and micromarketing has a high fixed cost relative to return."[7]

Obviously, Tyson's current focus on knowing market requirements at large is working. However, any attempt by Tyson to expand the range of value it provides or to increase its role in the consumer's value chain might require a shift in the level at which it develops consumer knowledge—to the segment level and perhaps even the individual level. At this time, this shift cannot be supported either economically or technologically.

Tyson's traditional mass-market approach does not imply an "all customers are equal" mentality. Indeed, Tyson has a clear profile of its highest-value consumer, and its marketing efforts are geared toward making Tyson products attractive to these customers. Its customer-knowledge management effort focuses on identifying what it takes to differentiate its product and on creating a differentiated position through its Tyson and Holly Farms brands. "Tyson—we're chicken" is a message delivered to the target audience via national and regional television and radio spots and through a multimedia in-store program.

GENERATING *the* RIGHT KIND *of* KNOWLEDGE

Once you have determined of *whom* you need knowledge, the next logical step is determining *what* you need to know. Customer-knowledge management activities should focus primarily on knowing what the customer wants. The details of how this should be accomplished are beyond the scope of this chapter; the task is complicated by the fact that people often don't know or have difficulty articulating what it is that they want. Nonetheless, there are three domains of knowledge about what customers want, and each is selected on the basis of the psychology associated with the offer (from highly rational to highly emotional) and its degree of visibility. The three domains are as follows:

- *Conversational knowledge:* understanding what customers want via *dialogue* (formal and informal) and interactions between customers and employees, employees and suppliers, and so forth.

- *Observational knowledge:* knowledge acquired through *observing* how customers use products and services.

- *Predictive knowledge:* knowledge based on *analytic* models designed to predict likely outcomes.

Conversational Knowledge

A conversation is one of the simplest, yet most misunderstood, sources for generating customer knowledge. Dialogue between two parties means that information exchange has occurred—but has a proper understanding been reached? Too often, we accept and act on surface-level responses to our inquiries without attempting to "reveal" the true meaning of the signal being sent.

Conversational knowledge, whether in the form of casual interactions or more systematic market research, offers the opportunity to develop deep knowledge of customer requirements, perceptions, and motives. Some new techniques, such as Gerald Zaltman's metaphor lab, seek to probe more deeply into customers' meaning by asking the customers to tell stories, draw pictures, or clip magazine pictures to express their feelings about a company or product.[8] Although we will not attempt here to describe all the research methods for acquiring deep knowledge, we present the following case to illustrate how generating deep knowledge of the customer can engender innovation and produce stronger customer relationships.

American Skiing Company
Having a Deep Conversation

For American Skiing Company (ASC), operator of Sunday River ski resort in Bethel, Maine, and of seven other New England ski facilities, knowing its customers—knowing what they really value—led to the development of a winning product, "signature snow," and enviable profits in an industry in which profits are elusive.[9] Ski resorts use many devices to attract and please their customers, among them modern lifts, snow depth, child-care facilities, aprés-ski activities, and special pricing packages. Resort managers can easily spend lots of money on any or all of these amenities, but there is only so much money to go around. Therefore, ASC President and CEO Leslie B. Otten and his management team decided to find out what *really* matters to skiers and to invest in that.

Skier Values, Rank Ordered

Priority	Needs
Primary	• Good snow conditions • Manageable lift lines • Variety of terrain
Secondary	• Friendly employees • Fun environment
Tertiary	• Competitive prices

Figure 2-6

The managers did this in the best tradition of market research: by asking questions of and observing customers. Using qualitative research and the feedback provided by their own mountain staff, Otten and his team studied their business through the eyes of its customers. They held focus group meetings with Sunday River skiers at the end of the day as skiers came off the slopes. Customer feedback was combined with information drawn from weekly department surveys, staff debriefings, credit card data, and other sources. Otten and his crew, avid skiers themselves, viewed this information through the lens of their own experience and passion for skiing.

Once they put together the many bits and pieces of information, they discovered that customers placed the highest value on aspects of the skiing experience that relate to being out on the mountain: the quality of the snow, the lifts that moved them up the mountain, and the terrain variety (Figure 2-6). A fun and friendly environment and competitive prices also were valued features. Skiers also offered plenty of suggestions about how parking, accommodations, and other amenities could be improved, but these alone clearly were not concerns that would entice people to drive far into the hinterlands of Maine.

Many managers would have stopped at this point, satisfied that they had identified the values that mattered most. However, the Sunday River crew asked the next question: What constitutes "good snow conditions"? Is it a deep base? Is it fresh powder? Is it a particular type of groomed snow? Not satisfied that they really knew what customers meant by good snow conditions, the management team did more research. They learned that good snow was *top* snow, not necessarily the deep base that ski resorts spend fortunes building with costly snow-making machines when nature is stingy. Armed with this insight and a bit of marketing ingenuity, ASC's Marketing Vice President Burton R. Mills and his staff set out to deliver what they now knew their customers wanted most.

Ski resorts (especially in the East) actually are manufacturers of snow. Recognizing the importance of the top snow led Sunday River's managers to rethink their entire manufacturing process, the type of machines used, the timing of applications, and the relative emphasis on laying down base snow versus grooming. In the process, they invented the notion of *signature snow*, which they differentiate from ordinary snow the way Evian differentiates itself from tap water. Sunday River's signature snow is more consistent on the surface and is groomed across the resort's eight peaks according to the skiing styles of thousands of weekly visitors. Skiers judge for themselves whether Sunday River has delivered good snow by means of a first-run guarantee. If skiers do not believe that skiing conditions are suitable, they can request and receive a voucher for a return visit.

In acting to meet another primary value, lift-line management, Sunday River invested in the greatest number of high-speed quad lifts as a percentage of total lifts in the business, such that the resort could offer an 8-minute lift guarantee. In terms of terrain variety, Sunday River took two actions: First, it developed an additional peak in 1994 and another in 1995 to accommodate skiers' desires for a more gladelike setting. Second, as a part of the newly formed American Skiing Company, Sunday River was able to offer a universal pass usable at any of the ASC's eight resorts.

Having addressed its guests' primary and secondary needs—snow, lifts, terrain, service, and fun—the company then could focus on refining its strategy by developing loyalty programs that reward guests for selecting ASC resorts. In addition to providing guest rewards, the programs help the company increase its customer knowledge of when, how often, and for what experience its customers are using the eight resorts within the ASC family.

As is true in many businesses, ASC customers fall into three categories of usage: very frequent participants, who ski or ride in excess of 20 days per season; moderately frequent participants, who ski or ride 7 to 10 days per season; and casual or infrequent participants, who ski or ride 5 or fewer days per season. The company created a program for each category. For the most active group (and those who prefer not to make regular trips to the ticket windows), the company offers an all-mountains pass, entitling the pass holder to ski all ASC resorts. For active skiers who don't reach the break-even threshold of a season's pass, the company created a program called the *Magnificent 7 Card*, which gives skiers / days of skiing at significant savings over the daily ticket rate. The card may be used at any resort for one full calendar year from date of purchase. For casual participants, the company provides a frequent-skier program called *The Edge*, which allows guests to earn a free lift ticket after as few as 5 days on the slopes. In addition to providing guests with extra value, the program compiles demographic information and data on the use of each product, allowing management to track results and learn what works and what doesn't.

One of the key lessons that Otten and his management team learned can be summed up in the motto, "Optimize the core before you do more"—that is, do a first-class job in satisfying the primary customer requirements before you start expanding offerings. Though such advice might sound obvious and simplistic, accomplishing this objective is very difficult, as it is predicated on deep knowledge of what customers value. "It's interesting that right now, in the so-called 'information age,' many companies don't stay on top of who their customers are or what they're looking for," says Otten. "It's the most fundamental aspect to running a business—*any* business—but it seems that lots of companies have let that part slip away."

This dedication to customer values has made it possible for Otten and his team to build a world-class ski resort. Between 1980 and 1994, Sunday River increased the number of skiers per year from 40,000 to nearly 600,000. More impressively, they more than doubled the return rate of first-time skiers. Along the way, Sunday River won a number of industry accolades: the number-one ski resort in the Northeast, the National Ski Area Design award, and best ski conditions and "snow quality" in the Northeast. In our view, the company's success is a direct result of the ASC's ability to know what its customers value, even when customers have difficulty articulating what they value and its commitment to setting priorities for investments to deliver superior performance against those values.

Observational Knowledge

In considering customer relationships, how much of the customer's purchase behavior is rational and how much is emotional? How deeply do you need to get inside the head of your customers, to understand their psychology, in order to relate to them and to forge the right connections? As with most of the principles in this book, the answer is a function of who your customers are, the range of value you are delivering, and the role you play in enabling your customers to fulfill their overall objectives. Accepting that every customer, whether a consumer or a businessperson, functions as a social being in combinations of rational and emotional states, on which side do you need to generate knowledge?

Next, consider whether the type of product or service offered is one that is intangible and, consequently, not very visible, or whether it is highly visible. As a general rule, the more the customers' emotional state matters, the deeper the knowledge that is required. Of course, the degree of emotion will vary depending on the customer or segment being targeted, and the more tangible the product, the greater the opportunity to observe what customers need.

Figure 2-7 is a handy guide to estimating where a particular value proposition falls in terms of observability and customer psychology. If you were an auto manufacturer, for example, you might plot your value proposition near the upper right-hand corner. For many people, a car is as much a personal statement as a form of transportation. It introduces emotional issues of status, self-esteem, safety, and so forth. It also is very visible. Because an automobile is a tangible product, knowledge of what the customer wants can be developed through both conversation and direct observation.

If you managed a life insurance company, however, you would locate your spot on Figure 2-7 at the lower right. Life insurance is both an intangible and an emotionally charged product that conjures up the inevitability of death, the responsibility for loved ones, and so forth. Building knowledge of the insurance customer requires digging below the surface and building knowledge of the psychology of the buyer and the unexpressed or latent values and needs that ultimately will affect the purchase decision.

The relative use of conversation, observation, and prediction to build customer knowledge is one of the major differences between Western and Japanese marketing. The Japanese are famous for watching customers in the act of using products and then interpreting their needs—in essence, applying informed judgment. U.S. companies, by comparison, tend to rely on quantitative measures of customer needs and preferences. In highlighting this distinction, Johansson and Nonaka make the following point:

> A scientific approach to marketing, coupled with the technical
> complexity of the standard texts, easily distances the marketer from the
> mind of the customer. It also puts hard limits on the marketer's
> imagination.…To the intuitive Japanese minimalist, the interesting
> consumer behavior question is simply, "What kind of products and
> services will our customers demand next?" The answer requires a lot of
> direct observation and talk with users, not advanced scientific methods.[10]

Our next case highlights a company that religiously pursues opportunities to observe its customers, using both informal techniques and scientific methods.

Building the Right Depth of Knowledge

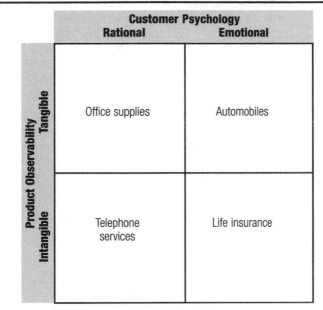

Figure 2-7

Executives who are squeamish about "touchy-feely" research and qualitative techniques can take heart from the identity of the practitioner.

Harley-Davidson
Hanging Out with "HOGS"

You've probably heard the story. Harley-Davidson, producer of America's most venerated motorcycle, an icon of American pop culture and the epitome of the free spirit, almost ran off the road in the 1980s.[11] The company lost touch with its customers, produced expensive yet low-quality bikes for which customers had to wait, and tarnished the halo that had long shone over one of America's strongest brand names.

Near bankruptcy in 1986, the company's new management team committed itself to rekindling the Harley-Davidson spirit by getting closer to customers and revitalizing the quality of the company's core product, the heavyweight motorcycle. In the words of Frank Cimermancic, Harley-Davidson director of business planning: "We had to remove the reasons for people to *not* buy a Harley."

Over the ensuing 5 years, Harley-Davidson gained 28 points of market share; since 1991, cycle output has increased 50 percent. During that same period, revenues grew 85 percent, and profits skyrocketed a whopping 130 percent. At the same time, the company expanded exports and launched a successful brand extension, Harley-Davidson clothing and merchandise. The operating philosophy underlying this turnaround can be summarized as follows:

- Perpetuate the heritage, tradition, and mystique of Harley-Davidson and seek to enhance it with new motorcycle products and services.
- Maintain an outward versus inward focus on products, services, and benchmarks of performance.
- Provide high customer satisfaction by supplying products that meet purchaser expectations.
- Maintain a close-to-the-customer philosophy with distributors, dealers, and customers.

Like most companies, Harley-Davidson relies on a number of traditional information sources to monitor its performance with customers: dealer and customer satisfaction indexes, R. L. Polk's market share information, and the company's own primary research of owners and prospects. Clearly, there is no shortage of information to indicate how well Harley-Davidson is performing.

Perhaps the greatest contributor to keeping the company in tune with its customers, however, is its "listening posts." Because the product is so observable, management has made a commitment to getting out of the office and living with its customers—not in the ceremonial way, in which the CEO becomes the "doorman for the day," but in a more profound manner. Customer events are the usual occasion for these interactions. Harley-Davidson sponsors more than 50 customer events each year, partly as marketing events but also as opportunities for listening to and observing customers. These Harley Owners' Group (HOG) events, which annually attract more than 400,000 riders, are attended by members of the management team. They provide a unique opportunity for managers to understand the culture of the motorcycle-riding public and to observe how human and machine interact. Supporting Von Hipple's assertion that the customer rather than the company often is the source of innovation,[12] HOG events and bike shows also allow Harley-Davidson personnel to observe how their bikes have been modified, thereby providing ideas for product improvement and new product development.

Ethnography is one way that Harley-Davidson builds knowledge of the shared characteristics and values of its customers. *Ethnography* is the scientific study of specific human cultures, typically through fieldwork by cultural anthropologists using the methods of participant observation. Two ethnographers on retainer to Harley-Davidson have conducted field studies of the Harley-Davidson subculture.[13] Their findings are interpreted from a product and marketing perspective. Management has used this knowledge successfully to walk the tightrope between maintaining the loyalty of its core franchise while expanding the appeal of the Harley-Davidson brand to additional demographic segments. This balancing act has proved easier than might be expected, as the cultural characteristics of Harley owners contained some surprises. It was found that more than 70 percent of Harley-Davidson customers have at least some education beyond high school, most are married, and almost half have children. Their median annual income exceeds $60,000. Armed with this knowledge, Harley-Davidson's management team plans to continue expanding the popularity of its products and services while maintaining the mystique of its brand and the unique ethos of its core customer base.

Predictive Knowledge

Whereas observational knowledge, as applied in the preceding case, has an important role in the process of understanding what customers want, we believe that marketing science also plays an important role in the customer-knowledge management process. Quantitative measures, taken from existing data sources or generated through research, are necessary to build what we call *predictive knowledge*, which uses analytic models to predict customer needs and responsiveness. AT&T Consumer Services is an example of a business using predictive knowledge techniques to reevaluate its entire customer relationship strategy.

AT&T Consumer Services
To Bundle or Not to Bundle—That Is the Question

Deregulation of telecommunications has shifted dramatically the competitive landscape for AT&T.[14] Today, its competitors are not simply long-line companies such as MCI and Sprint; regional Bell operating companies, cable companies, and even utilities now are vying to sell customers a menu of communications services.

Given this new environment, AT&T is committed to having the needs of its customers drive the shape of its future business. As it expands the scope of its offerings and customer reach, management realizes that both the complexity and risks of the business are increasing. Accordingly, AT&T Consumer Services is looking first to customer needs and then devising ways to outperform competitors in delivering services to meet those needs. Its focus is now on building relationships with customers and retaining them over time, as opposed to selling products.

Given more than 76 million customers and millions more prospects, relationship building promises to be daunting. This challenge is heightened by the changing nature of AT&T's business. Forced to defend its position in the long-distance market while developing the capability to offer each customer only the services he or she needs from a menu that includes long distance, local service, Internet access, wireless, and cable, AT&T puts a premium on having the right information to support decisions. The goal is to leverage this customer information to optimize the products and solutions offered to individual customers. Which customers and prospects are most likely to buy bundled solutions? Of these, which are the most profitable to acquire, and what will it take to win them over?

AT&T has begun to answer these questions by evaluating for every customer segment customer needs, competitive dynamics, economic attractiveness, regulatory factors, and geographic factors. The company is building targeting models to determine likely adoption behavior and future spending by running what-if scenarios according to geography, revenue, usage frequency, bundled versus à la carte services, share, and competitor. This modeling is helping to determine which customers AT&T should pursue. As it executes its strategy for each segment, the company is closely monitoring results and adjusting the segmentation and targeting models accordingly. The use of predictive knowledge is at the heart of AT&T's strategy, and the predictive power of that knowledge and the ability effectively to act on it ultimately will determine the success of the strategy.

LEVERAGING KNOWLEDGE

Clearly, information technology plays an important role in facilitating the development of a knowledge-intensive environment. Just as enterprise resource planning packages (such as SAP, Baan, and Oracle) now are being applied to operations and financial systems, technology can enhance customer information management.

Still, there is more to customer knowledge management than creating the right information technology infrastructure. Also essential are well-designed business processes and people trained to manage them. Consider customer complaints. Research by James Heskett has shown that a customer complaint process may be one of your best marketing opportunities.[15] When properly handled, a complaining customer can be converted into a more loyal customer. How does your firm handle complaints? Is there a formal process aimed at "recovering" the complaining customer? Does this process capture the nature of the complaint, determine the root cause, learn from the data how to improve the customer relationship, and track the outcome? Does your company even understand what drives customer satisfaction?

Surprisingly, our survey data indicated that more than one-third (36 percent) of Fortune 1000 companies are losing ground in their quest to satisfy customers. These companies reported that their satisfaction ratings had actually fallen over the past year.[16] Many of these companies know a great deal about who the customer is and what he wants, but customer knowledge must be more extensive and serve both as a measure of performance and a vehicle to drive that performance. The following case demonstrates how one company has used a closed-loop system in which its knowledge of what customers value is converted into an explicit service guarantee that provides a mechanism for ensuring that the company remains closely aligned with its customers' needs.

Delta Dental
This Won't Hurt a Bit

Assume for a moment that you are the head of employee benefits and that you're reevaluating health care policies for your company. An employee satisfaction survey has revealed a notable gap in your menu of benefits: dental coverage. Concerned both with employee contentment and with escalating health care costs, you begin to search for a dental coverage provider that offers both high quality and acceptable costs. If your business were based in Massachusetts, your search might bring you to Delta Dental, a provider of group dental insurance that pioneered the use of service guarantees in the health care industry.[17]

Even as a new business, Delta Dental recognized the need to stay close to customers. It formed two committees for this purpose: a professional advisory committee to keep current with dentists' needs, and a customer partnership committee to stay close to corporate accounts. Both committees meet regularly to discuss service, pricing, new products, and other matters that affect customer satisfaction. On the basis of feedback from the two committees, the company decided that its customer connection would revolve around its guarantee of service excellence (GOSE).

Delta Dental took the assurance of service excellence to the extreme, even to the point of guaranteeing year-over-year savings to customers. By making an explicit cost reduction promise, the GOSE program has galvanized the company's efforts simultaneously to improve service quality while reducing overall customer cost. This, in turn, has pushed the company to know everything it can about what customers expect, to know how well it is performing, and to share employee knowledge and best practices on delivering service more efficiently.

To accomplish these tasks, management instituted its keep it simple system (KISS) of suggestions to unlock what people knew or thought about improving the business. To date, more than 30 percent of KISS suggestions have been implemented, and each individual who submitted a suggestion—whether or not that suggestion was implemented—has received some token of appreciation.

Delta Dental currently is focusing on integrating its satisfaction and service databases to provide a single view of the experiences of the corporate client, the individual consumer, and the dentist. The payoff from these management practices has everyone showing a pearly white smile. The subscriber base grew by more than 20 percent in 1995, customer retention hovers around 96 to 97 percent, and overhead costs have been reduced to approximately 10 percent of revenues (down from roughly 14 percent in 1987).

In this chapter, we introduced the closed-loop model for the process of customer knowledge management. We discussed a taxonomy of knowledge types and techniques for acquiring, sharing, and leveraging customer knowledge. We illustrated how several companies managed their knowledge to deliver value to their customers and strengthen their overall relationships. In the next chapter, we address the role of technology in creating opportunities for electronic conversations, collaboration, commerce, and care.

chapter 3

Getting wired to your customer

CUSTOMER-CONNECTING TECHNOLOGY

You may have read about or used the sophisticated customer package tracking software provided by United Parcel Service (UPS) or Federal Express (FedEx). Perhaps you have made purchases through Internet shopping services from companies such as Peapod, Amazon, and Virtual Vineyards. A few of you may even have slipped into a "personal pair" of Levi's custom fit jeans. Each is an example of the successful application of customer-connecting technology. Customer-connecting technologies are the physical or electronic links between companies and customers; they support the development and ongoing management of a mutually beneficial, interdependent relationship.

Technology can be applied at various stages in the customer relationship to increase the value of relationships. It can reduce the costs of acquiring customers, expand the value provided to them, strengthen relationships with them, or create entirely new value propositions. At the front end of the relationship life cycle, connecting technologies can reduce the search time and costs necessary to bring buyer and seller together and can create a two-way conversation that ensures a good match between the needs of the customer and the capabilities of the provider. Technology can then be used to collaborate with the customer in the specification, acquisition, or production of the value proposition. Once a buyer has made the transition from prospect to customer, connecting technologies can be used to satisfy the customer's ongoing needs for information and support.

Longtime information technology (IT) industry analyst Patricia Seybold calls those technologies designed to help companies manage the total customer relationship *customer care systems* and argues that they have the potential to transform the provider-customer relationship:

> We are entering a new era in which total customer care transitions from slogan to reality, a reality enabled by advancements in infrastructure technology that connect the various systems and databases associated with managing the customer from "cradle to grave." In doing so, front-line employees are being empowered through more up-to-date and comprehensive information. Combining information access technology with on-line analytical processing tools and knowledgeable employees is becoming a potent recipe for delivering total customer satisfaction and loyalty.

Entire industries are being transformed through the strategic use of customer-connecting technology. Consider, for example, the banking industry. The automated teller machine (ATM), one of the pioneering technologies in customer connections, has helped change the complexion of the retail banking market. As bank customers have become more comfortable with unassisted service delivery, "virtual banking" is becoming reality. A recent study of banking technology[1] indicates some dramatic shifts in the nature of the consumer banking relationship. Consider the following trends:

- The proportion of total transactions processed by branches is expected to decline by nearly one-third by 1998. Branch banking will continue, but alternative channels are emerging. Remaining branches will be reconfigured to include in-branch kiosks and video conferencing.

- The average number of ATMs owned and operated by the top 100 banks will rise 36 percent by 1998. Thirty-two percent of these machines will be at nonbranch locations.

- ATMs will have significantly increased capabilities, offering mutual funds and insurance over the network.

- The number of transactions anticipated to be performed by telephone will grow by 50 percent.

- More than 80 percent of banks offer or plan to offer service through personal computers, and 60 percent are piloting or planning Internet services.

The on-line customer will look to the bank for a broader set of services such as account management, family financial planning, and security prospectuses. Clearly, in this industry as in many others, the role and value of technology is shifting from supporting the management of the business to enabling, and in some cases becoming, the essence of the business strategy. When targeted at the appropriate customers, the virtual bank will deliver real-time information, service, and transactions.

This rosy view of the future depends, however, on careful selection, effective deployment, and strategically focused use of customer-connecting technologies. In this chapter, we describe the strategic importance of these technologies that either interface with or provide direct benefit to the customer. It used to be that IT was all about management information systems. Today, it is all about value creation.

Every senior manager who strongly influences a P&L has an obligation to contemplate how she can apply technology most effectively to maximize the value exchange with the customer. In doing so, she must answer the following questions:

- What are the primary *objectives* of investing in connecting technologies—to reduce cost or improve efficiency, to generate new revenue streams, to solidify relationships with existing customers, to extend access to new customers, or to create an entirely new "informationalized" business?

- Which *performance metrics* should guide this effort and determine ultimate success? Should the metric be a single view of the customer; one call for whatever a customer needs; or customer retention, incremental revenues, or customer satisfaction measures?

- What *competencies* are needed to design, implement, and maintain these systems? Should they be built, bought, or outsourced?

- What role should the information systems department play in these initiatives?

The answers to these questions are no longer the sole responsibility of the chief information officer (CIO). Developing ways to apply technology strategically in order to create stronger connections to your customers transcends individual functions and is a responsibility shared by the entire management team.

Customer Connection: Primary Objective

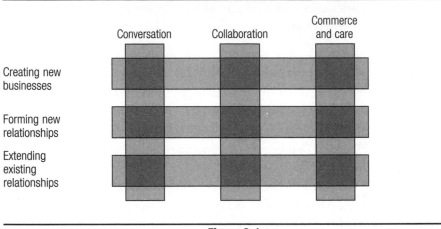

Figure 3-1

Technology now permeates every aspect of the customer relationship, providing new and exciting possibilities for two-way, real-time *conversation, collaboration,* and *commerce/care,* delivered via a spate of electronic conduits including the Internet and intranets, self-service (e.g., kiosk) systems, and mobile systems (e.g., laptop tools), as illustrated in Figure 3-1.

Operating in what Jeffrey Rayport and John Sviokla call the *marketspace,* managers are increasingly able to engage the on-line market cost-effectively with new customized value propositions.[2] We explore the dynamics and opportunities of these enablers of customer relationship management through a number of case studies.

CONNECTING *for* CONVERSATION

A key purpose of the customer connection process is to establish the company's brand as a preferred source in the minds of customers. Collectively, companies spend more than $150 billion annually in advertising, attempting to signal to the market that they are, indeed, the right choice.[3] Despite the calls of pundits to engage in one-to-one marketing, mass media channels continue to maintain a strong base. Television spending (including network and cable programming) has remained relatively constant over the last decade, despite the growing popularity of direct and interactive programs. Clearly, the reach-and-frequency approach to brand building still works—Nike, General Electric, Coca-Cola, and

IBM all still rely heavily on mass media. However, as markets continue to fragment and technologies continue to evolve, these powerhouse brands and many others are increasing their use of more interactive, real-time marketing channels.

The Electronic Connection

Our survey data suggest that most major companies already have recognized the potential and jumped into the new Web market space. Two-thirds of the companies surveyed currently have a Web page and, although World Wide Web ad revenues were a scant $71.7 million for the first half of 1996, or approximately 0.1 percent of the annual total, according to AdSpend data, the Internet is fast becoming a viable connection technology to support brand awareness. Unfortunately, many early users have treated the technology as no more than an on-line form of mass advertising, underexploiting the conversational and navigational power of the medium. Recent improvements in software tools and languages (such as Java Applets) have greatly increased the Web's potential power, creating new opportunities for communicating with and learning from the various types of customers attracted to Web sites. New database systems and "agent" technologies allow businesses to tailor their World Wide Web sites to individual customers or customer segments, to "push" information to them, and to track these customers' preferences. Collaborative filtering makes it possible for a company to adjust its message or offer based on how a customer reacts to the stimuli presented. A feedback loop then allows the marketer to build profiles of the customer over time and to deliver the right message to that particular customer.

Communication is an essential element of any relationship, and the more that you can engage and involve your customers (particularly your best customers) in a two-way conversation, the greater is the potential for a bond to be established. Although only 8 percent of the U.S. population currently is active on the Internet, a disproportionate number of educated, upscale consumers can be reached via the Net. Our next two cases illustrate how Lexus and IBM use the Net to engage customers in conversations.

Lexus
Staying in Touch

Let us assume that, like many people, you don't view an automobile as mere transportation but as an extension of who you are.[4] You appreciate both style and performance, and you have been drawn to the Lexus SC 400. Unfortunately, the closest dealer is 40 miles away. In addition, you're uncertain about your ability to manage the purchase financially and about whether you fully understand the differences between the SC 300 and SC 400 models. What are your options? You could go to the Yellow Pages, find the dealer's number, and call to speak with a salesperson, or you could ask that product information be mailed to your home. Another alternative, however, that would enable you to educate yourself at any time and at your own pace would be to access the Lexus Web site. The "Lexus Centre of Performance Art," a stylishly laid-out Web site complete with your own personal concierge, Alex, offers many different halls for you to explore:

- *Model Gallery*: allows you to obtain information on vehicle performance, luxury, safety, accessories, and specifications.
- *Dealer Grande Hall*: allows you to search for a Lexus dealer by area code, state, or dealership name, and to link to that dealership's Web site.
- *Tech Center*: gives you a glimpse of the technical innovations engineered into Lexus vehicles.
- *Events Centre*: enumerates Lexus-sponsored sports, cultural, and automotive events.
- *Reading Room*: provides up-to-date information including awards, articles, and reviews.
- *Patrons' Circle*: a room reserved exclusively for Lexus owners that offers special privileges available only to such owners.
- *Financial District*: helps you to decide whether to buy or lease a vehicle through Lexus Financial Services.
- *E-Mailbox*: allows you to request brochures and complete a marketing survey to communicate directly with Lexus.
- *Wishing Well*: describes Lexus's commitment to various charities.

The Lexus home page is not unique in its presentation or functionality; BMW and Ford use similar environments. Nonetheless, this particular site is distinctive as an example of effective customer connection in that it projects an image very consistent with the image Lexus conveys through its other brand-building efforts. In addition, it presents an effective and reinforcing blend of information that is well aligned with the company's attempt to support the total car-owning experience. The company entices viewers to share information about past and prospective auto purchases, making the site a learning device and providing an additional opportunity to "converse" with these high-value customers. Finally, the site differentiates existing from prospective customers, thereby allowing Lexus to tailor the type and depth of interaction for each. By inserting their vehicle identification numbers, customers also are given access to privileged information, such as new model information. A playful feature of the Patrons' Circle enables a customer to send an e-mail postcard to a friend or relative displaying the model of his or her choice on the front and a personalized message on the back, thereby increasing word-of-mouth association with the brand.

Lexus's 176 dealers are independently owned enterprises, which means that they are not obliged to follow corporate initiatives beyond their franchise agreements. However, every Lexus dealer has a basic Web site that includes the dealership's address, phone number, geographic map, and a link to the new model information. Many dealers have gone so far as to include photographs of staff and directions to the dealership. Increasingly, many dealers also are listing their inventory of preowned Lexus vehicles. This allows potential customers for preowned Lexus vehicles to search the entire inventory for vehicles by Lexus certification, color, mileage, year, dealer geographic location, and the like. Specific vehicles can then be traced to specific dealers, which the potential customer can contact directly to obtain further information, to arrange a test drive, and even to negotiate a price.

Lexus's use of the Web aligns well with the company's overall customer connection strategy. Moreover, given the long interval between product purchases in the auto industry, Lexus's ability to sustain a dialogue with the customer throughout his or her total car experience is likely to increase the probability of a repeat purchase.[4]

IBM
Casting the Net

Recognizing that the tremendous momentum behind and expectations for the World Wide Web were overwhelming to many of its business customers, IBM established the e-business Advisor program to assist its field force, business partners, and corporate customers in understanding how to take maximum advantage of this evolving environment.[5] The company sought to present to its customers a value-added service that defined how customers can incorporate the Web effectively into their business and produce an information exchange that delivers mutual benefit (Figure 3-2).

By accessing the new IBM home page and answering a series of questions, a customer immediately receives a customized assessment that indicates how the customer's company is positioned relative to a three-phase model of Web development:

- *Business foundation*: highlights early-stage development focused on basic launch and links.
- *Business extension*: demonstrates use of interactive techniques, an advanced repository and database.
- *Business transformation*: demonstrates ability to provide mass customization, commerce, closed-loop knowledge management, and the like.

Depending on how involved the customer elects to become with the e-business Advisor, there are three levels of interaction: a base implementation planner, an advanced implementation planner, and an ROI tool. The base implementation planner analyzes the customer's answers against key indicators and provides a perspective on his strategy, resources, and Web function design. Results can be compared to the population in general or to the customer's specific industry. The base planner also displays future Web directions that the customer could take.

Whereas the base planner primarily assesses the customer's Web development from a technical perspective, the advanced planner evaluates the customer's deployment from a business process and integration point of view. The idea is to encourage customers to think of the Web as a transformational tool. As such, the advanced planner analyzes the customer's approach to the business processes associated with the deployment effort. Additionally, the customer can interact with a tool called the *E-Commerce Assistant* to understand better what it takes to market a product or service successfully on the Internet. Once again,

IBM e-business Advisor Web Tools Service

Customer Benefits	IBM Benefits
Provide output to customers, tailored to their needs, that they can use now to implement net solutions.	Establish ongoing dialogue with e-business Advisor visitors.
	Build databases of interested customers.
Provide customers the ability to measure progress in Web development.	Provide a practical way to handle, in volume, customer questions about Internet.
Support customer efforts to calibrate ROI associated with Web investments.	Create a path to providing e-business Advisor solutions to customers.

Figure 3-2

through a series of questions and answers, the customer is provided with an assessment, this time measured against key marketing indicators including target market, brand, distribution, price, promotion, and marketing environment. The output identifies strong and weak elements of the customer's approach and provides a quick reference snapshot that offers suggestions to consider.

The ROI tool estimates baseline costs for developing and implementing an intranet. Three reports are generated that identify the potential impact that an intranet can have on an organization in terms of implementation costs, break-even point, and 5-year savings.

Customers can store the initial results obtained by using each of these three tools (the planners and the ROI tool). They then can revisit the site to obtain an updated assessment of their progress.

Clearly, altruism is not the motive for the significant investment that IBM has made in its e-business Advisor. The company hopes that by adding real value to the customer in terms of education and performance assessment, the Advisor will, over time, position IBM as a leading provider of solutions and result in "pull-through" consulting, hardware, and software revenues. Nonetheless, as a customer-connecting system, the e-business Advisor facilitates an invaluable two-way conversation between the company and its customers.

The Human Connection

Not all conversation takes place over wires. Many high-involvement products and services always will require some form of face-to-face interaction. Even so, new technology in the area of sales force automation and opportunity management are producing not just more efficient sales processes but a more effective selling environment. This new environment allows reps to transform the nature of the dialogue from transactional to consultative, thereby increasing the value delivered to the customer. Sales automation tools are not new in the realm of business-to-business marketing. Road warriors selling everything from consumer packaged goods to computers have long relied on laptops as their link to the home office. However, increasingly these systems are being used as much (if not more) for customer consultation and conversation as they are for purchase order management.

Technology has facilitated the evolution of the traditional sales role from order taker to relationship manager. In the MCI case discussed in Chapter 1, we described how the growing complexity of relationships led to the use of large, dedicated client teams composed of specialized industry and functional knowledge experts. Later, we'll discuss how the UPS national and global accounts managers define their role to include working with customers to develop business solutions. These are examples of a broader trend. David Jones of Jones Consulting in Atlanta, who has studied and tracked the evolution of account managers, reports that the duties of key account managers at leading firms now include many activities, such as the following:

- Acting as a single point of contact.

- Developing and extending customer relationships.

- Understanding customers' decision-making processes.

- Identifying added-value opportunities.

- Providing competitive intelligence.

- Negotiating sales.

- Orchestrating customer service.

Obviously, these roles cannot be performed by operating in isolation. Rather, technological means are required to tap into and coordinate with the firm's expertise and to convey that knowledge to customers in a useful way.

In many commercial markets, the value associated with intangibles (i.e., response time, better access to information, and the ability to configure an order to the buyer's satisfaction) is an increasing proportion of the total value of the good or service. Consequently, the ability to inform and educate in real time is increasingly important. Thanks to improvements in computer disk capacity, communications technology, and database management, field personnel can play the role of knowledge broker rather than simply that of product representative. One of the most sophisticated practitioners of this art is Pioneer Hi-Bred, a company we met in Chapter 2.

Pioneer Hi-Bred
Down on the Farm

Though undoubtedly there is still an art to and a feel for what it takes to coax the greatest yield from a given acre of land, the farming business is undergoing a transformation to what many call *precision agriculture*.[6] The science of farming now is heavily weighted toward genetic engineering (on the seed and chemical side) and advanced agronomy. Farmers are using global positioning satellite systems to take the guesswork out of chemical and fertilizer placement, tillage strategies, and so on. This change affects both the requirements of the farmer and the skills and expertise needed by the suppliers' sales organization as these parties enter into a discussion of whose seeds will do the best job.

For Pioneer Hi-Bred, knowledge, as much as high-yielding seeds, has become the basis of differentiation. In response to this trend toward precision agriculture, the company has made substantial investments in arming its farmer sales reps with the on-line information and data necessary to engage its customers in knowledgeable discussion. The need to become more involved in the customer's business has caused sales reps to shift their time allocation from mostly selling to mostly counseling. Pioneer supports its reps' counseling efforts through its knowledge management system (as described in Chapter 2) and the development of technologies to bring that knowledge to the farmer.

Creation of the customer and prospect system (CAPS) database and field information system (FIS) provides a basis for a more robust conversation between farmer and sales rep. CAPS arms the rep with a current account status and farm-specific information including last year's yield by crop, acreage, farm ownership structure, and so on. The broader FIS provides remote access to a wide variety of information and facts that the rep can download in real time, including side-by-side competitive product comparisons, 2,000 articles on various agricultural topics, product updates, hybrid profiles, and performance data. *Crop Insights*, a newsletter that can be downloaded, provides helpful facts and tips on topics such as row spacing and no-till techniques. This knowledge technology is complemented by access to on-staff agronomists. With these tools, the Pioneer sales rep can work closely with the farmer, analyze options in real time, and make a true contribution to the farmer's planning process.

The Pioneer, IBM, and Lexus cases illustrate the interplay between knowledge and technology management in communicating with customers and conducting a conversation with them. You need to determine whether you are fully leveraging what you know about the market, customer needs, and the competitive performance of your value proposition to engage your target customers. Are you using connecting technology primarily to increase your efficiency and productivity, or are you attempting to use it as a conversational device to educate your customers further and to deliver more value to them?

CONNECTING *for* COLLABORATION

The notion of connecting for collaboration focuses on the direct involvement of the customer in the process of needs specification and value delivery. Customers who are given the opportunity to influence the design or delivery of a product usually will be loyal purchasers. This premise is at the heart of the movement toward mass customization, one-to-one marketing, and relationship marketing.

Involving the Customer at the Product Design Level

Custom Foot
If the Shoe Fits...

Because no two feet are truly the same, footwear is a perfect subject for mass customization. How many times have you tried on a pair of shoes and found that the one-half-size measurement just doesn't deliver the right fit? Perhaps your right foot is just slightly longer or wider than the left.

At Custom Foot, an in-store scan of a customer's feet is made, and then a sales associate assesses the customer's fit type and selects a few prototypes for her to try on.[7] The customer determines her fit preferences, collaborates with a sales agent, and uses a personal computer to select the desired colors, styles, types of leather, and other features; she also is given the price. Custom Foot's Italian manufacturers receive these directions and employ a "mass customization assembly-line" process to craft the shoes. The shoes, which the customer receives in approximately 3 to 4 weeks, sell for only slightly more than off-the-shelf high-quality but mass-produced shoes and for far less than the price that traditional hand-crafted shoes command.

Interestingly, Custom Foot's approach to meeting consumer demand depends less on innovations in technology—although these are critical—than it does on marketing and customer handling, according to former CEO Jeffrey Silverman. For example, in response to customer requests, the original electronic scanning process was modified so that both the operator and the customer can view the computerized image of the customer's feet on separate computer monitors.[8]

Custom Foot's original target market was 30- to 55-year-old consumers with incomes in excess of $75,000. It was forecast that the 50-50 mix of men and women would be college-educated, savvy consumers, and residents of affluent communities. However, Custom Foot quickly discovered that it had tapped into a pent-up demand for well-fitting, custom-made shoes from people who had long histories of shoe discomfort. The company found that this market was very emotion-driven. According to Laureen Kirsch, Custom Foot's director of marketing, the company discovered a market in which people are "willing to try anything, pay any price, and to drive or fly any distance" to address their shoe problems.

Custom Foot has found that only 40 percent or so of its customers are men. Men seem to be attracted to Custom Foot because of the new concept and fit, whereas women apparently are attracted to the potential for comfortable fit in stylish shoes. Market information suggests that two-thirds of the country's women own at least some shoes that do not fit well. Surveys suggest that at least 80 million women are likely to have a foot problem. Custom Foot's concept accommodates a variety of foot types with appropriate styles and supplies those styles in a large number of lengths and widths.

Without the use of press releases, Custom Foot's unique marketing concept was featured on Cable News Network, in the *New York Times* (and its syndication throughout the country to local markets), and on the front page of the *International Herald Tribune.* It was largely this free publicity that tapped into the unanticipated demand of customers in need of well-fitting shoes, a demand Custom Foot was forced to meet directly and quickly by hiring two full-time podiatrists. The podiatrists now assist with customer inquiries via an 800 number, review orders that in-store sales personnel flag as needing special attention, and consult directly with the manufacturing staff in Italy. They also help train the sales staff.

Not surprisingly, Custom Foot spends considerable time recruiting and training its sales staff. The work involves knowledge of in-depth technical and consultative dimensions that sales personnel in other shoe stores do not need. Special training includes sessions about foot anatomy and the fabrication process in Italy. Recruiting is aided by the fact that the sales and marketing staff are enthusiastic about the innovations offered by their stores.

From information gained through the fitting process, Custom Foot assembles specialized mailings unique to each customer. This targeting of each customer's interests and needs helps Custom Foot to offer appropriate styles and to develop its products. Kirsch explains that Custom Foot is a "learning-based company that asks a lot of questions that have value to the customer, not immediately to us. The more you learn from the customer, the better you can deliver what the customer is actually asking for."

The Custom Foot example illuminates the very real opportunities today to use technology to deliver a new form of value to the customer, one for which customers typically are willing to pay a premium. Collaboration with the customer to design more customized offerings allows companies to create a deeper connection, thereby increasing the probability of a sale and the potential of an ongoing relationship. This case also shows how a collaborative design process may attract unforeseen customers and lead to changes in the business model to deliver the promise of mass customization.

Involving the Customer at the Marketing and Merchandising Level

Even when a product cannot be totally customized, still it often is possible to collaborate with customers to involve them in some aspect of the order-to-delivery process. Many products such as cars and computers are inherently configurable, but the economics of traditional retailing places limits on the range of choices that can be displayed and puts pressure on the customer to buy what is available. A number of computer manufacturers (e.g., Dell, Gateway 2000) offer configurability but at a distance. Plymouth, a division of Chrysler Corporation, has developed an interactive presale environment that allows customers to navigate their way through the process of researching and selecting a new automobile.

Plymouth Place
Driving to the Customer

In 1993, Chrysler decided to refresh its sagging Plymouth product line, which had lost more than 50 percent of its sales volume since 1973.[9] The Plymouth Renaissance Team, a 23-member multidisciplinary group, was created to formulate and implement an innovative marketing strategy to revive the Plymouth brand image and differentiate it from the other Chrysler lines. One of the strongest facets of the new approach was the creation of the Plymouth Place information displays.

Located in the walkways of shopping malls, each Plymouth Place display includes automobiles, an advisor to answer questions, and the Plymouth Tech

Cart, an interactive computer kiosk that visitors can use to access vehicle and pricing information tailored to their needs. The key to the success of this customer-connecting innovation is not the technology itself but its ability to effectively support a strong, customer-focused strategy.

The team set out to define a new product line and market positioning for the "new" Plymouth brand. In turn, this commanded a shift in the target group to a younger demographic. The Renaissance Team determined that the prime market for Plymouth is composed of people from 20 to 40 years of age, a substantial number of whom are first-time buyers. This group represents a drop of 15 to 18 years in the median age of the former target market for Plymouth products such as the Acclaim and Sundance. This target group of buyers, of which 65 percent are women, has a complex set of requirements for an automobile, due to the buyers' busy schedules and varied lifestyles. These potential customers are concerned with affordability, dependability, versatility, and safety. They tend to conduct more prepurchase research, prefer to do it outside of the dealership environment, and are comfortable using a computer and other forms of technology. They also tend to be more loyal to a brand than to a specific dealer. Through focus group research, the Renaissance Team confirmed its belief that this target market still has a negative perception of the process of buying an automobile and is frustrated with dealerships.

Instead of adopting Saturn's approach to reengineering the sales *experience* within a traditional dealer setting, the Renaissance Team elected to reinvent the *environment* in which customers shop for a car. Facts from earlier market research indicated that a gap existed in supporting customers' search process—namely, the need to assist customers in conducting their prepurchase research. Piloted at two regional malls in February 1995, Plymouth Place displays the information in a location and format that is easily accessible to potential customers, who can shop or browse for a car within the context of their daily routine. The entire package (including the cars, stage, and Tech Cart) is portable, affording Plymouth Place the ability to travel wherever potential customers may be. Plymouth Place has been set up at hundreds of events around the United States.

The Plymouth Place site offers convenience and information but none of the sales pressure of the dealership. Each automobile is displayed with its doors and hood open to encourage consumers to explore. The on-site advisor provides as much information as would a salesperson but cannot make sales.

At the Tech Cart, visitors are invited to peruse product features such as drive, design, and safety specifications. The Tech Cart provides side-by-side comparisons of each model and competing vehicles, according to a comprehensive list of features and equipment. Other available information includes current incentives, accessories, and leasing and warranty information. A customer can even "spec" out a model, choosing from standard equipment, option packages, features and available discounts, and can view running footage of the vehicle that he creates. The Tech Cart generates a summary of the chosen vehicle and calculates the manufacturer's suggested retail price. This summary and a list of dealers can be printed out, thus preparing the customer for the buying process and cutting down on his transaction time at the dealership. The average visitor spends 20 to 30 minutes at the Tech Cart, and Plymouth has found that customers who invest this research time have a higher propensity to purchase a Plymouth. This blending of human interaction with technology allows Plymouth Place visitors to make the transition easily from the salesperson-assisted environment of the dealership to an environment in which they are encouraged to explore options on their own. Consumers who are comfortable with the technology also can use the Plymouth Place Web site. For additional support and information about Plymouth vehicles, an 800 number is also available.

In the first 4 months of 1995, 66,700 consumers visited the Plymouth Place sites, and 14,200 obtained Tech Cart printouts. More impressively, retail sales increased significantly in the two pilot markets, as compared to the national increase in Plymouth sales in that same period. The Plymouth Place program was launched nationally in early 1996, coinciding with the introduction of the compact Plymouth Breeze. By the summer of 1996, there were more than 100 Plymouth Place mall locations. According to Jim Holden, executive vice president of sales and marketing for Chrysler, 22 percent of the early buyers of the Breeze learned about the product through Plymouth Place.

In November 1996, Chrysler opened a 15,000-square-foot store in the Mall of America in Minnesota, in which all Chrysler vehicles will be showcased using the same environment (albeit expanded) as is used in the Plymouth Place displays. In addition, Chrysler is working with a software company to design a program that will link updated information from company headquarters to any outside location, including dealerships, kiosks, home computers, and even factories.

This is just the beginning of a major transformation of the automobile sales and distribution model. Improved capabilities could allow Chrysler to use customers' input, feedback, and preferences in developing, forecasting, and manufacturing the product. With value-added information tools, it is not difficult to imagine the future integration of Plymouth Place into the entire order management and supply-chain process. When asked about enhancements to the Plymouth Place concept and its potential migration toward transaction management, Steve Bruyn, an original Renaissance Team leader, said simply, "Let your imagination be your guide."

Involving the Customer at the Service Level

Our third example of a collaborative connection technology involves the use of customer terminals. Early examples of this connecting technology focused on inventory replenishment and order management, as in the highly publicized example of the Baxter/American Hospital Supply ASAP system. More recently, companies have taken customer terminal systems to new levels, making them an integral part of the supplier-customer relationship by involving the customer in the service delivery process. Consider the case of UPS's investment in customer automation technology.

UPS
Connecting at the Speed of Business

UPS is responsible for ensuring that billions of packages each year reach millions of customers spread across 200 countries. The only way to manage a business and customer base of this scale and complexity is through the effective use of IT. The parcel movement business is not merely about logistics management; it is about information management.

Along with its competitors—FedEx, Airborne Express, DHL, RPS Services, and, to a lesser extent, the Postal Service—UPS has just about reached the logical limit of competition on the "core" value proposition of parcel movement: reliably delivering the goods at the specified time (e.g., next day, 10:30, 8:30, same day). The battleground of the future, therefore, will be the customer relationship, and the weapon of choice will be customer-connecting technology. Intending to win this war, UPS, which spends upwards of a half billion dollars annually on information systems and technology, shifted a large percentage of its IT budget to systems that directly interface with or benefit the customer. The company plans to spend more than $150 million (approximately 30 percent of its IT budget) on customer automation processes. Using the very latest technology, the company is building a wireless package-tracking system that will make today's state-of-the-art systems obsolete and probably will consume in excess of $2 billion in investment capital by the time it is completed. UPS views this decision as vital to its strategic position. According to Frank Erbrick, the company's recently retired CIO:

> Today it isn't good enough just to move packages from Place A to Place B quickly and efficiently. You have to be able to move *information* quickly and efficiently. For instance, some companies connect to their customers through our VANS [value-added network]. They get in an order electronically; we ship the order; when the package is delivered, we tell them it is okay to send the invoice.

UPS's strategy is interesting and quite progressive in that the company's focus is on aligning its customer-connecting technology with the type and value of customers being served. UPS reserves its On-Line Host Access system for top global accounts. UPS On-Line Professional serves the information needs of the midtier customer, and UPS On-Line Maxiship is available to any customer through the Internet. In this way, UPS meets the special needs of its most valuable customers while still providing added conveniences to all customers. In all cases, the company is extending and opening its systems and processes to the customer in a collaborative spirit, in the hope that providing customers with better information and increased control will extend the duration of the relationship and the amount of business conducted with UPS.

Although the specific objectives and knowledge deployed across the UPS, Plymouth, and Custom Foot cases are very different, the common denominator is the investment made in technology to collaborate with the customer at some stage in the order-to-delivery process. Plymouth Place is essentially a marketing and merchandising system designed to simplify the customer's search process. Custom Foot engages the customer in the specification and configuration of the actual product, whereas the UPS tracking system allows the customer to monitor the execution of service delivery.

CONNECTING *for* COMMERCE

In the months between completion of this manuscript and its arrival in bookstores, a number of the problems currently hampering increased Internet commerce, such as security, network performance, and transaction standards, may have been solved or displaced by increased use of virtual private networks. However, for the full potential of this medium to be realized, clear customer benefits will have to converge with improved technological capabilities and favorable economics—a tall order. Nonetheless, pundits envision a $5–10 billion Internet consumer market by the year 2000. Business-to-business commerce has already, by some accounts, passed $50 billion with companies like GE using the Internet as an important part of their supply chain management strategy.

Use of the Internet as a money-making connection technology will most likely take two forms. One form will be use of the Web to *extend the value proposition* of existing businesses. The other will involve the creation of *entirely new businesses* with new value propositions, such as auction marts and community-of-interest networks (COINS), designed specifically to take advantage of the unique characteristics of the Web—real-time contact, networked access, and the capacity for large transaction volumes. Both types of use are being attempted today, albeit with modest transactional volumes and financial results, but each portends what is to come.

Extending the Value Proposition of Existing Businesses

Airlines
Getting Ready to Take Off On-Line

The airline industry continues to tinker with its customer management process, from priority check-in service and self-service ticketing to end-to-end transportation, on-the-ground concierge services, and new reservations systems. It seemed only logical that, having built proprietary reservation systems for the travel agent community, the major carriers would make use of this experience to jump into the Web market space with direct connections for the individual traveler.

American Airlines is one example. Rather than constructing its Web site as a brand-building and communications-oriented tool, as did Lexus, American decided to focus its initial development squarely on the transaction-related services currently dispensed through its 800 number. Using this approach, the company designed a site optimized for customers already skilled in the mechanics of airline travel. The airline focuses its efforts on improving the access, ease of use, and convenience of the services customers need most. The site provides flight times, airport logistics information, special services, frequent-flyer status, and reservations capabilities.

As business travelers increasingly access the Internet, more and more companies are following American Airlines' lead and launching on-line reservation systems to try to capture a portion of this market.[10] For example, American Express and Microsoft announced a joint plan to develop an on-line reservation system for corporate travelers, to be available early in 1997. Performance Quest International, a company based in Scottsdale, Arizona, has initiated Travel Quest, a Web site that allows business and leisure travelers to book airline, hotel, and car reservations in one step. The site claims to be garnering nearly 15,000 "hits" per day. Meanwhile, Direct Travel, Inc., of New York has been gathering converts to DirectLink, an on-line booking service also aimed at business travelers. DirectLink, which is available to clients of Direct Travel (one of the largest U.S. travel agencies), allows corporate employees to make their own arrangements but offers only reservations that comply with those employees' travel policies. For example, the system can be programmed to search for the cheapest fare within a 2-hour window of a requested departure time. Through DirectLink, the executive submits an e-mail request detailing when and where she wants to go and, within 6 minutes, DirectLink sends back a report of available options. The traveler then confirms the selection on-line. In addition, DirectLink will check the itinerary against current rates every few hours so that the traveler will be alerted and reticketed if favorable fare changes occur.

Many large corporations face the age-old conundrum of how to cost-effectively penetrate the middle market for products and services. In the aggregate, small and mid-sized companies represent enormous market potential. However, individually, such companies often are not economical for large providers to pursue, at least not directly. Customer-connecting technologies, such as the Web, are changing the economics of small-market penetration, providing new opportunities to previously unserved market segments.

Small Business Problems
Just Ask ERNIE

Many small, entrepreneurial companies don't have the resources to obtain top-notch consulting advice on tax, accounting, and technology issues, or don't generate sufficient volume to be served in the usual way by major professional service firms. To fill this gap, Ernst & Young launched ERNIE, an on-line consulting service aimed at companies with less than $200 million in revenues. This segment includes almost 9,000 clients as well as the entire market of recent initial public offerings.

Based on a fixed subscription price, customers gain access to a private site on the Internet's World Wide Web to submit direct questions to the firm. Via the Internet, users give ERNIE the topic, the question, and some background information. Questions arrive at ERNIE, are sorted by broad subject category (i.e., tax, audit, consulting), and then are routed through an internal knowledge web, or intranet, to the business professional who is most knowledgeable about the industry, topic, or issue at hand. Answers are routed back through the intranet and are posted to the user's e-mail account within two business days.

For instant information, subscribers can scroll through a database of answers to previously asked questions. Analysis of question volume resulted in the launch of Trendwatch, in which experts offer perspectives on the larger issues raised in the most frequently asked questions. ERNIE, in conjunction with Farcast, also offers a news clipping service that subscribers can custom-design for their own interests. The Farcast service allows for 24-hour, unlimited search and text retrieval, access to more than 70 industry information broadcasts, and personal electronic agents called *Druids* that filter and deliver specific information customized for the customer.

"With ERNIE, the way businesses make decisions is being dramatically altered," said Roger Nelson, deputy chairman of consulting services. "Over time, the electronic delivery of professional services will become a fundamental component of the overall service delivery paradigm in our industry."

This type of on-line service provides a useful example of how companies—in this case, professional services—can extend the traditional business model to make a firm's know-how available cost-effectively to a wider audience than ever before.

New Businesses, New Value Propositions

Virtual Vineyards
Uncorking Opportunity

The California wine market has experienced phenomenal growth over the last 15 years, taking its place alongside the great wine-growing regions of the world. Some 9,000 wineries operate across the state, producing some of the finest varietal and blended wines available. However, given the limited scale of most of these operations, particularly those producing fewer than 10,000 cases per year, many of the wineries lacked access to the broader consumer market.

In late 1993, Robert Olson came up with a solution to this problem—marketing wines of small California vineyards over the Internet.[11] Teaming with sommelier Peter Granoff, he launched a Web site in January 1995 that serves as both an educational resource for wine consumers and a distribution channel for more than 65 small wineries. All wines presented on the site are described by Granoff, "the Cork Dork," who has 20 years' experience assessing wine quality. The site provides detailed information about each wine, the winery, and the winemaker, along with a tasting chart to assist site visitors in making their selections. A site visitor can order on-line the wine he wants and have it shipped to his front door. The site thus elevates what was a cottage industry to a position in which it can compete with the distribution systems of large wineries. Granoff and Olson recently have added specialty food products to the Web site to complement the wine selections.

Marketing programs using Internet technology require extensive back-office support to succeed. This back office must manage all the nuts and bolts of direct marketing: establishing complete electronic integration with the warehouse, developing and sustaining a professional fulfillment process, and maintaining a just-in-time inventory program.

Once these critical elements are in place, however, the Web offers almost unlimited potential for growth. For example, Virtual Vineyards recently has translated portions of its Web site into Japanese, resulting in large orders from Japanese customers. Other international sales are growing rapidly (currently representing approximately 10 percent of all customers and an even greater share of revenues), and Granoff has plans to translate Web information into other languages in the near future to expand sales further.

As of October 1996, Virtual Vineyards represented 65 vineyards, and many more were being evaluated. The first selections in an imported wine portfolio also were added in October 1996.

The personal nature of the Web site permits close customer interaction. Several thousand Web users visit the Virtual Vineyards site daily, and sales have been compounding at approximately 20 percent per month. Granoff and Olson have designed the site so that they can track where each of these visitors goes on the Web site and how long each browses there. Virtual Vineyards is able to remind regular customers via e-mail of the arrival of new wines that might meet their tastes (as evidenced by purchase histories) and to offer prepackaged food and wine gift baskets tailored to seasonal events. In addition, Virtual Vineyards' database of purchases allows customers to add their own notations as to what they liked or disliked about previous purchases, making it possible for customers to call up favorite selections even when they cannot recall wine names or years.

Virtual Vineyards is one example of the broad array of entirely new businesses poised to emerge as a result of the unique properties of the Internet. With the Web's ability for easily building COINS, it is highly likely that "network managers" will emerge in every industry that depends on high search or assembly costs to bring buyers and sellers together.

Virtual Vineyards demonstrates the capacity of electronic commerce to broaden a market and build a community of interest. The next case goes further and illustrates the ability to actually create a market on-line.

Onsale Inc.
Who'll Start the Bidding?

One of the Internet's most dynamic businesses is Onsale Inc., an on-line auction service that brings together buyers and sellers of used computers.[12] Onsale Inc. attracts people with its low prices and a gamelike experience that mimics a live auction. Refurbished computers are natural products for on-line auctioning. Jerry Kaplan, Onsale founder, exclaimed in a *Wall Street Journal* interview, "Old computers rot faster than fruit!" The constant change in technology means retailers frequently are stuck with excess inventory. The U.S. market for refurbished computer goods is estimated to be nearly $7 billion.

Unlike most of the nearly 100,000 commercial Web sites at which only the buyer and seller interact, Onsale's auction site accommodates many people, as does a live auction. Noted computer industry observer Esther Dyson remarked in the *Wall Street Journal,* "It's a community built around commerce. It moves. It's alive."[12] Users can see and respond to one another's bids only seconds after the bids are placed on-line. It is this interplay of the Internet's strengths—real-time communication and virtual community—that Onsale exploits. As with real auctions, the experience can be addictive for some users: "It's the technocrat's answer to the Home Shopping Network," says Scott Ignacio, a California computer consultant. "I like the haggle."

Approximately 36,000 of the nearly 750,000 weekly visitors to Onsale's Web site actually bid on or buy computer goods. As of the summer of 1996, Onsale was grossing $700,000 in weekly revenues. During 1996, its first year in business, Onsale expects to post $35 million in revenues. Gross profit margins approach 15 percent, with net profits expected to be approximately 10 percent.

Our final case illustrates the possibilities of moving beyond commerce and providing ongoing customer care on-line.

Cisco
The Router to Success

Cisco Systems is a company built literally on the concept of connecting customers.[13] It was founded in 1984 by the husband-and-wife team of Leonard Bosack and Sandra Lerner to capitalize on technology that Bosack, then manager of Stanford's computer science laboratory, had created to link different computer networks within the school. In classic Silicon Valley fashion, Bosack and Lerner mortgaged their house, bought a used mainframe computer, put it in their garage, and began developing a commercial network router.

Cisco's first sale was in 1986. Since then, the company has grown at an extraordinary pace, earning revenues in excess of $4 billion by 1996 (an 83 percent increase over 1995). Through a number of acquisitions and partnerships, the company is now able to offer total solutions and one-stop shopping for customers linking their own networks, using the Internet or World Wide Web (what Cisco calls "internetworking").

Cisco Connection Online, launched in 1991, has enabled Cisco to provide superior customer care and support despite breathtaking growth in the number of customers served and products offered. Today it logs more than one million contacts per month. Cisco delivers three levels of on-line service. For its largest customers, Cisco Marketplace provides on-line ordering with current product line and price lists. This produced $120 million in on-line sales between August 1996 and January 1997. Second, Cisco Commerce Agents allow customers to track the order fulfillment process. Third, the Technical and Support Library provides access to on-line diagnosis and problem solving.

In addition to offering sophisticated customers an on-line order service, the system has produced a number of benefits. More than 70% of the log-ins save a call to Cisco, reducing the need for sales and service personnel. An on-line "bug toolkit" automatically notifies customers of software problems and suggests potential work-arounds. Since implementing the Cisco Connection Online, customer satisfaction scores have increased more than 20 percent (3.4 to 4.2 out of 5.0). Cisco now guarantees that if a problem is not resolved within 48 hours, they will personally contact the customer.

Cisco has also moved toward closing the loop of customer information and knowledge. The Customer Advocacy Response Engine (CARE) system integrates customer interactions by phone, fax, and e-mail. E-mails are sent to reps automatically if customer log-ins suggest a problem.

Cisco's experience shows that intelligent use of electronic commerce and care technology can enable a business to improve service quality while undergoing rates of growth that would strain traditional service operations.

The applications of technology are moving beyond the automation of traditional marketing, sales, and service functions to provide strategic capabilities and the potential to transform a firm's approach to the market. In this chapter, we have discussed and illustrated the current application of technologies to conduct conversations with customers so that companies can understand and serve customers better, collaborate with them to create mutual value, and strengthen bonds to engage in electronic commerce for the purposes of extending market penetration for existing products and creating entirely new businesses. We also showed how the ongoing relationship can be conducted on-line, at least in part. This rapidly evolving area promises to be increasingly important for demand-side strategy by expanding the number of potential customers, permitting more precise value propositions, and allowing for new forms of reward and risk sharing. In the next chapter, we outline the third foundation of customer-connected strategy, customer economics.

Finding out where the money is

CUSTOMER ECONOMICS

Willie Sutton, a prominent member of the U.S. financial community in the 1920s and '30s, had two distinctive competencies: robbing banks and escaping from jail. In a famous but apocryphal story, when asked why he robbed banks, Willie replied, "Because that's where the money is." No better advice can be given to businesses searching for sources of shareholder value than to find out where the money is.[1]

Why do two firms such as competing local TV stations, with comparable technological and physical assets serving the same market, often have widely disparate market value? If you were buying the more valuable station, for what would you be paying a premium? If you bought the lesser station, how would you go about adding value? Most people don't have much trouble solving this problem: Clearly, one station has a larger or more valuable audience. The value of businesses such as TV and radio stations is determined by the number and quality of their customers and, when such businesses are sold, their value often is calculated on a per-customer basis. This relationship between the value of a firm and the number and quality of its customers holds not only for such obvious cases but also is true of almost all businesses. Indeed, the closer we look at the valuation of businesses, the more we become convinced that there are few exceptions to the rule that the value of a firm is equal to the aggregate value of its customer relationships.

Customer economics is the analysis of the value of a business in terms of the number and quality of its customer relationships. Of course, all of microeconomics is concerned with the way customers and firms make decisions, but most discussions of shareholder value focus on the firm's selection and management of its portfolio of financial and physical assets. We are concerned instead with the use of economic concepts and tools to build a portfolio of valuable customer relationships and to maximize the value of those relationships. Our approach will be to explore a firm's search for shareholder value from the perspective of managing that firm's customer portfolio.

Viewing a business as a customer portfolio manager enables us to establish the link between efforts to create customer value and the shareholder value those efforts produce. Because a firm's shareholder value can be calculated as the present value of its expected net cash flows, and those cash flows are derived from the firm's customers, it follows that the aggregate value of that firm's shares equals the present value of the net cash flows that the market expects the firm to earn from its current and future customers. The future value of the firm therefore depends on how effectively the company acquires profitable new customers, develops the profitability of existing customers, and retains existing profitable relationships.

In this chapter, we outline the basic tools necessary to evaluate customer relationships and to deploy resources on customer acquisition, development, and retention to maximize the value of the customer portfolio. We discuss the following concepts:

- *The value of customer relationships*: We show how to use the volume, margin, and duration model and the probability-of-purchase model to estimate individual relationship and customer group value.

- *The distribution of customer relationship value*: We explore the insights gained by understanding the customer value frequency distribution, cumulative customer value function, and the relationship between the variance of relationship values and value concentration.

- *Managing the customer portfolio for maximum growth*: We introduce the concept of economic segmentation, which is based on customer value and responsiveness, and show how it is applied to develop an optimal portfolio growth model.

This chapter necessarily involves some mathematics, which we present in figures that include graphs and formulas we think all readers will be able to understand. Most of the concepts also are illustrated arithmetically using the case example of ScrubaDub Car Wash.

THE VALUE *of* CUSTOMER RELATIONSHIPS

If customer relationships are a firm's most valuable assets, how can a firm estimate these relationships' value and decide how much to invest in getting and keeping them? As we mentioned in the introduction, the asset value of a customer relationship is called *customer equity*. Like any asset, the value of customer equity depends on the net cash flow over time.

The task of calculating customer equity involves identifying the cash flows received from a particular customer or group, the outflow of cash necessary to establish and maintain the customer relationship, and the period over which the relationship will continue. We can think about customer value as comprising two components: inflows produced by the relationship, and outflows necessary to establish and maintain the relationship. *Intrinsic* customer value is the stream of net cash flows you receive from the customer. The size and value of this cash flow stream depends on the customer's *volume* of purchases per period, the *margin* on those purchases, and the *duration* of the relationship or number of periods over which these purchases are made. Discounting this cash flow stream by the firm's cost of capital represents the value of the relationship if it were costless to establish and maintain.

Of course, relationships are not costless. To receive the customer revenue stream, a firm incurs acquisition, development, and retention (ADR) costs. *Acquisition costs* refer to the investment made to attract and qualify customers and include the marketing, advertising, and selling expenses associated with acquiring new customers. *Development costs* are those expenditures made to increase and maintain the value of existing relationships, such as learning more about the customers' needs, increasing their probability of purchase, or responding to their requests and servicing their accounts. *Retention costs* involve expenditures to increase the duration of relationships, to reduce customer defections, or to reactivate customers.

Customer equity, the net value of the customer relationship, is simply the difference between intrinsic value and the ADR costs. Figure 4-1 illustrates graphically how customer equity is calculated. Increases in three of the variables—volume, margin, and duration—raise the value of customer equity. For a given level of volume, margin, and duration, increases in ADR costs and the discount rate reduce the value of customer equity. In principle, if you know the

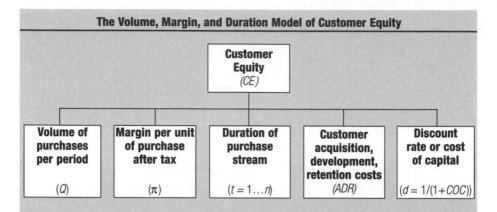

The Volume, Margin, and Duration Model of Customer Equity

This relationship can be expressed mathematically as the volume, margin, and duration model of customer equity:

$$CE = \sum_{t=1}^{n} Q_t \pi_t d^t - \sum_{t=1}^{n} (D_t + R_t) \, d^t - A_1$$

From this formula, the basic rules for maximizing customer value can be readily derived:

- **Invest in acquiring a customer if the expected net present value of cash flows from the customer is equal to or greater than the acquisition costs.**
- **Acquisition costs are sunk costs and irrelevant after the customer has been acquired.**
- **The value of a customer can be raised by increasing the volume of purchases, the margin on purchases, or the period over which the purchases are made.**
- **Invest in customer development and retention until, at the margin, the increases in customer value attributable to changes in volume, margin, and duration are equal to the costs of achieving them.**
- **An increase in any one of volume, margin, or duration will increase customer value so long as there is no offsetting decline in one or both of the other variables.**

Figure 4-1

values of these variables, you can determine the value of any customer relationship. Although historical data are sometimes useful, it is critical to estimate the future or expected values of these variables. In practice, there sometimes are significant computation and estimation issues. However, for many companies, the effort to nail down workable estimates of the value of these variables is amply repaid in the form of better focus in the search for shareholder value.

As those of you who glance at the equation below the graphic in Figure 4-1 will notice, the customer asset valuation formula is essentially the same as that for a bond or any financial asset. The first term, volume × margin, is analogous to a bond coupon or stock dividend, the cash you receive from the asset. The second, customer development and retention costs per period, represents the costs that you incur in serving and keeping these customers; these are similar to financial management fees. The last term, customer acquisition costs, is comparable to the price and commission paid to acquire a financial asset.

The customer equity model enables us to identify valuable customer relationships, to understand and select among alternative means of increasing the value of these relationships, and to avoid simplistic prescriptions about what determines the most valuable customer relationships. Obviously, a customer relationship is valuable only when the present value of the net cash flows received is greater than the expenditures made to acquire, develop, and retain the customer relationship. Beyond this point, the value of a customer relationship may be raised by increasing margin, volume, or duration, as long as one does not suffer an offsetting decline in one or more of the other variables.

Because volume, margin, and duration respond to the same factors, maximizing the value of a relationship involves carefully balancing the elements of the value proposition and considering long-term as well as short-term factors. For example, increasing current prices may produce short-term gains in margin but may reduce the future volume of purchases and the duration of the relationship. Depending on the customer's price elasticity, switching-related costs, and the discount rate, the net effect on customer relationship value of changing one variable may be positive, neutral, or negative.

The volume, margin, and duration model of customer relationship value is immensely useful for businesses that have continuous customer relationships of discrete duration, such as insurance companies, telephone service providers, and magazine publishers. With this model we can rank customers by the expected value of the relationship, determine how much we can afford to spend on getting and keeping their business, and test ideas for increasing the value of the relationship.

The volume, margin, and duration model also is extremely useful in assessing popular prescriptions for increasing customer value and determining whether they fit the circumstances faced by a firm. Just as financial markets are full of people with pet theories of stock and portfolio selection, the manager trying to grow his customer portfolio will encounter many appealing shortcuts to building customer value. One such axiom is, "It costs 5 to10 times as much to get a new customer as to keep an existing one." On the surface, this seems to be a powerful argument to throttle back on customer acquisition and devote more resources to retention, which may, in fact, be the right course for many companies. However, once you are familiar with the customer equity model, you will appreciate that even if this estimate of the relative costs of acquisition and retention were true in all cases (and it is not), such evidence would be irrelevant, because what matters is not the *cost* of acquisition but the *return* on the investment. As long as the value of the customer relationship, properly calculated, exceeds the cost of acquisition, the firm should acquire the customer.

The value of an individual customer relationship is determined by all the factors in the customer equity formula. You wouldn't buy a bond just because your broker told you it had a longer term to maturity, any more than you would buy a stock simply because it had a high dividend. Rather, you would consider all the factors that together determine a financial asset's value. Similarly, without making the customer equity calculation, it often is difficult to identify the most valuable customers. For example, consider two customers. One, Big Spender, is expected to purchase 10 units per year for the next 6 years; the other, True Blue, is expected to buy 7 units per year for the next 10 years. Which is more valuable, Big Spender, with the higher rate of purchase, or True Blue, with the longer relationship? If the after-tax margin per purchase in both cases is $5.00 per unit and we use a 10-percent discount rate, then these customers, despite 30 percent and 40 percent differences in annual volume and duration respectively, have net present values within 2 percent of one another. No variable by itself is an infallible indicator of value. Volume may be overwhelmed by duration and vice versa; margins may be different and overwhelm the effects of purchase rates and duration. Even if product margins are uniform for all customers, different ADR costs will result in different customer values.

Although we ignored ADR costs in our example, we know that in the real world these costs can be substantial. If it costs $50.00 to acquire Big Spender and only $10.00 to acquire True Blue, it becomes immediately obvious which relationship is more valuable.

Probability-of-Purchase and Customer Relationship Value

The volume, margin, and duration model of customer equity (just described) portrays the customer relationship as if it were continuous and uniform over some discrete relationship duration. For example, you are either a cable TV subscriber or you are not; if you are, the revenue stream from your subscription is uniform over the period of your subscription.

However, many relationships are not continuous; instead, they represent a series of probabilistic events. In these cases, we need to take account of the probability that the customer will buy from the seller in any particular period. For instance, you may prefer Coke to Pepsi, but, for a variety of reasons, the probabil-

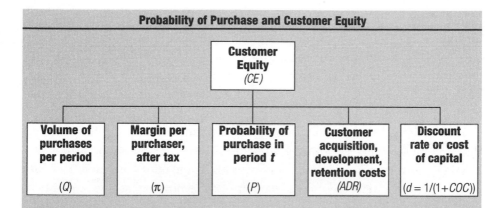

Algebraically, the relationship between customer equity and these variables can be expressed as the sum of expected cash flows over time (t = 1...n):

$$CE = \sum_{t=1}^{n} P_t\,(Q_t\pi_t)\,d^t - \sum_{t=1}^{n} (D_t + R_t)\,d^t - A_1$$

Since *d* is less than one, this geometric series converges to the much more convenient form below, which can be used when the factors are constant over a relatively long time:

$$CE = P\,[\frac{Q\pi}{(1-d)} - Q\pi] - [\frac{(D+R)}{(1-d)} - (D+R)] - A_1$$

which is equivalent to:

$$CE = P\frac{Q\pi}{COC} - \frac{(D+R)}{COC} - A_1$$

Figure 4-2

ity that you will buy Coke at any given time may be only 80 percent. Despite your preference for Coke, it may account for only 80 percent of your total soft-drink purchases. Similarly, business buyers rarely purchase all of their requirements from a single seller but instead patronize several suppliers, varying the percentage of business given to each to provide incentives for the suppliers to offer better deals or to reward them for good service. In these cases, which represent the bulk of consumer goods and many other business purchases, the simpler notion of continuous duration and its relationship to the retention rate must be modified.

Figure 4-2 illustrates the calculation of customer equity when the purchase stream is a series of probabilistic events. When the duration of the relationship is fairly long and the expected probability of purchase is relatively stable, the formula reduces to a very simple ratio that provides an easy way to evaluate options. The probability-of-purchase (or repurchase) coefficient enables us not only to estimate individual customer values but also to forge links to buyer behavior models and to estimate potential market size and the yield on efforts to change customers' probability of purchase.

In addition, the probability-of-purchase model can provide insights into the firm's allocation of resources to acquire more customers or to develop existing customers more fully. In many cases, companies have acquired customers but have captured only a fraction of their purchases. Looking only at product category share can obscure the trade-off between acquisitions and development.

Garth Hallberg has reported that in 1992, Folger's commanded 25 percent of the coffee category compared to Traditional Maxwell House's 15-percent share, but Folger's penetration of heavy coffee buyers was only 6 points higher than Maxwell House's (58 versus 52 percent). However, Folger's heavy buyers had (using our terms) a 38-percent probability of buying Folger's, whereas heavy buyers bought Maxwell House only 24 percent of the time.[2]

Let us assume that heavy coffee buyers purchase, on average, 20 cans per year, with a net margin of $1 per package, or $20 per year, and that they maintain this purchase stream for a relatively long time. Using a 10-percent cost-of-capital rate ($d = 0.9091$), the intrinsic value of a heavy coffee buyer is $200 [20 ÷ (1 − 0.9091) − 20]. Folger's heavy-coffee-buyer customer equity is 38 percent of this, or $76.00. Maxwell House's customer equity is only $48.00 because of the lower, 24-percent probability of purchase.

Should Maxwell House try to acquire more high-value buyers or develop the value (i.e., increase the probability of purchase) of those with whom the firm already has a relationship? Unless there is an overall budget constraint, the decisions about whether to acquire new customers or to develop existing ones are essentially independent of one another. The amount devoted to each activity depends on its respective costs and yields. If there were no budget constraints, Maxwell House should try to acquire new heavy coffee buyers up to the point at which these customers cost approximately $48.00 to acquire. Because each percentage-point increase in probability of purchase is worth nearly $2.00 per customer, Maxwell House would also gain by developing existing heavy buyers until the cost of the last point reaches $2.00.

The probability-of-purchase model can also be applied to estimate the expected duration of a relationship. In many cases, companies find it difficult to assess the length of time that the relationship will endure. Historical data on cohort groups and customers with similar characteristics may be helpful but often are unreliable guides to future behavior. However, many companies can, by survey or through their sales force, estimate a customer's current or near-term probability of purchase or repurchase.

Let us assume that the sales force reports that a customer has an 80-percent probability of repurchase. If the decision to purchase is made annually, and we assume that the repurchase rate will remain constant (or, equivalently, if we have no reason to believe it will change), then the likelihood that the customer will remain for 4 years is approximately 41 percent [(0.8) (0.8) (0.8) (0.8)]. Similarly, if we have some reason to believe that the probability of purchase will decline or increase regularly over time (due to, say, experience or increased knowledge of needs), the estimates of likely duration may be adjusted accordingly.

Estimates of the value of acquisition and retention efforts can be tied to changes in relationship value due to increases in probability of purchase. For example, if current probability of purchase with a $5.00 annual margin is 30 percent and the cost of capital is 10 percent, the intrinsic value of the relationship is approximately $15.00. If research indicates that a customer development program costing $2.00 per customer would result in a 10-point increase in probability of purchase to 40 percent, the intrinsic value would rise to $20.00 and net customer equity would be $18.00.

The Value of Customer Groups or Segments

Up to this point, we have discussed the value of individual customer relationships. All other things being equal, understanding the value of individual customer relationships always increases the *potential* value of the customer portfolio and, hence, of the business. This is because the firm can target only those customer relationships that are valuable and avoid or disengage from those that are not. Though this is conceptually true for all firms, there are many situations in which knowledge of the customer at the individual level is impractical or prohibitively expensive to acquire.

Many consumer packaged and nondurable goods, although purchased regularly by millions of people, do not generate sufficient *individual* customer value to warrant extensive investments in customer-specific knowledge. Advances in connecting technologies (see Chapter 3) are continually reducing the costs of achieving individual customer knowledge but, for some time into the future, many companies will have to manage their customer portfolios in terms of groups, based on statistical profiles of representative customers.

The value of a customer group is estimated similarly to that of individual customers, but in these cases we need to take into account segment size and use

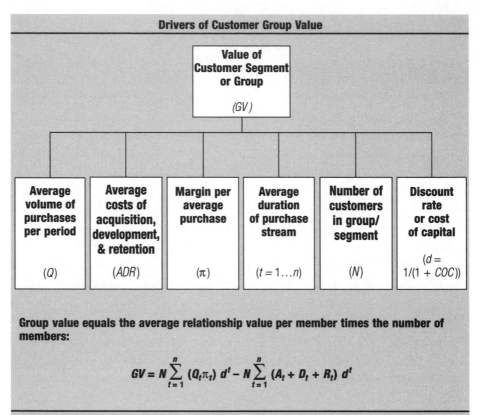

Drivers of Customer Group Value

Value of
Customer Segment
or Group

(GV)

Average volume of purchases per period	Average costs of acquisition, development, & retention	Margin per average purchase	Average duration of purchase stream	Number of customers in group/ segment	Discount rate or cost of capital
(Q)	*(ADR)*	(π)	$(t = 1 \ldots n)$	*(N)*	$(d = 1/(1 + COC))$

Group value equals the average relationship value per member times the number of members:

$$GV = N \sum_{t=1}^{n} (Q_t \pi_t)\, d^t - N \sum_{t=1}^{n} (A_t + D_t + R_t)\, d^t$$

Figure 4-3

average values for volume, margin, and duration (Figure 4-3). For most applications, it is necessary also to aggregate expenditures on acquisition, development, and retention. The use of average values introduces some imprecision into the estimates of firm value and calls for careful analysis of the grouping scheme used. As we will show, the effectiveness of a segmentation scheme as a basis to increase firm value depends on the quality of the customer value distributions that are generated.

Acquisition-Cost Ratio and Customer Duration

In many cases, we don't have precise estimates of expected customer duration and need to make informed judgments about how much to devote to the acquisition of particular customers or groups. The acquisition-cost ratio and a simple table of the values of dollars received in the future provide a useful way of assessing acquisition costs.

The acquisition cost is important in the initial assessment of prospects. The higher the acquisition cost is relative to annual net cash flows, the longer the customer duration must be to generate a positive value. This is the same as a financial "payback" analysis.

The break-even duration period is the number of years necessary for the value of the annual cash flow stream to equal the acquisition cost. If there were no discount factor, it would simply be the ratio of acquisition costs to annual cash flow $(A/Q\pi)$. For example, if the acquisition cost were \$4 and net cash flow each period were \$2, it would take 2 years to break even. The acquisition-cost ratio relates the number of current dollars spent to get dollars in the future. Because the value of future dollars diminishes the further out in time that they are received, it takes more of these dollars to equal a current dollar and we have to find the cumulative *discounted* equivalent, as shown in Figure 4-4. For example, if the acquisition cost were \$30 and annual cash flows \$10, the acquisition-cost ratio of 3 indicates that the customer tenure must be at least long enough for each dollar of annual cash flow to generate a future value of 3, which occurs just before the fourth year if a 10-percent discount rate is used.

The relationship between acquisition costs and duration explains why some people assert that modest increases in retention rates cause dramatic increases in customer relationship value: For instance, it is sometimes asserted that a 5-percentage-point increase in *retention rates* may increase the value of a typical customer relationship by 35 to 95 percent. In those industries that have relatively high acquisition-cost ratios, such as insurance and credit cards, the net value of a customer relationship does increase dramatically as the duration of the relationship crosses over the break-even period and for the first several years thereafter. However, this is an *acquisition*-related consideration that underlines the importance of targeting customers whose expected relationship durations exceed the break-even period.

Once you have a customer relationship, investments in development and retention must be evaluated against the *incremental* yield, which generally will be much less dramatic. The increase in value of extending an existing customer relationship equals the net present value of the added cash flows over the incremental years of the relationship. It can be very misleading to talk about increases in relationship value in terms of retention rates, as the following example demonstrates. The retention rate is equal to 1 minus the reciprocal of the average customer duration. If the customer base turns over, on average, every 10 years, then, on average, 10 percent of the customers leave each year. The reciprocal of 10 is $^1/_{10}$, or 10 percent, which is the defection rate. The average retention rate is 1 minus the defection rate—in this example, 90 percent. Clearly, an increase in retention rate—say, 5

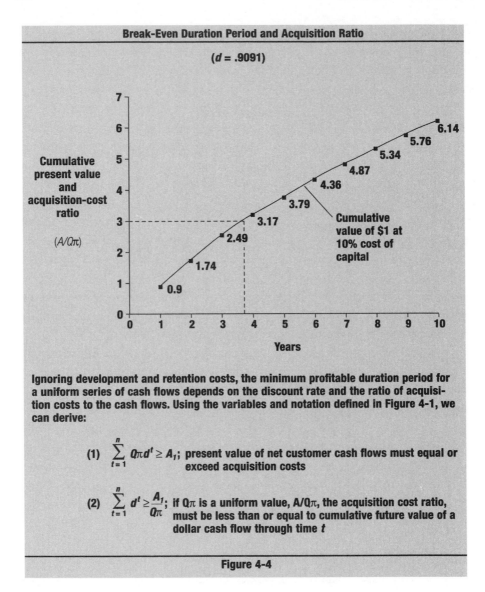

Break-Even Duration Period and Acquisition Ratio

$(d = .9091)$

Cumulative present value and acquisition-cost ratio

$(A/Q\pi)$

Years

Ignoring development and retention costs, the minimum profitable duration period for a uniform series of cash flows depends on the discount rate and the ratio of acquisition costs to the cash flows. Using the variables and notation defined in Figure 4-1, we can derive:

(1) $\sum_{t=1}^{n} Q\pi d^t \geq A_1$; present value of net customer cash flows must equal or exceed acquisition costs

(2) $\sum_{t=1}^{n} d^t \geq \dfrac{A_1}{Q\pi}$; if $Q\pi$ is a uniform value, $A/Q\pi$, the acquisition cost ratio, must be less than or equal to cumulative future value of a dollar cash flow through time t

Figure 4-4

points—will increase the intrinsic value of the relationship—but how much? A 5-point increase in retention rates can come about in an infinite number of ways. For example, a shift from a 4-year to a 5-year average duration is equivalent to moving the average retention rate from 75 to 80 percent. Shifting the average duration from 10 to 20 years is the same as moving from a 90-percent to a 95-percent retention rate. Both examples represent 5-point increases in retention rates, but which results in a more dramatic increase in customer value?

First, notice that the modest-sounding 5-percentage-point increase in retention rates turns out to require hefty 25- or 100-percent increases in average customer duration. In the case in which the relationship was extended from 4 to 5 years, the increase in relationship value is the discounted value of the net cash flows realized in the fifth year. Assuming a uniform net cash flow and no acquisition costs and using a 10-percent discount rate, the additional value attributable to changing the number of years is approximately 20 percent: This is not bad, although it is well below the increases sometimes claimed. Moving from a 10-year to a 20-year average duration under the same assumptions results in nearly a 38-percent increase in value. The reason that the 25- and 100-percent increases in duration yield only 20- and 38-percent increases in intrinsic value is because the cash flows in the future years have lower present values. Of course, it may be less expensive to increase the average duration by 1 year than 10, resulting in a greater net relationship value.

The customer equity model demonstrates that the optimal retention rate is a function of the relative costs of acquisition, development, and retention. Businesses in which acquisition costs are relatively small compared to annual net cash flow (low acquisition-cost ratio) find that the minimum or break-even customer duration is lower and, hence, customer retention and loyalty are relatively less valuable. These businesses can afford to pursue customers with lower expected durations or loyalty.

The acquisition-cost ratio also determines the minimum customer relationship value that businesses can pursue profitably. For any given level of customer duration, the lower the acquisition cost, the less intrinsically valuable a customer relationship must be to warrant acquisition. This fact can be used also to explain the use of multiple marketing channels in businesses characterized by a broad range of customer values. In Chapter 5, we'll discuss how Staples employs different channels to reach customer groups with different values.

Higher-value customers naturally warrant higher acquisition investments, but they also attract more attention from rivals, so the acquisition (and retention) costs will likely be higher. Because they have more avid suitors, these customers have more bargaining power. Therefore, firms must devote more specialized and dedicated resources to them if they are to win and hold such customers.

Customers of more modest intrinsic value generally will be more numerous, and less costly acquisition strategies are appropriate. Competitive advantage can be gained by matching the acquisition strategy to the customer value distribution, as illustrated by the case of Staples Direct, which is discussed in more detail later.

ScrubaDub
Polishing the Customer Base

This case affords us a look at how the customer equity and ADR concepts introduced thus far provide strategic insights to a business and shape its customer portfolio.[3] Even in the seemingly straightforward car wash business, understanding the relative values of customer groups can fuel the development of a distinctive relationship strategy and a new business model. To an outsider, the economics of the car wash industry seem pretty simple: Wash more cars and sell more high-margin extras such as hot wax. In fact, most car washes do emphasize traffic-building strategies aimed at attracting anyone with a car: high-traffic locations to catch impulse buyers, heavy coupon distribution to draw people in, and drive-time commercials on the most popular radio stations. A car is a car, right? All cars need to be washed sometime.

Traditional car wash companies pursued a basic product-driven model. All customers were viewed as essentially equal, the core product was differentiated only modestly, pricing was strictly market-based, with little or no performance-based risk sharing, and the operator assumed a product manager role that stressed cost control. However, ScrubaDub, a family-owned eastern Massachusetts chain, has achieved superior results by using its knowledge of customer value to build a valuable customer portfolio, extend the range of its value proposition, and offer performance-based reward sharing to its customers.

In 1991, ScrubaDub was recovering from a disappointing year of bad weather and slow growth. Marshall Paisner, ScrubaDub's founder and president, suspected that the key to greater profits was not attracting more cars but attracting more valuable car wash customers. Marshall, his wife Elaine, and their sons Dan and Bob began analyzing the usage patterns of their customers to find out which customers spent the most per visit and who made the most frequent visits to the car wash.

The Paisners found that the population of car wash buyers varied substantially in the number of car washes purchased each year and the amount spent at each visit. Nearly half the population patronized a car wash less than once per year. The other half visited more frequently. As illustrated in Figure 4-5A, the distribution of car wash customers is skewed to the left because of the large proportion of low-frequency buyers. This situation is typical of many service businesses, such as hospitals, restaurants, and dry cleaners, in which a large number of infrequent users dominate the customer count.

Distribution of Car Wash Buyers

A. Percentage of Car Wash Buyers at Each Frequency Level

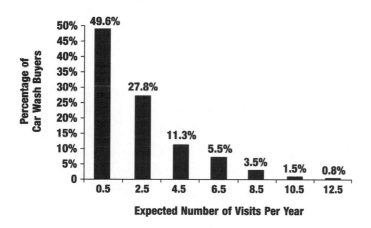

B. Percentage of Visits by Each Frequency Group

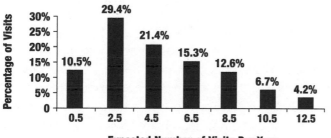

C. Percentage of Total Revenue by Frequency Group

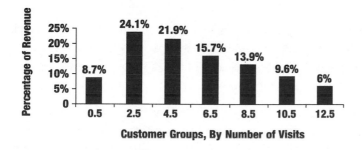

Figure 4-5

Looking at just these data, one might conclude that the traditional car wash strategy of trying to build traffic across all customers was justified. After all, half of all customers visit less than once yearly. However, experience had shown that it was nearly impossible to alter the buying behavior of the infrequent buyer. Taking a closer look at the data from a customer-relationship value perspective suggested a more fruitful strategy. As shown in Figure 4-5B, the distribution of total visits was far less skewed. Although the very-low- and low-frequency buyers accounted for more than 75 percent (76.4) of the customer count, they accounted for only 40 percent of total annual visits. Roughly a quarter of the customers accounted for 60 percent of total visits.

In addition to studying frequency of visits, ScrubaDub determined that the amount spent per visit also was directly related to frequency of visit. Very-low- and low-frequency users tended to buy the basic car wash and to spend, on average, approximately $5.25 per visit. The moderate users bought a mix of basic and higher-end products, averaging $6.50 per visit. The high- and very-high-user groups averaged $7.00 and $9.00 per visit, respectively. As shown in Figure 4-5C, the spend-per-visit data reinforced the value of the higher-use customers, as the margins on the special services are much higher.

From the revenue distribution data, it appeared that five groups of customers were representative of the market: very-low-frequency customers, representing almost 50 percent of customers and 8.7 percent of revenues; low-frequency customers, accounting for roughly one-fourth of all customers and revenues; moderate-frequency customers, representing 16.7 percent of customers in the 4.5- and 6.5-visits-per-year range, who account for nearly 38 percent of revenues; high-frequency customers who, while only 5 percent of the customer count, generate almost one-fourth of the revenues; and the outlier group of very-high-frequency users.

As they did not have access to customer duration or retention rate data, the Paisners estimated the duration for all groups at 4 years (75-percent retention). Customer acquisition and development costs were allocated on a per-customer basis because the efforts were targeted broadly to all customers. The customer information, together with cost data, enabled ScrubaDub to develop customer relationship values, as shown in Figure 4-6.

Looking at the results of their customer profitability analysis, the Paisners could see that a mass-market approach overinvested in acquiring low-value customer relationships and underinvested in high-end relationships. A car-wash customer portfolio that was weighted with the same proportion of customer values as the

Car Wash Customer Value Customer Groups (Total Market)

	Very Low	Low	Moderate	High	Very High
Average purchase per visit	$5.25	$5.25	$6.50	$7.00	$9.00
Margin per purchase (AT)	5%	5%	10%	20%	30%
Number of visits per year	0.5	2.5	5.2	7.1	12.5
Gross contribution per year (AT)	$0.13	$0.66	$3.38	$9.94	$33.75
Development and retention cost per customer/year (AT)	$1.00	$1.00	$1.00	$1.00	$1.00
Net contribution per year (AT)	$(0.87)	$(0.34)	$2.38	$8.94	$32.75
Average duration (years)	4	4	4	4	4
Discount rate (10% EOY)	0.9091	0.9091	0.9091	0.9091	0.9091
Pre-acquisition cost value	$(2.75)	$(1.08)	$7.54	$31.51	$106.98
Acquisition cost (AT)	$1.00	$1.00	$1.00	$1.00	$1.00
Net value of relationship	$(3.75)	$(2.08)	$6.54	$30.51	$105.98
Customers in group	49.6%	27.8%	16.7%	5.0%	0.8%
Revenues, by group	8.7%	24.1%	37.6%	23.6%	6.0%

Figure 4-6

entire market was a little better than a break-even proposition, with an average customer equity of just more than $1.00.

Clearly, there were tremendous gains to be made by focusing ADR efforts away from the low end of the relationship value distribution and toward the higher-value end. The only questions that remained were who were the high-use customers and how could ScrubaDub reach them. Surprisingly, the highest margin per visit came not from Lexus and Acura owners but from owners of sport utility vehicles (Jeep, Bronco, etc.) and (we are *not* making this up) Hyundai owners. Frequency of visits was, less surprisingly, related to distance from the car wash, age of the cars owned (cars 3 years old or newer being washed more often), and high income.

By understanding the parameters of customer value, the Paisners were able to develop an integrated strategy across the dimensions of the value chain. Their customer portfolio strategy focused on the high-value end of the market distribution. Based on their understanding of these customers' relationship value, the Paisners could justify using direct mail (unusual for a car wash at the time) and

ScrubaDub Relationship Model

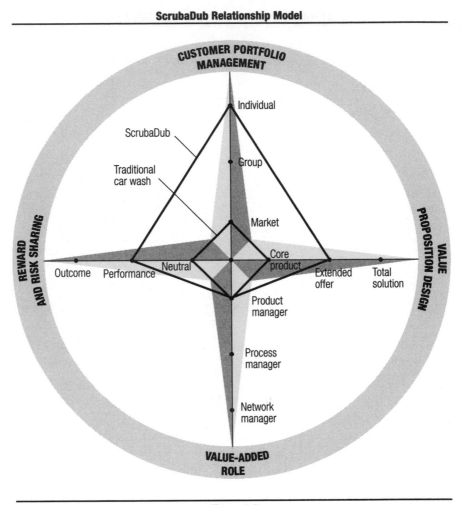

Figure 4-7

inviting high-potential customers to join the ScrubaDub Club, with an offer of free car washes. Relationships with active club members were managed on an individual basis. The Paisners also extended their value proposition to attract affluent owners of relatively new cars. They created an attractive environment at their facilities, sprucing up landscaping and the waiting rooms at ScrubaDub facilities and providing free gourmet coffee, peanuts, and other snacks. They also stressed personalized service, "advertised" on National Public Radio to raise brand awareness among their target population, and scheduled personnel to minimize peak-time waiting periods. Knowledge of customer value even influenced the development of technology. To ensure a competitive advantage in locating near the source of afflu-

Change in Customer Portfolio Weighting

Customer Group Value ($)		% of Market	% of ScrubaDub Customers
Very low	(3.75)	49.6%	40%
Low	(2.08)	27.8%	22.0%
Moderate	6.54	16.7%	25.0%
High	30.51	5.0%	11.0%
Very high	105.98	0.8%	2.0%

Figure 4-8

ent customers, ScrubaDub invested in environmentally friendly technologies, such as wash-water recycling, that enables it to put facilities in towns closed to many competitors. ScrubaDub also altered its reward- and risk-sharing policy away from neutral prices and broad promotional discounts, instead offering frequency-based discounts in the form of free washes and a 3 day clean car guarantee to the buyers of premium washes. The greatly expanded ScrubaDub relationship model relative to the traditional car wash is illustrated in Figure 4-7.

Results have been dramatic. Whereas northeastern U.S. car wash volumes from 1994 to 1995 increased by 7.0 percent, ScrubaDub's volume was up 12.5 percent. This increase is attributable largely to the high-volume, high-margin ScrubaDub Club members, who represent only 18 percent of the customer count but generate almost 40 percent of revenues and a somewhat higher share of profitability. Redirecting customer ADR efforts away from low-value to higher-value customer relationships has increased the value of the infrequent buyers and modestly reduced that of the higher value customers, although this has been offset by the much higher proportions attracted. Figure 4-8 compares the current ScrubaDub portfolio to the market.

THE DISTRIBUTION *of* CUSTOMER RELATIONSHIP VALUE

All customers are not created equal. If all relationships were profitable and a firm had no constraints on the resources available to invest in relationships, the inequality of customer relationship values would not matter much. After calculating customer relationship value, many firms find, however, that their customer base

Customers Are Not Created Equal

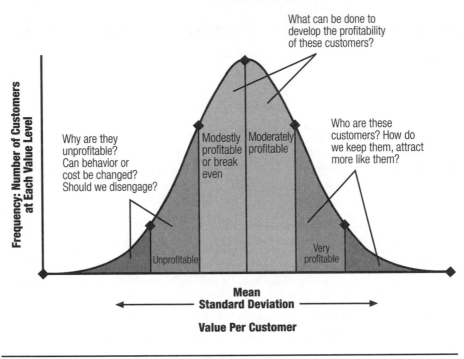

Figure 4-9

exhibits a familiar bell-shaped or normal frequency distribution similar to that illustrated in Figure 4-9. There is no theoretical reason for a firm's customers to be normally distributed as illustrated, and many different distributions are encountered, but this is the most familiar form and is suitable for illustrating the importance of understanding the mean and the variance of the customer distribution.

As with all statistical distributions, the key factors are the mean and the variance. By definition, some customer relationships are more valuable than the *mean* (or average). The *variance* is a measure of the spread of values around the mean. It also is an indicator of the potential yield on "de-averaging" the firm's treatment of customers by gaining additional customer knowledge or connecting with them in different ways. The goal of strategically managing the customer portfolio is to increase the mean and reduce the variance of the firm's customer-relationship value distribution. The key questions that must to be answered to accomplish this are:

- Which are the most valuable customer relationships, and what can we do to keep them and find more like them?

- What can be done to increase the value of the modestly profitable and moderately unprofitable customer relationships?

- What factors account for the unprofitable customer relationships? Can these factors be changed, or should we disengage from the unprofitable customer relationships?

Value Concentration

Value concentration refers to the proportion of the total portfolio value represented by the most valuable customer relationships. Many businesses find that a relatively small percentage of customers account for a disproportionate share of total profits (the so-called 80/20 or Pareto rule) but do not understand why this occurs or the implications for managing their customer portfolios. Two tools outlined in this section, the cumulative customer-relationship value function and the value concentration function, can help you to understand the factors that have a bearing on value concentration in your customer portfolio.

Cumulative Customer-Relationship Value Function

The data developed for the relationship value frequency distribution can be arrayed in ascending order, from least to most valuable, to create a cumulative profitability function. Many companies find that their cumulative customer-relationship value curve reflects the popular 80/20 rule (80 percent of the effect is accounted for by 20 percent of the causes). Although the cumulative customer-relationship value function is not always that extreme, a general power rule seems to hold: A relatively small number of customers usually accounts for a disproportionate share of total value or profit. In our example, we've illustrated in Figure 4-10 the cumulative value curve of ScrubaDub customers derived from the data in Figure 4-6. Although the very large proportion of customers with negative relationship values is partly an artifact of the allocation of ADR costs, the curve is representative of many we have observed.

Many firms accept that a small set of their customers are disproportionately profitable but find it harder to eliminate the drag on firm value caused by their unprofitable customer relationships. Nonetheless, customers whom it is unprofitable to serve are a significant factor, especially in businesses in which acquisition costs are relatively high, per-unit margins are low, and customer profitability is therefore sensitive to both volume and duration. For example, many insurance products have high up-front costs for marketing, selling, and setup, and require a number of years of premium payments to break even and

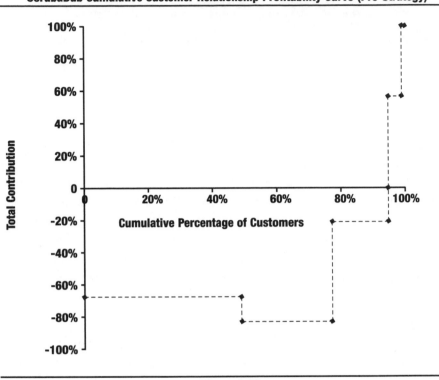

Figure 4-10

earn a return. High turnover or "churn" means that many insurance customers do not maintain their policies long enough to become profitable. This is why customer duration or loyalty is such an important strategic factor in the insurance business. Similarly, the early days of cellular phones were marked by generous promotions aimed at building the customer base. These drew in large numbers of people who, on receiving their first bill, dropped the service, resulting in turnover rates of 30 to 40 percent. As a consequence, initial profits were low. Over time, cellular phone service providers learned to better target their offers and to require minimum service periods. However, a great deal of value could have been saved had cellular phone firms anticipated the turnover problem and avoided the pursuit of market share for its own sake.

VARIANCE AND THE VALUE CONCENTRATION FUNCTION

The shape of the customer value distribution curve is important in determining which customers to target and how much to invest in customer information or knowledge. As the standard deviation increases, identifying and attracting higher-value customer relationships becomes more important to growing the value of the business. This is so because, while the customers one or more standard deviations from the mean still represent the same proportion of customers, their relative value is much higher, and so they account for a larger proportion of the total value. If customer relationship value is distributed normally, increases in the standard deviation indicate that total value becomes more concentrated in the relatively few customers (15.87 percent) one standard deviation or more from the mean.

Figure 4-11 illustrates the proportion of total value concentrated in customers one or more standard deviations from the mean as the standard deviation increases from one-half to three times the mean value. As shown, 15.9 percent of the customers account for only 27.97 percent of the total value when the standard deviation is 50 percent of the mean. However, as the standard deviation increases to 300 percent of the mean, these customers account for more than 88 percent of total value. It is important to remember that one reason for this concentration of total positive value is that the number of customer relationships with a negative value also is increasing. When the standard deviation equals the mean, 15.87 percent of relationships have a negative value; when the standard deviation is three times the mean, more than 37 percent of relationships have negative value.

MANAGING *the* PORTFOLIO *for* MAXIMUM GROWTH

The analogy of the customer relationship as a financial asset can be carried further by viewing the customer mix as a portfolio to be managed for maximum yield. This allows us to introduce comparisons to the broader market and to gauge the effectiveness of strategies to build firm value.

Managing the customer portfolio involves deploying customer ADR resources to achieve the highest possible overall yield. As with financial portfolio management, *relative* success depends on the degree to which the customer portfolio manager "beats the market." It is rare for a financial portfolio manager to outperform the market over long periods because financial markets are extremely efficient processors of information. Only by taking on additional risk can a financial portfolio achieve a higher expected return but at the cost of greater variance about the mean value and, therefore, higher possibility of loss.

The market for customer knowledge often is much less efficient than the market for financial knowledge, and the customer portfolio manager can, by creating and using superior customer knowledge, establish a strategic edge. Our research shows

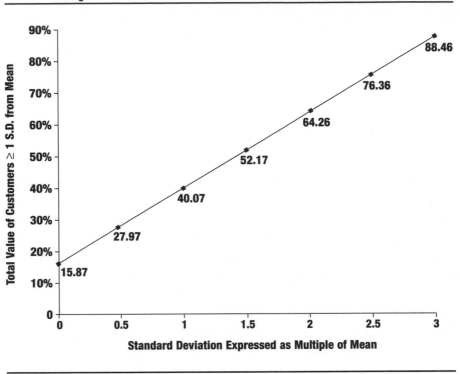

Change in the Value Concentration as the Standard Deviation Increases

Figure 4-11

that higher-growth companies typically have a clearer view of and more knowledge about their most valuable customers than do lower-growth companies. The ability to gain this edge depends on the efficiency of the market for customer knowledge, the value of additional knowledge, and the cost of acquiring it. As customer knowledge becomes more widely held by members of the industry or as its cost of acquisition declines, the potential edge declines. Nevertheless, many industries are very far from being efficient customer knowledge markets, so there is tremendous opportunity for those who get there first to gain significant competitive advantage by effectively employing such knowledge in managing customer relationships and portfolios. Even when customer knowledge becomes readily available to all sellers, a business with superior ability in applying that knowledge can maintain a strategic edge.

Using Economic Segmentation to Focus on Valuable Customer Relationships

No idea is more ingrained within marketing circles than the dictate to segment, segment, segment! Ever more powerful tools are employed to determine the mathematical centers of gravity among people on the basis of demographics, attitudes, needs, and behaviors. Some companies employ as many as 15 to 20 segments to describe their markets. This balkanization of markets is undertaken to define customer needs and more accurately to target appeals to various groups.

The problem with noneconomic segmentation schemes is that they often do not distinguish among customers in terms of relationship value. In many cases, customer relationship value varies as much or more *within* segments as it does *across* segments. In other words, a business looking for valuable customers is likely to find them distributed across several segments rather than bunched together in one or a few clearly defined groups. Though it is true that valuable customers might be slightly or even considerably concentrated in some areas, on inspection this often is discovered to be a fortunate coincidence.

The greatest challenge to the traditional segmentation perspective has come from direct and database marketers, who begin from the fairly straightforward premise that the best predictor of a person's future purchasing behavior is her past behavior and that the next best predictor is that she closely resembles other people who have purchased previously.

The database marketer casts his neural nets over the population of known customers and searches for patterns that connect buyers regardless of their membership in various demographic or psychological segments. Like Kepler's discovery of the elliptical orbits of planets, the neural netter essentially is engaged in a curve-fitting exercise, and although this process often works, in many cases the marketer hasn't a clue about why he catches what he does. We can't argue with the results of many neural-netting exercises, but we prefer to understand the reasons that some customer relationships are more valuable than others.

In grouping customers, we follow Willie Sutton's dictum by asking two questions: Where is the money, and what are our chances of getting it? This idea can be expressed more formally as a method of grouping customers on the basis of *customer relationship value* and *responsiveness*. This approach involves estimating the intrinsic relationship value of existing and potential customers and then estimating their responsiveness or probability of responding favorably to our offer. Once value and responsiveness have been estimated, it is often helpful to develop additional knowledge of such things as attitudes and behaviors to the extent that this information is useful in reaching target customers. The approach is the reverse of most traditional segmentation schemes, which define groups first in terms of their characteristics and then, perhaps, estimate their value. We call this approach of first estimating value and responsiveness *economic* segmentation to distinguish it from behavioral, demographic, needs-based, and other types of segmentation.

In Figure 4-12A, we've illustrated a simplified economic segmentation map to reinforce the importance of understanding both value and responsiveness. Customers in the *Right Stuff* quadrant, being both valuable and responsive, should be the business's primary targets, because efforts toward them are likely to yield the greatest return.

Odd Couples are customers who, while inherently valuable, are not inclined to purchase your product or establish relationships with you. Understanding the cause of the mismatch can be very valuable, because in some cases it may be reversible. For example, ScrubaDub learned that many luxury-car owners feared that car washes would damage finishes. With this knowledge, ScrubaDub undertook to educate luxury-car dealers about the new technology and persuaded them to include trial coupons for new car buyers.

Fatal Attractions are customers who are very responsive to your value proposition but who are relatively unprofitable to serve. Understanding the reasons for their responsiveness to your offer sometimes can provide a basis for fine-tuning your message and avoiding them, redesigning your value proposition to align more precisely with the target group, or changing the pricing policy to discourage unprofitable customers.

Ghosts are both of relatively low value and unresponsive. In some cases, such as the roughly 50 percent of car owners who rarely use car washes, these customers may be a large part of the market and promote a kind of wishful thinking that Clancy and Shulman call "the myth of the non-users."[4] Companies that succumb to this myth often waste resources trying to convert unresponsive customers, resources that would be much better directed at higher-value, more responsive customers.

Optimal Customer Portfolio Weighting

The value of the customer portfolio is equal to the weighted value of the customer groups, where the weights are the proportions of each economic segment. The optimal proportions of the various economic segments are achieved by investing in acquiring customers up to the point at which the incremental value and acquisition costs are equal. Figure 4-12B illustrates a simplified portfolio weighting model based on the value-responsiveness matrix. Customer relationships are assumed to have one of two intrinsic values, indicated by V_1 and V_2. For simplicity, we've shown two acquisition cost schedules, one for the two unresponsive groups and one for the two responsive groups, which indicate the number of customers in each group attracted as a function of investment in acquisition. In the case illustrated, the maximum portfolio value is achieved

Economic Segmentation

A. Grouping by Customer Relationship Value and Responsiveness

	Customer Responsiveness (Probability of Positive Action)	
	Low	**High**
High	Odd Couples (O)	The Right Stuff (R)
Low	Ghosts (G)	Fatal Attractions (F)

Intrinsic Customer Relationship Value

B. Optimizing the Customer Portfolio Weighting

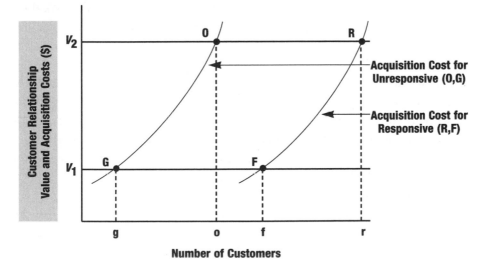

Figure 4-12

when the number of customers shown by points g, o, f, and r on the horizontal axis are represented in the portfolio.

The Portfolio Growth Model

The simple linear model of portfolio value growth illustrated in Figure 4-13 can be used to examine the dynamics of growth. The firm's total growth is expressed as the sum of new portfolio value from acquiring new customers plus the additional value from developing existing customers (after defections) minus the value of defecting customers.

Holding aside the ADR costs, we can illustrate the basic dynamics with a simple example, using the data presented in Figure 4-14. Assume that our firm has a customer attraction rate of 6 percent (new customers represent 6 percent of the available prospects), that the development rate is 2 percent per remaining customer, and that the retention rate is 95 percent (equivalent to a 5-percent defection rate). For simplicity, assume that in the initial year the relationship value of both prospective and existing customers is $1.00 each. The company starts with 300 customers and 1,000 prospects.

Though you may be tempted to sum the acquisition and development rates and then subtract the defection rate to obtain a growth of 3 percent, in fact, this example yields a positive 16.9-percent growth in portfolio value. Breaking down the growth by component, we find that we have added $60.00 in value through acquisition, added $5.70 through developing the value of nondefecting customers, and lost $15.00 through defections (or kept $285.00, depending on how you look at it).

Even in this greatly simplified form, the portfolio growth model demonstrates that the growth rate, G, is a function not only of the ADR rates but of the relative size of the prospect and existing customer base. For example, a very low acquisition rate in a very large prospect pool may overwhelm the effect of high development and retention rates in a small customer base, and vice versa.

To determine the maximum profitable growth, it is necessary to add ADR functions to the model. The maximum profitable growth rate occurs when the increases in value attributable to the ADR activities are, separately, equal to the marginal costs of each activity. In other words, invest in acquisition up to the point at which the last customer's relationship value equals the cost of acquiring him or her, and so on for development and retention. There is no reason a priori that the incremental yield on ADR activities will be equal. It is best to think of each activity as operating on a separate demand curve.

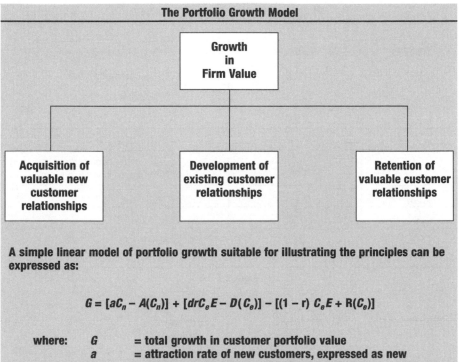

The Portfolio Growth Model

Growth
in
Firm Value

| Acquisition of valuable new customer relationships | Development of existing customer relationships | Retention of valuable customer relationships |

A simple linear model of portfolio growth suitable for illustrating the principles can be expressed as:

$$G = [aC_n - A(C_n)] + [drC_eE - D(C_e)] - [(1 - r)\ C_eE + R(C_e)]$$

where:

	G	= total growth in customer portfolio value
	a	= attraction rate of new customers, expressed as new customers divided by potential customers
	C_n	= number of potential new customers
	$A(C_n)$	= acquisition cost function
	N	= value of each new customer
	d	= development rate (increase in value) of remaining customers
	E	= value of an existing customer
	C_e	= number of existing customers at beginning of period
	$D(C_e)$	= development cost function
	r	= retention rate of existing customers
	$(1-r)$	= defection rate
	$R(C_e)$	= retention cost function

Growth in portfolio value is maximized when investment in each activity (acquisition, development, and retention) is made up to the point where the value of the last customer relationship acquired, developed, or retained equals the cost.

Figure 4-13

Illustrative Portfolio Growth Variables

Variable	Value	Meaning
a	0.06	6-percent acquisition rate
C_n	1,000	1,000 potential customers
N	$1.00	Value of new customers
E	$1.00	Value of existing customer
d	0.02	Development rate or increase in value of a non-defecting customer
C_e	300	Existing customer base
r	0.95	Retention rate
$(1-r)$	0.05	Defection rate

Figure 4-14

In this chapter we have shown that customer relationship value is a function of the volume, margin, and duration of the purchase stream, and we have provided algorithms to measure and track the value of relationships. We have shown how an appreciation of the distribution of relationship value can guide investment decisions in customer knowledge and connecting technology as well as in the ADR of customers. Acting as a customer portfolio manager, a firm can maximize its rate of profitable growth by deploying its resources in proportion to the value of relationships and the costs of ADR. The next four chapters explore the four axes of relationship value in more depth, applying the principles developed in this and the two preceding chapters.

chapter 5

Getting together

BUILDING THE RIGHT CUSTOMER PORTFOLIO

Harley-Davidson treats all of its customers the same—as *HOGS*. Staples provides four different levels of relationship, depending on the amount of office supplies purchased. Wachovia Bank assesses the potential of every individual and tailors its investment in relationship building accordingly. Each of these companies manages its customer portfolio very differently. In this chapter, we explore how the interaction of customer economics, knowledge, and technology influences the management of customer portfolios.

Customer portfolio management consists of three processes: selecting the target customer base, determining who the relevant buyers are, and designing the appropriate means for interacting with these buyers. The first of these, selecting target customers, is one of the most important strategic decisions a firm must make, as the other elements of the relationship—value proposition, role, and reward and risk sharing—will evolve dynamically in response to the needs and preferences of this targeted customer base. Even the identity of competitors and their range of possible actions will be defined by a firm's choice of customers. As customers change, learn, and evolve in response to the pressures they face, businesses that serve them must change with them or lose out. In addition, even if a business is successful in choosing its customers and coevolving to meet their changing needs, that business must keep a wary eye on its competitors, whose strategies also are evolving over time.

The second process, determining who the relevant buyers are, involves defining the customer and determining the amount and type of knowledge required to interact effectively. In some cases, the customer is relatively easy to identify as the final consumer or household. In other cases, particularly in business markets, the customer may be several people involved in or affected by the buying decision.

Finding the appropriate means of interacting with buyers requires consideration of all the various points of contact, whether they are direct or indirect. A firm may manage all of its relationships vicariously through various media; it may assign to individuals responsibility for particular customers; or it may interact differently with parts of the buyer organization. The appropriate relationship management process and level of interaction depends on the additional value created by greater interaction.

In Chapter 1, we introduced the notion of managing the customer portfolio at the right level and illustrated a firm's choices with three representative positions: market, group, and individual. As we pointed out, the potential value of the portfolio increases directly as the level at which a firm manages its relationships moves toward the individual end of the spectrum. However, the cost of acquiring the necessary knowledge and taking action on the basis of that knowledge precludes most firms from achieving, across their entire customer base, idealized one-to-one relationships. A business may "know" its customers at many levels, ranging from a statistical abstraction of the average or typical customer to extensive profiles of individuals. The appropriate amount and type of customer knowledge depends on its contribution to efforts to increase customer relationship value.

THE DISTRIBUTION *of* CUSTOMER RELATIONSHIP VALUE *and* RETURN *on* KNOWLEDGE

How much knowledge is enough? Because knowledge building is expensive, it is essential to understand the distribution of customer relationship value in a potential or existing market, as well as the number of customers in that market. Analysis of this information will show how worthwhile further knowledge building would be. Although many companies invest substantial resources in developing and maintaining customer information, and two-thirds of the respondents in our survey develop some customer relationship value measures, far too many companies do not calibrate their information development efforts against the relative value of their customer relationships or the costs of different ways of interacting with customers.

Portfolio Management Strategies

	Variance of Customer Needs and Tastes	
	Low	High
Variance of Relationship Values — High	Group, by value	Individual, by value and proposition
Variance of Relationship Values — Low	Market	Group, by proposition

Figure 5-1

It is important to emphasize that investment in customer knowledge is worthwhile only to the extent that it enables the firm either to identify or to create more valuable customer relationships. The value of knowledge equals the incremental change in the value of the relationship that that knowledge makes possible. Such a value change comes through an improved ability either to select customers or to align more effectively with customers.

The yield on knowledge for customer identification and selection depends on the variance of intrinsic customer relationship values. The greater the variance, the more significant is knowledge in identifying valuable relationships and avoiding unprofitable ones. The yield on knowledge for creating more valuable relationships depends on the variance of customer needs, tastes, and preferences. The more customers vary in needs or tastes, the greater is a firm's opportunity to tailor propositions and achieve greater alignment. Figure 5-1 illustrates how these two dimensions of variance interact to determine the level at which customer portfolios may be managed most profitably.

We will discuss three types of distributions of customer relationship value, defined according to their mean value and degree of variability, as illustrated in Figure 5-2. *Tight value distributions* are those that, regardless of their specific

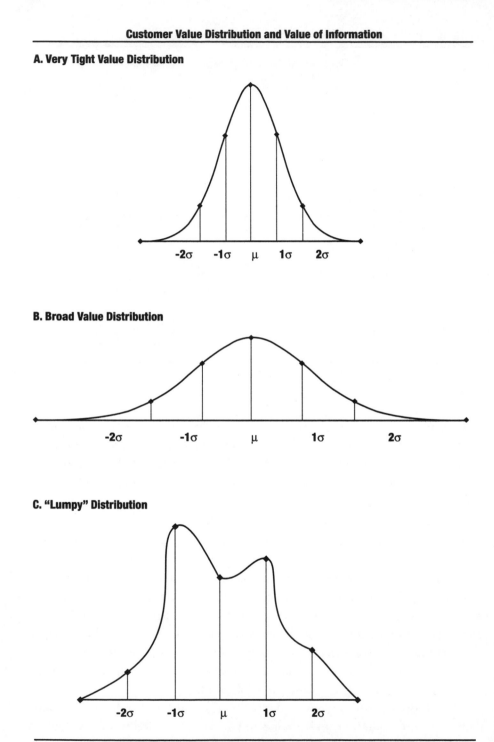

Customer Value Distribution and Value of Information

A. Very Tight Value Distribution

B. Broad Value Distribution

C. "Lumpy" Distribution

Figure 5-2

statistical form, show relatively little variance about the mean. *Broad value distributions* vary broadly but smoothly about the mean. *Lumpy value distributions* are those that vary widely and unevenly about the mean. Lumpy distributions do not exhibit the familiar, single-peak, bell-shaped form but instead look more like a series of peaks and valleys. This form often indicates that several distinct distributions may exist within the larger distribution. In these cases, it usually is best to treat each distribution separately.

It may help to recall that under a normal distribution curve, the *proportion* of the total area between any two points measured in standard deviations is the same for every normal distribution. This means that 68.2 percent of the values in any normal distribution will fall within one standard deviation of the mean, and 95.4 percent will fall within two standard deviations. The mean and the standard deviation may, of course, vary, but the proportion of observations within any number of standard deviations is constant. This handy fact makes it possible, once you have plotted the distribution of value in your customer base, to draw useful conclusions about the value of different levels of customer knowledge as well as to assess the potential value of your customer portfolio. Although the same proportions of customers are found one, two, and three standard deviations from the mean in Figure 5-2A and B, the larger standard deviation of distribution (B) implies that the absolute differences in value are much greater. The implications of this fact for the relative value of customer relationships were discussed in detail under Value Concentration in Chapter 4.

One of the most important factors determining the usefulness of customer-specific knowledge is the size of the standard deviation of customer relationship value compared to the mean. The smaller the standard deviation, the less valuable more detailed information will be in identifying target customers. This is because, if the distribution is very tight around the mean, any customer acquired is likely to fall close to the mean value, as shown in distribution A in Figure 5-2. Therefore, statistical information about the targeted customer group will often be sufficient for developing strategy, and little or no added value would be gained from information about specific individuals or subgroups, as none of them is significantly more valuable than any of the others. If the distribution broadens and flattens out, as in distribution B in the figure, the potential value of information increases because the consequences of customer selection will be more important. In a distribution with a large variance, the most valuable customer relationships may be 5 to 10 times more profitable than the average, so learning how to identify and attract those more valuable customers will pay off handsomely.

Of course, customers may have very similar relationship values but very different tastes and preferences. In this case, the seller may need additional information about the distribution of tastes, but it would still be uneconomical to invest in customer-specific knowledge beyond the value of the relationship. Customers of individual grocery items such as toothpaste or shaving cream may have fairly compact distributions with low average relationship values, for example. Hence, knowing and managing them on an individual basis would be very uneconomical.

The expected value or mean itself is the second factor bearing on the usefulness of customer-specific knowledge and the level at which the portfolio may be managed. If the mean value is substantially greater than the cost of information, it suggests that investment in customer-specific knowledge for a large part of the customer base may be worthwhile, and vice versa.

Businesses in which customer-relationship value distributions have both low means and low standard deviations generally do not invest heavily in customer-specific information but can rely instead on statistical profiles of "typical" customers. A firm in this situation usually manages its customer portfolio at the market level, pursues relatively nonselective targeting, and gears acquisition efforts toward attracting large numbers of customers. Brand development often plays an important role in the strategies of this type of firm.

Companies that do not have direct connections with their customers often find themselves at a disadvantage compared to intermediaries such as retailers, who have easier access to customer-specific knowledge, better means for developing and using it, and more opportunities to employ sophisticated connecting technologies. This is due in part to the retailer's proximity to customers, which reduces the cost of research, and in part to the broader relationship enjoyed by the retailer. Viewed as a customer for toothpaste, a customer's relationship value might not support substantial investment in knowledge, but viewed as a customer for groceries and a wide range of general merchandise, investment in knowledge of the customer might be considerably more profitable. This accounts in part for the relatively high investment by retailers in scanner and other point-of-sale technologies. The intermediaries' greater customer knowledge often provides them with tremendous leverage in dealing with manufacturers.

In contrast, businesses that face a customer landscape of relatively valuable customer relationships with a lumpy distribution and significant variance can benefit greatly by developing and leveraging customer-specific information about particular groups of customers. The lumpy distribution of relationship value suggests that increasing the portfolio's weighting of customers from specific groups could have a significant effect on the profitability and value of the business. The problem, of course, is figuring out which groups should be targeted for such "special treatment" without investing in expensive customer-specific knowledge about everyone. Businesses in this situation frequently partition their customer bases into subgroups and employ different means of interacting with individual groups, depending on value. For example, MCI employs large, dedicated account teams for its very largest business customers and uses telesales and telemarketing techniques with the lower-value segment of the business market.

Markets with a very high average relationship value and a great deal of variance often are found in business-to-business settings. Even the smallest customers for commercial aircraft warrant some investment in customer-specific knowledge, for example.

In the next few sections, we'll discuss some of the factors affecting the appropriate level of customer portfolio management and illustrate these factors with case studies of three companies—Harley-Davidson, Staples, and Wachovia—that pursue very different strategies.

CREATING *and* MANAGING RELATIONSHIPS *at the* MARKET LEVEL

Periodically, someone forecasts the end of mass marketing or one-size-fits-all approaches to the market and suggests a future of one-to-one relationships, segments of one, and universally intimate customer relationships. Nonetheless, many successful companies still approach their markets very broadly, making few (if any) distinctions among the customers for their products. Coke appeals to all consumers with the same recipe; Microsoft's operating systems and applications seek to dominate their markets; Stanley's tools are promoted universally. The degree of customer closeness, or intimacy, may be thought of as an economic good and, like any other good, it has a price or opportunity cost and is truly worthwhile only when the benefit in terms of increased relationship value outweighs its costs.

The market portfolio manager is relatively indifferent to the particular customers he attracts and usually seeks to attract the largest share of the company's potential customer base. This type of market strategy may be attractive when one or more of the following conditions exist:

- The customer relationship value distribution is relatively narrow and therefore a small number of statistical representations serve to characterize the customer population.

- Customer needs and tastes are reasonably uniform and can be satisfied with a modest level of variety, or differences can be incorporated within a standardized product.

- Scale economies in production, distribution, or promotion can only be achieved at levels that are large relative to the size of the market.

- The market demonstrates a strong disposition to adopt a standard product or technical configuration.

- Increasing returns operate over a large range of output levels.

If customers are all basically the same, it doesn't pay to treat them differently. When the customer relationship value distribution is relatively narrow, there are no economically distinguishable groups, meaning most customer relationships are of roughly equal value. If the mean value of the customer relationship is low relative to the cost of acquiring and executing against customer-specific knowledge, it will not pay to manage customer relationships at an individual level. (You wouldn't pay $10.00 to get to know better a customer whose lifetime relationship value is likely to be $8.00.) Either of these conditions alone—a relatively narrow customer relationship value distribution or a low mean value of the customer relationship—may suggest a broad portfolio strategy; together they almost compel it.

Of course, it is possible for customers with similar economic profiles to have substantially different needs or tastes. However, different customer tastes and needs are not in themselves reasons to manage relationships at a more intimate level. Needs and tastes that vary significantly might indicate a need to redefine the market or to define groups within the market. However, if tastes are reasonably uniform, the firm probably will do best by managing its customer portfolio at a broad level. Offering a moderate level of product variety may be more effective than fragmenting the customer portfolio. For example, toolmakers manufacture hammers of various weights and composition to accommodate different needs and preferences. Given the relatively low retail price of most hammers, the toolmaker will maximize the firm's value proposition by defining the firm's customers broadly as professionals or as do-it-yourselfers rather than defining them according to their individual preferences for specific tool types or characteristics.

If a firm determines that its most efficient scale of production, distribution, or promotion occurs at a level that is a significant proportion of the total market, that firm might reasonably pursue broad market portfolios. Despite the promise of and recent advances in flexible manufacturing, many businesses still achieve their most efficient levels of operation when producing a fairly uniform product in large volumes. This is the case not only in heavy manufacturing sectors such as paper, chemicals, or automobiles but also in many retail and service businesses. For example, Home Depot's superstores must attract customers from across a wide spectrum that includes serious craftspeople, general jobbers, and inexperienced homeowners. All these groups benefit from the economies of the superstore's scale, and the stores can meet the customer groups' specific needs by offering a selection of merchandise rather than a focused channel.

The phenomenon of increasing returns, or markets that exhibit what economists call *positive feedback,* may also prompt firms to pursue broad, share-based strategies. In a traditional diminishing-returns business market, equilibrium is achieved through negative feedback. For example, in response to rising demand, firms whose production is subject to diminishing returns incur higher unit costs; to recoup, they raise prices, then customers respond negatively by reducing demand, and equilibrium is restored. In a diminishing-returns business, customer selection is important in part because limits on the efficient scale of output make it important to direct that output to those who place the highest value on it.

In an increasing-returns business, unit costs may continue to fall as demand and output increase: Positive feedback from price reductions leads to more output, lower costs, and so on. The first copy of a software product may cost millions to create, but subsequent copies cost pennies to produce. Acceptance of a system often is self-reinforcing. In this situation, being first to gain acceptance or build volume can be critical. In cases where establishing standards turns out to be necessary, such as in the early years of VCR manufacturing and computer operating systems, the firm that first achieves scale in customer adoption will have a good chance of becoming the industry standard. The firm that hesitates or invests too much time trying to select exactly the right customers may find itself locked out of the market.

A firm pursuing a market portfolio strategy does not distinguish among its customers based on relationship value. A firm may pursue *the* market (very broadly defined) or *a* market (more narrowly defined). We already have alluded to companies such as Coke and Stanley that pursue very broadly defined markets. Some firms, while not distinguishing among groups or individuals, define their markets more narrowly. What is important is that the portfolio is managed nonselectively, relying on brand image and customer self-selection.

For our case example of customer portfolio management at the market level, we return to Harley-Davidson, a firm that defines its market narrowly as customers for heavyweight or cruiser motorcycles. This company has refocused its customer portfolio on this particular market and manages its relationships uniformly within this market. Harley-Davidson's experience shows that in some cases, trying to distinguish and manage relationships with several different customer groups can blur a firm's image and erode its relationship with its franchise

customers. Treating all of its customers the same reinforces the customers'
identification with one another as HOGS.

Harley-Davidson
On the Road Again

The ultimate sign of brand equity, Harley-Davidson is in the unique position of having
its corporate logo literally tattooed onto some of its customers.[1] So strong is the market pull of this brand that the market comes to Harley-Davidson. Moreover, first-time
buyers have a 95-percent probability of purchasing another Harley-Davidson motorcycle. In the words of Harley-Davidson CEO Richard F. Teerlink, the company "sells
excitement and a way of life." The company holds a special place in the hearts,
minds, and lifestyles of its customers. To sustain that position, it focuses on delivering superior product quality, styling, and reliability in combination with brand imagery
that "connects" to the special psychology of heavyweight-motorcycle enthusiasts.

Not long ago, the company was at severe risk of losing its franchise position.
Having been acquired by AMF, a conglomerate of leisure-related companies,
Harley-Davidson pushed too rapidly to increase production, expand product line
variety, and grow its dealer population, reaching a point at which product quality
and brand image began to erode. The company became product- rather than
customer-focused and attempted to appeal to several market groups rather than
to focus on the heavyweight-motorcycle market that had built the brand into
such a powerhouse originally. It lost touch with the needs and expectations of
its customers while simultaneously underinvesting in the manufacturing and
dealer infrastructure required to deliver quality product efficiently to market.

After Harley-Davidson's divestiture from AMF, a new management team identified
product quality as the prescription that would speed the company toward recovery. Throughout the 1990s, Harley-Davidson methodically attacked every link in
the supply chain to restore luster to its brand. The company also invested heavily in strengthening its manufacturing, distribution, and logistics efficiency to
ensure that product reached dealers on time and defect-free (the current defect
rate is 0.03 percent, compared to an industry average of 1.5 percent).

Figure 5-3 illustrates the difference between the AMF and post-AMF relationship
strategies. Under AMF, Harley-Davidson tried to build a broader customer portfolio. Since regaining its independence, the company has refocused on improving the quality of its core product and extending its brand to areas that reinforce

Harley-Davidson Relationship Model

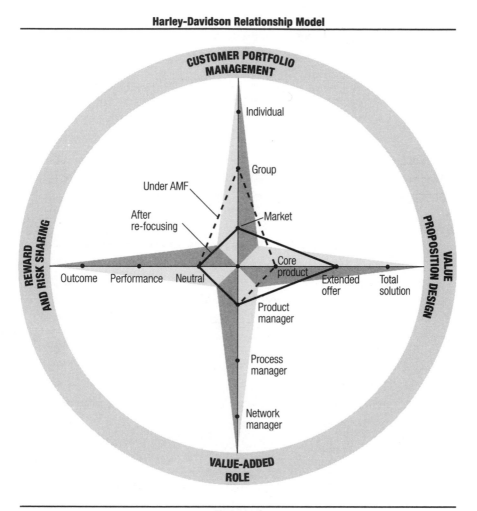

Figure 5-3

the company's affinity with its customers. Rather than broaden its product line to appeal to several groups of motorcycle buyers, Harley-Davidson has extended its brand (Harley-Davidson MotorClothes, Harley-Davidson Cafés, etc.) in ways that reinforce the firm's image and customers' identification with that image. Recognizing that over the course of the ownership experience, customers would spend approximately 50 percent of the initial cost of the motorcycle on parts and accessories, Harley-Davidson worked hard to make the dealer experience more appealing and extended its value proposition in new directions, offering motorcycle casualty insurance, a Harley-Davidson credit card for all purchases at the dealership, motorcycle leasing programs, and the like. Revamping its distribution to achieve the right ownership experience involved reducing the domestic dealer network from 750 to 600 dealers, despite surging demand.

Harley-Davidson does not attempt to create individually tailored relationships with customers. Instead, it supports and reinforces their collective sense of being a special group, as evidenced by the 300,000 passionate members of the Harley Owners Group. An incredible proportion of its owner population—nearly 50 percent—belongs to its affinity group. As described in Chapter 2, Harley-Davidson engages in many conversational and observational techniques (including the use of ethnography) to develop deep customer knowledge.

This formula appears to be working, as the company has garnered a 48-percent market share within the U.S. heavyweight-motorcycle market. Demand has far outstripped supply, prompting the company to increase capital expenditures substantially to support a new manufacturing facility and a state-of-the-art product engineering center. Harley-Davidson realized revenue growth of approximately 13 percent in 1996.

That Harley-Davidson does not have to spend many dollars on advertising to sell out its entire inventory suggests that the "build-it-and-they-will-come" approach to doing business might actually apply when the right market is targeted with the right product and image.

CREATING *and* MANAGING RELATIONSHIPS *at the* GROUP LEVEL

Firms manage their customer portfolios at the group level when there is substantial variation in customer relationship value and needs, which makes it profitable for the firms to distinguish among groups of customers, and when individual customer relationships are not valuable enough to warrant individualized relationship management. Managing the customer portfolio at the group level is attractive under two conditions:

- *Customer relationship values vary significantly*. This makes it worthwhile to invest in understanding these differences and even in developing tailored value propositions.

- *Customers' needs or tastes vary substantially.* This may require separate value propositions or approaches for different groups.

Under these conditions, treating all customers alike would suboptimize the portfolio. Instead, a firm must determine how many groups it will pursue within the total population and how many different relationship management models are appropriate. Executing multiple relationship models depends on a business's ability to calibrate models to the value of different groups of customers and on customers' responsiveness to different models.

Group-level portfolio management strategies tend to fall into three broad categories: (1) betting on the blue chips (i.e., focusing on the high end of the customer relationship value distribution), (2) dominating the middle, and (3) stratifying the market. The first two are discussed briefly in the following sections, and the third is illustrated by the experience of Staples.

Bet on the Blue Chips

Why does *PC Week*, which has only 300,000 subscribers, generate almost $200 million in ad revenues, whereas *PC World*, with almost 1 million subscribers, pulls in only $67 million?[2] How did Capital One (née Signet Credit Card) and MBNA achieve spectacular growth rates and higher-than-average profitability?

Each of these businesses strategically targeted the most valuable customer relationships in their markets. *PC Week* is very profitable because it has targeted readers who are very valuable to advertisers. *PC Week* doesn't even charge for its magazine; most readers are "permitted" to receive the magazine because they are buyers of computer equipment, software, or services. *PC World*, on the other hand, targets a much more general and relatively less valuable (in the eyes of advertisers) customer base. Capital One invested heavily in computerized customer qualification software that allowed it to screen for the most valuable high-balance, low-risk credit card customers.[3] MBNA grew profitably by targeting affinity groups that could be readily identified, thus reducing acquisition costs, and by focusing on customers who would be more likely to stay with the issuer.

The strategy used by these firms involves tailoring the relationship and business model to the highest-value end of the customer value distribution. It works best in markets in which value is relatively concentrated in a small proportion of the customers and in which competitors in the market pursue undifferentiated relationship strategies. ScrubaDub's discovery of the value concentration in the car wash business enabled it to focus on attracting valuable, high-frequency, high-margin customers.

Dominate the Middle

A strategy geared toward dominating the middle involves focusing on the often-neglected second tier of customers, who may be only modestly valuable as individuals but who are two to four times more numerous than the very-high-value customers. This strategy is most successful when the existing players in the market are focused on the high-end customers and are relatively indifferent to mid-value customers.

Successful examples include Southwest Airlines, which does not offer the first-class seating or assigned seats beloved by expense-account business travelers. Southwest positions itself as the fun, economical choice, whereas American, United, and others compete to be first among the same group of high-value corporate travelers. Similarly, Enterprise Rent-a-Car focuses on the very large group of infrequent renters not targeted by the airport-based majors, making up in numbers of customers what it sacrifices in individual customer value.

Stratify the Market

Stratification of the market differs from traditional segmentation that defines customers along noneconomic criteria. Stratification can be combined with knowledge of other customer characteristics, but the essential defining characteristics of stratified groups are economic in nature.

This strategy works best when a portfolio contains customer groups with distinctly different economic values and needs that can most profitably be served by different relationship models. In addition, it should be possible to leverage some common competency or connection—such as brand—to all customers in all groups. This is akin to the mutual fund practice of including several families of funds with different risk and return characteristics. As with mutual funds, stratification often involves assigning different portfolio managers for each relationship model.

Staples
Aligning the Business Models

Staples is an excellent example of a business that recognized the differences in relationship values and customer needs and hence the need for different relationship strategies for different groups within its overall market.[4] As a result, Staples evolved from managing its portfolio on a broadly defined market basis (small businesses) with essentially a single self-service value proposition to operating four distinct portfolios—retail, direct, regional, and national—each managed according to a different relationship model and by a separate organization within Staples.

In many cases, a firm will find that creating significantly different relationship models for different customer groups enables it to achieve better alignment with customer needs without blurring or diluting its position. Staples stratified its relationship models to align itself better with the needs of different customer groups.

Staples Retail

The original Staples Retail model, which defined the target customer portfolio very broadly as small businesses and the self-employed, provided a very focused core product that consisted of wide selection and self-service and shared the rewards of the relationship in terms of market-based, discounted prices. Staples Retail played the role of product manager, emphasizing supply-chain management and careful control of fixed costs associated with the super-stores and their inventory.

The original Staples Retail relationship model is indicated by the most interior solid line connecting its position on each dimension shown in Figure 5-4. Over time, as Staples learned more about its customers, it created three additional models to align itself better with the needs of larger customers.

Staples Regional and Staples National

To reach large regional customers and very large national accounts, Staples created Staples Regional and Staples National, respectively. Each employs the relationship model illustrated by the most exterior position in Figure 5-4. Accounts are targeted and managed on an individual basis. For these large accounts, Staples will provide a total solution that relates to office supplies, including, if requested, the operation of stockrooms and internal distribution. In some cases, Staples' role is that of a process manager responsible for the entire process.

Staples Direct

Our detailed discussion of Staples Direct illustrates how the stratification process can be applied within a market. Staples Direct manages a customer portfolio specifically targeted to the group of small businesses employing 5 to 50 people. These larger customers are provided an extended-value proposition that includes credit and delivery. The increased specificity of customer targeting and the extended-value proposition of Staples Direct are shown in Figure 5-4.

Multiple Connection Strategies Within the Same Company

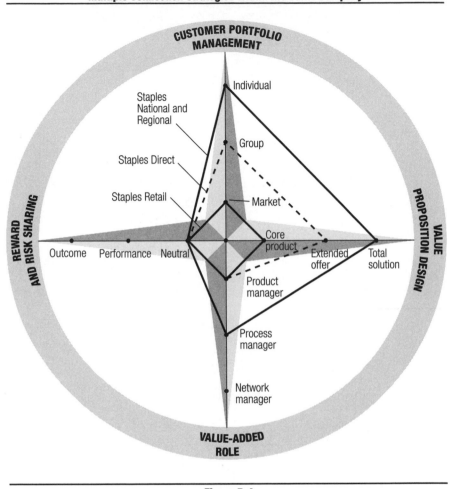

Figure 5-4

Meeting these customers' needs involves significantly different economics, moving from the high fixed cost–low variable cost environment of the superstore to the low fixed but higher variable costs of direct marketing.

Staples Direct, the direct-marketing division of Staples, is an outstanding example of a business managed with a keen sense of customer economics informed by extensive customer knowledge. Since its introduction in 1991, Staples Direct has grown at an annual rate of 55 percent to $350 million in sales and handles more than 25 percent of Staples's small-business volume.

Staples Direct was born of the recognition that the original Staples relationship model (self-service superstore), while extraordinarily successful, did not align precisely with the needs of some important customer groups. As discussed in Chapter 2, the original superstore concept was targeted broadly to small businesses and the self-employed, who were very responsive to the low-cost, full-line offer and who accepted self-service as part of the package.

By tracking customer buying patterns, however, Staples discerned that once businesses reached a level of approximately 10 employees, the probability of purchasing from Staples declined. Deeper analysis indicated that as the level and frequency of purchases increased, these customers placed a higher value on extended services such as delivery, ordering by phone or fax, itemized billing and credit—services that generally are inconsistent with the superstore concept. Jim Forbush, senior vice president of marketing, pointed out, "Customers put us into the delivery business; they were the impetus. It's one thing for the proprietor of a two- or three-person firm to stop by the superstore and load the supplies into his trunk; it's another thing to do this to keep 15 people stocked with office supplies."

As businesses enlarge, Staples realized, they not only buy more office supplies, but they buy in different ways. The result is changes in the economics of the business model for efficiently meeting the needs of these businesses. Staples determined that for its market, an appropriate stratification method was by number of employees. The chart in Figure 5-5 shows the distribution of U.S. businesses by number of employees and the coverage of this market by the four Staples divisions: retail, direct, regional, and national. This stratification is not rigid, however; there is some overlap between divisions, and customers frequently distribute purchases across channels, buying more of certain items (such as printers) from the retail stores, for instance, because it is important to see and touch them.

Staples has learned that annual office supply purchases per white-collar employee are reasonably uniform within broad industry categories. Therefore, the company concluded, if Staples knew the industrial classification of a customer and the proportion of white-collar workers at a location, it could develop a workable estimate of that location's annual demand for office supplies.

Because the precise purchase rates and margins are proprietary, we will use representative figures to illustrate the connection between customer value and the different customer portfolio management approaches and value propositions offered by each of the Staples divisions. If we assume that, on average, 80 percent of the

Staples Market Stratification by Employee Count

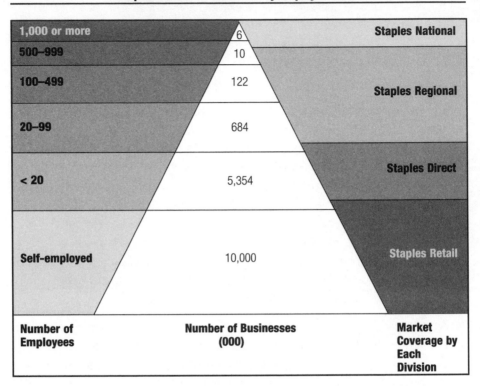

Number of Employees	Number of Businesses (000)	Market Coverage by Each Division
1,000 or more	6	Staples National
500–999	10	
100–499	122	Staples Regional
20–99	684	
< 20	5,354	Staples Direct
Self-employed	10,000	Staples Retail

Source: Rolf Anderson, *Atlas of the American Economy*, 1994, Congressional Quarterly, Inc., Department of Commerce data

Figure 5-5

employees of a representative customer are white-collar or clerical workers and that the average annual office supply requirement is approximately $100.00 per white-collar or clerical worker, with a 12-percent operating margin, we can develop rough market potential estimates to illustrate the connection between customer economics, the customer relationship, and the business model. Using these assumptions, the self-employed market, while very large at nearly $800 million per year, is made up of customers with an annual purchase rate of approximately $80.00 ($9.60 margin) and an intrinsic lifetime value of approximately $96.00 at a 10-percent discount rate. Clearly, the value of these customer relationships cannot support extensive marketing and relationship investments; therefore, the mass marketing and efficient distribution associated with the superstore aligns well with the large-number, low-individual value characteristics of this group of customers.

Moving up in size to the 15-person business with 12 white-collar workers, we find that annual purchases approach $1,200.00, with a margin of approximately $240.00 and an intrinsic value of approximately $2,400.00. At 50 employees, annual margins are approximately $480.00, leading to an intrinsic value of nearly $4,800.00. At these levels, the customer economics will support a very different level of service and justify a substantially larger investment in customer acquisition and development. Direct's business design is almost the opposite of the superstore model. Whereas the store has relatively high fixed costs and low variable costs, the cost structure of the Staples Direct operation is dominated by variable costs.

Probing deeper into its customer data, Staples discovered that not only the volume but also the frequency of purchases increased directly with customer size, further reinforcing the value of extended services such as phone ordering and delivery.

Within its target customer base of businesses with 5 to 50 employees, Staples Direct has stratified its customers into three subgroups based on value and frequency of purchase. Staples Direct employs very different customer acquisition methods for groups of different value. Telemarketing and direct mail are used predominantly for smaller customers, whereas a direct-sales force concentrates on acquiring the larger, more valuable customer relationships.

Acquisition costs also vary directly with customer size and value, for two reasons. At the lower end, there is a minimum acquisition cost associated with contacting and selling to each prospect by mail or phone. Because of the lower lifetime value of these lower-end customers, this cost represents a higher percentage of that value. At the higher end, it is worthwhile to employ more expensive acquisition techniques such as a direct-sales force. However, even employing the more expensive sales force, the acquisition-cost ratio for the higher-value customers still is lower than for the smaller-volume, less-frequent buyers.

By tracking its acquisition-cost ratio (Staples measures acquisition costs as a percentage of estimated lifetime value), Staples Direct was able to justify an increase in its marketing budget from 7 to 9 percent of sales. It also discovered that, in many cases, customers acquired by the sales force became more profitable than similar customers acquired by direct mail, which suggested increased use of salespeople to acquire larger customers. These insights provided Senior Vice President of Marketing Jim Forbush with the justification to increase his marketing budget as a percentage of sales by more than 20 percent.

....

CREATING *and* MANAGING RELATIONSHIPS *at the* INDIVIDUAL LEVEL

Managing the customer portfolio at the individual customer level involves making customer-specific decisions about the amount and type of investment in each relationship. Because customers may have similar needs, the nature of the individual relationships need not be unique; each follows from an assessment of the value and potential of the specific relationship. Managing relationships at the individual level may be an effective strategy when one or more of the following conditions apply:

- The value of individual relationships is high relative to the cost of developing and acting on customer knowledge.

- The needs, tastes, and preferences of individuals vary significantly.

- The value proposition lends itself to tailoring sufficiently to accommodate individual needs or tastes.

- The buyer has sufficient incentive to collaborate and share information.

Wachovia illustrates the application of these conditions in the banking business.

Wachovia Bank
Checking All the Accounts

In the last 20 years, heads of U.S. households have made substantial changes in selecting those with *whom* they save, *where* they borrow, and *how* they conduct financial transactions.[5] A plot of the flow of U.S. household savings from the mid-1980s reveals massive outflows from commercial banks almost exactly matching the inflows into mutual funds. In less than two decades, the share of U.S. financial assets held by commercial banks fell from approximately 40 percent to less than 25 percent, while that of mutual funds rose from a negligible base to more than 12 percent.

During the same period, new competitors seized much of the loan business once dominated by banks and their savings and loan cousins. By the early 1990s, more than half of mortgage lending originated with nonbank mortgage companies. The banks' short-term business-lending market was diminished by the growth of efficient, worldwide commercial paper markets.

In the same short time, people changed substantially how they interacted with their banks. Although automated teller machines (ATMs) and call centers often are viewed as substitutes for branch banking, in practice the emergence of new channels appears to have increased the overall number of bank customer interactions. Thus, while the proportion of total transactions handled by branches has dropped, the branches remain an important channel and serve an important part of the customers' total experience.

The greatest challenge faced by banks has been to recast their relationship with customers. Traditionally, banks viewed customers (depositors) as a low-cost source of funds and provided relatively low-risk, secured lending services. Banks were saying, in effect, "Leave your money with us and we'll keep it safe." In contrast, mutual funds were telling people, "Give us your money and we'll make it grow."

The erosion of their deposit base and increased competition in traditional lending areas pushed banks increasingly toward fee-based services and higher-risk credit card income. These income sources place a higher premium on customer knowledge, as a number of banks found out through poorly targeted efforts to build credit card bases. To secure a greater share of customers' business and replace lost revenue streams, many banks adopted a product-driven or *financial supermarket* approach and attempted to cross-sell a range of financial services. These efforts often were unsuccessful because customers did not have confidence in banks' ability to offer extended services and because of the difficulty of matching a particular offer to the specific needs of customers.

People do not buy financial services in the same way that they buy groceries. Wachovia's research found that, in general, people don't have time to monitor their financial needs: They need expert help from someone they trust, want access to a team of specialized experts, and will consider switching to a new institution if they believe that institution is truly working in their best interest. On the other hand, people are skeptical of banks and consider them too conservative. Therefore, banks need to build on the trust they enjoy (based partly on their conservative reputation) while demonstrating their competency to play a larger role in managing customer finances.

Wachovia's strategy is to build on trust-based relationships that keep its customers' best interests in mind by developing personalized solutions. Achieving this goal requires that systems be built to evaluate the needs of individual customers. In addition, it requires that the company move beyond treating each customer roughly the same and that it engage customers with the right professional resources and channels. Wachovia's experience demonstrates the importance of aligning knowledge management, connecting technologies, and customer economics to focus on the right customer with the right product at the right time.

Customer Portfolio Management

Wachovia has recognized that to manage its customer portfolio effectively on an individual basis, it needs to take relationship banking to the next level. The new process described here is in proof-of-concept testing at the time of this writing, but it illustrates the direction of individual relationship strategies.

Wachovia was a leader in personalized service and, as a result, had attracted an above-average customer portfolio. Traditionally, Wachovia had managed its customer portfolio in terms of groups. The very affluent were handled by *private* bankers. All mass-market customers were assigned a *personal* banker and were encouraged to work with this individual on all matters. Although popular with customers, providing personal service to everyone was extremely expensive. Wachovia became a victim of its own success. Customers liked the idea of a single point of contact and, as a result, the personal bankers found themselves tied down, performing routine tasks for customers at all levels of customer relationship value.

In planning its new relationship strategy, Wachovia built on its customer knowledge to align its connecting technologies (broadly defined to include branches and relationship managers as well as ATMs, call centers, etc.) with its customer economics. The driving factors were the concentration of customer relationship value, the diversity of customers within various profitability groups, and the recognition that customers' situations and needs change over time in a reasonably predictable way.

Value Concentration

The value of banking customer relationships is very concentrated. In Wachovia's case, the top decile accounts for roughly half of all revenues and profits. The top three deciles account for more than three-fourths of total profitability. Given the high value concentration, it follows that a large number of customer relationships are marginally profitable or unprofitable. Clearly, there is a tremendous payoff to being able to assess relationship profitability and then to align acquisition, development, and retention efforts effectively.

The emerging relationship process is designed to sort or stratify *all* customers into categories based on potential profitability, to assign each customer to a tiered set of relationship channels, and to manage those relationships proactively as customer needs evolve or new information is gained. Although the planned relationship process described here addresses development and retention of existing customers, the new acquisition process is very similar.

However, estimating customer relationship potential is not as easy as one might think. Membership in both high- and low-value groups is diverse and not fully explained by simple demographic characteristics. As David Pope of Wachovia points out, "We're as likely to find doctors as factory workers in our lowest or highest deciles." This fact calls for fairly sophisticated customer profiling models that use multiple factors to predict potential relationship profitability. What is distinctive about Wachovia is that it profiles or scores its *entire* customer base, in contrast to the more common practice of assuming that a particular group—say affluent professionals—is a priori the most promising target. Wachovia classifies individual accounts as having similar potential on the basis of a number of factors, which were identified through prototyping tests.

Wachovia's focus on *potential* profitability is important in overcoming a common problem among banks that use current profitability or economic status as a targeting criterion. Almost everyone opens a checking account early in his career, thus giving banks a head start in relationship building. However, banks that wait to invest in developing a relationship until the client obviously is affluent or receptive to extended services are likely to find that the customer already has established a financial management account with a broker or an IRA with a mutual fund. The problem then is to estimate the future value of the relationship on the basis of current information. Wachovia, while still far from its ideal position, has begun to create predictive knowledge by developing customer life-cycle analyses. Using these analyses, the bank can align its customer development efforts more closely with each customer's current and potential needs.

Wachovia has planned to implement its new relationship strategy in three phases. First, it is repositioning and reoptimizing its market network, including branches, ATMs, and the call center, to reflect current and expected patterns of channel usage. Customer channel preferences vary both within and across profitability groups. These preferences also change over time, as people become more comfortable with new technologies. As mentioned earlier, the total number of

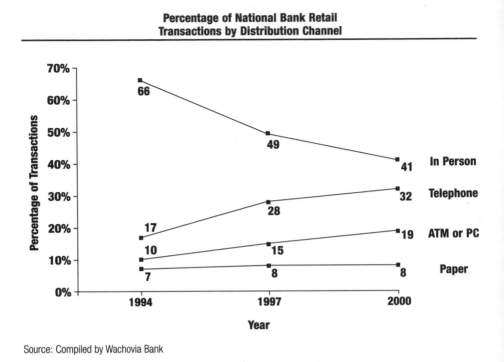

**Percentage of National Bank Retail
Transactions by Distribution Channel**

Source: Compiled by Wachovia Bank

Figure 5-6

interactions per customer is expected to increase but the mix, as shown in Figure 5-6, will change. The percentage of transactions conducted in person is projected to decline from more than two-thirds to approximately 40 percent by the year 2000. Both telephone and electronic (ATM or personal computer) transactions are expected nearly to double. The expected persistence of in-person banking may surprise those who anticipate the almost total eclipse of branch banks by electronic channels. Approximately 76 percent of customers use branches regularly (averaging about 2.5 visits per month), and channel usage by major demographic groups is fairly uniform. There are some differences, however: Older mass-market customers use all channels relatively less frequently, whereas young affluent customers, not surprisingly, tend to be somewhat more intensive users of telephone and electronic channels. The implications are that consumer banks will continue to offer a blend of channels and must calibrate carefully the introduction of new technologies.

To match the deployment of new connecting technologies (such as video kiosks) with customer utilization, Wachovia analyzed the timeline or wave of acceptance. Although a number of branches are being closed, a significant

**Managing Lead Flow by
Profitability and Potential**

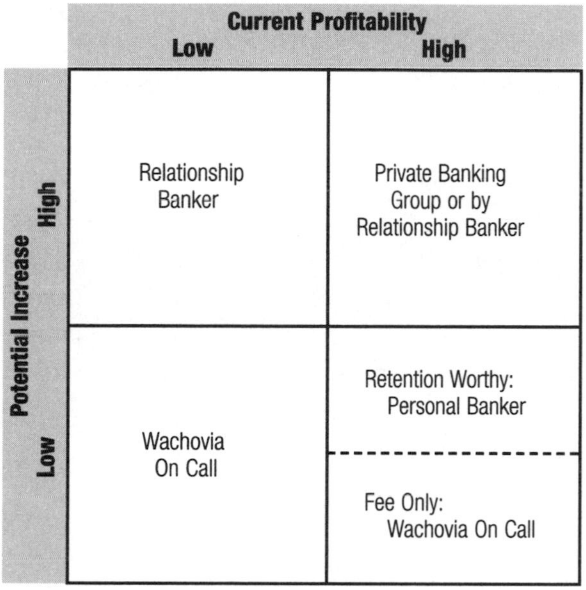

| | Current Profitability | |
	Low	High
High (Potential Increase)	Relationship Banker	Private Banking Group or by Relationship Banker
Low (Potential Increase)	Wachovia On Call	Retention Worthy: Personal Banker / Fee Only: Wachovia On Call

Figure 5-7

number of new branches are being built but, importantly, with an updated, modular design that provides flexibility to incorporate future changes in technology.

The second phase, which is under way as of this writing, is to develop a more rigorous customer-profiling capability. The objective of this knowledge management system is to be able to anticipate accurately customer receptivity to various financial offers. To build this capability, Wachovia had to expand greatly the amount of information on each customer and, in some cases, to append outside data. In addition, it had to develop, prototype, and test predictive models of customer profit potential and responsiveness. The output of these models is used to assign customers to one of three tiers of relationship management. The very affluent customers are assigned to the private banking groups. The top customers in the mass consumer market will be assigned to the new relationship managers, who are responsible for developing the value of several hundred customer relationships. The much larger group of lower current or potential profitability relationships is assigned to the branches or is handled by the call center.

The distribution of leads by channel is illustrated in Figure 5-7. The profiling and lead management systems try to ensure that the relationship bankers are working only with high-potential customers. In addition, the banker is responsible for selling and initiating fulfillment but, unlike his role in the previous model, does not perform the fulfillment process. This frees up time for relationship building and sales. Importantly, this more refined customer portfolio management process has enabled Wachovia to be more proactive and to substantially increase share of wallet among pilot customers.

The third phase, which Wachovia calls *financial integration,* will involve using information technology to deliver higher value-added financial planning services to the mass consumer market. A set of models will be employed that uses questionnaire data to develop cost-effective financial plans. This set of tools allows Wachovia to move beyond the typical cross-selling approach and to individualize offers based on an understanding of the customers' objectives.

Although it is too soon to be certain, early tests of this new relationship model have been very encouraging. Preliminary results seem to indicate that customers appreciate the proactive approach when it is based on thoughtful, professional analysis of their personal situations.

In this chapter, we've shown how the distributions of customer relationship value and customer characteristics influence the level at which firms can manage their customer portfolios most profitably. In the Harley-Davidson case, all customers are treated equally and are offered a fairly narrow range of products that appeal to their sense of common identity. Staples has found that distinguishing groups of businesses largely on the basis of employee count leads to significantly different propositions and business designs. Wachovia Bank, with broad distributions in both relationship value and customer needs, is moving toward individual relationship management across its entire portfolio. Of course, over time, as the power of information and connecting technologies increases, the boundaries of what constitutes significant and actionable differences in value and characteristics will continue to shrink, moving more and more companies toward customer-specific portfolio management strategies.

chapter 6

Creating customer value

DESIGNING THE RIGHT RANGE OF
VALUE PROPOSITION

A large proportion of new products fail. Generally, such failures do not occur because companies don't try to find out what customers want and then deliver it to them. In many cases, they occur because companies approach customer value creation too narrowly and don't truly understand the context in which the customer uses a given product—how it fits together with other products to achieve the customer's final objective. By understanding the customer's value chain and total experience, a company can better assess the value it is creating for the customer and can identify opportunities to increase that value.

The value proposition is the seller's half of the exchange of value with the buyer. It involves both the tangible and intangible factors embodied in the offer as well as the buyer's expectations of the exchange. As outlined in Chapter 1, the potential range of the value proposition is defined either by the buyer's value chain or by what we call the buyer's *total experience*. There are a number of approaches to represent the ways buyers combine factors and intermediate products to achieve a final purpose; among these are production and utility functions, process maps, value chains, and total experience maps. We will use a simplified form of the value chain developed by Michael Porter to indicate a flow of value-added activities. In cases in which there is no flow or direct combination of products to achieve the customer's objective, we will use total experience maps.

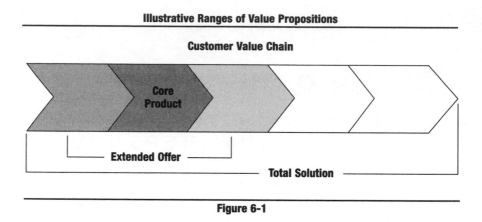

Figure 6-1

The seller's position on the value proposition dimension of the value compass refers to the extent of the seller's involvement with the buyer's value chain or total experience. The seller's level of involvement can be illustrated by one of three points along a continuous spectrum of value: core product, extended offer, or total solution. The spectrum of potential value propositions can be mapped against the set of activities undertaken by the customer to achieve his objective (known as the *customer's value chain*), as illustrated in Figure 6-1.

The *core product* position involves a clearly defined package of attributes that addresses a specific part of the customer's value chain or total experience. Most consumer goods (e.g., breakfast cereals, baseball bats, and shoes) are core products. A firm such as Pioneer Hi-Bred, a seed producer, might stick to its tangible core product but increase its involvement in the buyer's value chain by using information and knowledge to enhance its value proposition.

An *extended offer* involves the seller in a greater part of the customer's value chain or total experience. In this position, the seller extends the value created for the buyer by combining into an integrated offer additional elements of the value chain or total experience. For example, the core product of an automobile frequently is combined with financing services. American Skiing Company, as we'll show later in a case study of this firm, has extended its value proposition to include several parts of the skier's total experience.

A *total solution* provider offers an integrated solution that either covers the entire customer value chain or addresses the customer's total experience. Unlike the core product and extended offer, which are delivered at a particular time (e.g., all facets of a ski trip), elements of the total solution might be purchased at different times. *Inc.* magazine has expanded its value proposition to include the delivery of information in several forms, offering direct counsel on business issues and serving as an advocate for small-business interests.

Expanding the range of your value proposition to cover a larger part of your customer's total experience or value chain is an attractive strategy when there is a significant gap between the value of your current offer and the customer's total expenditures to meet his underlying need. In principle, the potential value of a relationship always increases directly with extensions of the value proposition because the seller is capturing more of the buyer's total expenditures. For example, a ski-lift operator, aware that his customers' expenditures for equipment, apparel, lodging, and food greatly exceed their expenditures on lift tickets, might aspire to become a full-service destination ski resort. However, the ski operator's business will become more valuable only if the additional revenues exceed the incremental costs of offering the expanded value proposition. Customers will gain by and be responsive to an extended-value proposition if it increases the total utility they receive or lowers the total costs of achieving the result they desire.

The temptation to extend the range of one's value proposition is great and has seduced many bright executives into offering end-to-end service or one-stop shopping. Though it often is possible to accomplish such full service, the business highway is littered with the wreckage of failed attempts, many of which threatened the companies' core product. One of the most prominent is Allegis, an unsuccessful attempt to combine an airline, a hotel chain, a rental car agency, and a reservation system. The Allegis experience and others like it explain why so many experts advise businesses to "stick to their knitting" and concentrate on their core competencies. Although we agree with the sentiments underlying this advice, many firms have moved well beyond their core products and successfully increased the amount of value they create for their customers and capture for their shareholders.

Businesses often must go beyond their original core competencies to realize the full potential of their customer relationships. Sunday River, today a destination ski resort, began as little more than a lift operator. Pioneer Hi-Bred successfully—and profitably—provides farm operators with both seeds and valuable information to make the appropriate seed-related decisions. *Inc.* has become much more than a magazine; it provides a wide range of developmental services to managers of growing businesses as well as customized marketing services to the advertisers who want to reach those businesses. United Parcel Service has migrated from offering a core product of one-size-fits-all package delivery to offering a full suite of distribution and logistics services.

What distinguishes successful extensions of value proposition from others that have failed? We believe a combination of the following factors is involved:

- Expanding from the core competency into only those areas where customers see a clear connection.

- Focusing, at least initially, on customers whom the firm already understands and with whom the firm already maintains relationships.

- Communicating a clear and common message across the extended range of the value proposition.

In this chapter, we discuss, in terms of the general factors that lead to success, representative strategies at each point along the value proposition dimension, illustrating these points with examples and case studies.

ENHANCING *the* CORE PRODUCT

Enhancing the core product often works when one part of the customers' experience has a disproportionate influence on the customers' perception of value. Redesigning this part or combining it with the core product might greatly increase the value to the buyer. There are numerous examples of this popular strategy. Saturn adopted a no-haggle sales environment, greatly reducing buyer transaction costs (and anxiety). British Airways treats Club-level flyers to a meal on the ground so that they can sleep longer while airborne and offers them a shower and suit press at Heathrow Airport so that they can go directly to their meetings.

In many cases, a buyer's costs of gathering information and assembling the components of his or her value chain are a significant part of total costs. In these cases, the core product often can be enhanced by what Stan Davis calls "informationalization."[1] Pioneer Hi-Bred has remained focused on seed but has greatly expanded its value to buyers by serving as a source of valuable information.

"Everyone thinks that the corn seed business means wallowing in the mud, but Pioneer is absolutely the most high-tech company I'm associated with. In many ways it's similar to an aerospace company."[2] This assessment by Warren McFarlan, a Harvard Business School professor specializing in information technology's role in creating competitive advantage, neatly captures the contrast between the perception many people have of agriculture and the reality of one of the United States's highest-tech businesses.

Pioneer's experience exemplifies the many pressures faced by companies whose core product is being threatened by rivals operating on the same and adjacent sections of the customer's value chain. Rather than extend its tangible product, Pioneer undertook to increase its value to its customers and deepen relationships by leveraging information and knowledge.

Pioneer Hi-Bred International
Harvesting Knowledge

In 1970, Pioneer and its major rival, DeKalb, each controlled approximately 23 percent of the U.S. hybrid seed corn business.[3] Today Pioneer sells nearly 45 percent of all U.S. hybrid seed corn and DeKalb, in second place, holds on to less than 10 percent. Pioneer's original core product—hybrid seed—provided added value by increasing the yield on the growers' other inputs of land and labor. Land planted with hybrid rather than varietal corn seed would yield almost 20 percent more corn. Initially, growers were almost exclusively interested in yield per acre but, recently, other factors such as drought and disease resistance have also become important. The seed itself represented the delivery vehicle for Pioneer's knowledge of genetics and agronomy.

Nonetheless, Pioneer's once commanding lead in technology took a significant dip in the mid-1980s. A number of well-funded chemical and oil companies entered the seed market, competing with Pioneer not only by challenging its technological advantage but also by offering farmers a full suite of products, including fertilizer, crop protection chemicals, and seeds.

At the same time, Pioneer's customer base was becoming heavily consolidated. Nearly 1 billion acres are farmed in the United States today, almost the same amount as in 1926 when Pioneer was founded, but those acres are farmed by far fewer people working on far fewer farms. When Henry Agard Wallace founded Pioneer, there were more than 6 million farms; today there are only approximately 2 million. Even this number is deceptive; total agricultural output and therefore opportunity for suppliers such as Pioneer are highly concentrated in a very small percentage of farms. Nearly half, or almost 1 million farms, have annual sales of less than $10,000, whereas the 6.5 percent of farms with sales in excess of $200,000 account for almost two-thirds (62 percent) of total sales (Figure 6-2).

Of the 2 million working farms in the United States today, approximately 25 percent grow corn and are potential customers for Pioneer's leading product, seed corn. The distribution of value for these potential customers is concentrated in roughly the same proportions as it is for all farms.

Value Concentration in U.S. Agriculture

Farms	Number	% of U.S. Total Sales
14.1%	282,000	75%
6.5%	130,000	62%
1.5%	2,600	40%

Source: Rolf Anderson, *Atlas of the American Economy,* 1994, Congressional Quarterly, Inc.

Figure 6-2

The concentration of value into a small proportion of farms presented a dilemma for a company founded by a man who was a populist secretary of agriculture under Franklin D. Roosevelt and who ran as the Progressive Party's presidential candidate in 1948. Philosophically, the company had always been attached to the family farmer and still believed it was important, in the words of one executive, to "give every grower an opportunity to plant Pioneer products." Pioneer's extensive sales force of 4,000 independent sales representatives began as a network of farmers who sold seed to their neighbors. Many companies might react to the growing concentration of customer value by focusing only on the high end, but Pioneer worked hard to continue to serve smaller growers while responding to the demands of the very large growers. To maintain its presence across the entire spectrum of growers, Pioneer invested heavily in databases and communications systems that would enable it to track individual growers and provide focused information to the firm's sales representatives and customers. However, though reluctant to reduce service to or disengage from its smaller customers, Pioneer recognized the implications of the growing concentration of farm value.

Having regained its position as overall technological leader in the seed corn business with patented hybrids that yielded 5 to 10 percent more corn than its major competitors, which permitted Pioneer to capture a modest price premium, Pioneer knew it needed to increase the value of its offer to match the sophisticated needs of the modern grower. Believing that, in the future, growth might depend as much on its knowledge of its customers as on its technology, Pioneer set out to increase the intangible value it delivered to its customers both through continued research and, increasingly, through sharing its extensive knowledge about issues affecting the farm operator's total experience.

We will examine how Pioneer concluded that this would be the best approach. Today's larger growers operate businesses in which an understanding of the com-

Representative Mega-Farm Process

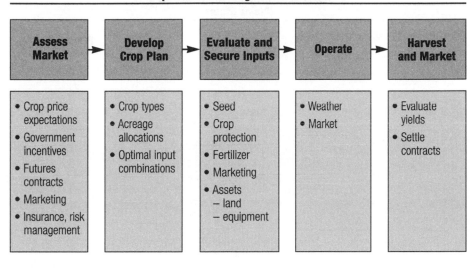

Assess Market	Develop Crop Plan	Evaluate and Secure Inputs	Operate	Harvest and Market

• Crop price expectations
• Government incentives
• Futures contracts
• Marketing
• Insurance, risk management
	• Crop types
	• Acreage allocations
	• Optimal input combinations
		• Seed
		• Crop protection
		• Fertilizer
		• Marketing
		• Assets
		  – land
		  – equipment
			• Weather
			• Market
				• Evaluate yields
				• Settle contracts

Figure 6-3

plex interactions of many variables is required to produce the optimal output. Figure 6-3 illustrates the complex decision-making and operating issues facing the modern "mega-grower." Output must be planned several months before production is complete, markets for output often are volatile, inputs must be carefully balanced with one another and, even with the best planning, capricious factors such as the weather and the fluctuations of commodities markets can adversely affect the outcome. By understanding this process and optimizing its seed offering within the specific context of individual buyers, Pioneer is able to add value to its core product.

A simplified value chain representing the major activities of acquiring land and fixed assets and planting, protecting, and nurturing the crop is shown in Figure 6-4 in terms of the major cost elements. As shown, a Plains-states corn farmer who received $2.33 a bushel in 1993 spent $0.21 or 9 percent of revenues on seed. This chart roughly indicates the opportunities to increase the range of Pioneer's value proposition or, for that matter, of any other party serving the farm operator. Three principle routes are open to Pioneer: substitution, bundling, and informationalization.

The Substitution Route

The substitution route would involve increasing Pioneer's value to the farmer by reducing the total costs to produce a bushel of corn. If, for example, Pioneer produced a seed that was naturally resistant to insects or disease, the operator could reduce his

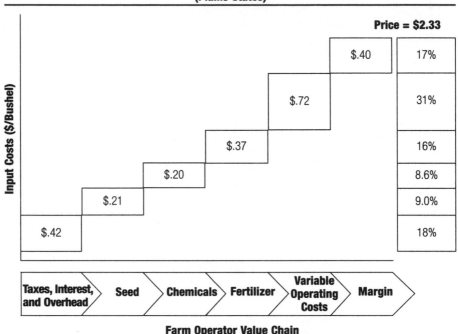

Farm Operator Expenditures Per Bushel of Corn
(Plains States)

Price = $2.33

Input Costs ($/Bushel)

				$.40	17%
			$.72		31%
		$.37			16%
	$.20				8.6%
$.21					9.0%
$.42					18%

| Taxes, Interest, and Overhead | Seed | Chemicals | Fertilizer | Variable Operating Costs | Margin |

Farm Operator Value Chain

Source: Economic Indicators of the Farm Sector: Costs of Production, 1993; Major Field Crops and Livestock and Dairy, USDA, 1994

Figure 6-4

use of crop protection chemicals. If Pioneer developed a seed that increased the yield per acre and required less fertilizer, then the farm operator could reduce his use of land and fertilizer (or, equivalently, produce more corn using the same amount of land and less fertilizer). Historically, most of the value created by Pioneer had come through the substitution route, largely through the development of products that substitute yield for acreage, which is a major reason that farmers produce so much more corn on nearly the same number of acres as were farmed 30 years ago.

It is important to note that a seller's gains from substitution are limited to the amount of the buyer's incremental decrease in expenditures on the complementary product. For example, if the improved seed reduced the use of crop protection chemicals by 10 percent, Pioneer could, at most, capture that 10 percent of value in a price premium for its seed. In practice, Pioneer would be likely to capture substantially less because part of the savings must be shared with the buyers and the chemical company might retaliate by lowering its price.

The Bundling Route

The second route available to Pioneer for increasing its value to the operator is bundling. For example, Pioneer could leverage its sales and distribution network to offer a full range of crop protection chemicals, such as fertilizers and insecticides, in addition to seed. This, in fact, was the route apparently being taken by many chemical and fertilizer companies, who were buying up smaller seed companies. The potential gains from this strategy appear to be much greater than the gains from substitution, because instead of capturing only the efficiency gains from substitution, Pioneer could, in theory, capture the total margin associated with the complementary good.

To evaluate the potential gains from the bundling strategy, we need to add two dimensions to our representation of the farm operator's value chain—the competencies required to operate at each point on the chain and the margin earned on the complementary product. In Figure 6-5, we've added a vertical axis of illustrative competencies that correspond to each point on the value chain. For example, seed production involves competencies in genetics and plant biology, whereas fertilizer production requires chemical- and process-manufacturing capabilities. Seed and fertilizer producers typically have more than a working understanding of the other's sphere of knowledge because of the interrelated and complementary nature of the products, and both must know a fair amount about farming or agronomy; however, only the specialized or distinctive knowledge required for each type of production is crucial to competitive success.

For any firm to move deeper into the growers' value chain, it would need to build or acquire the additional competencies. Accomplishing this would increase the value of that company's relationship with the grower only if the total margin on the bundled products exceeded the firm's existing margin on the core product. Such an increased margin might occur if the grower saw an advantage in the bundled product or if substantial channel economies resulted from the same sales and distribution network's handling of more products.

Still, it remains far from clear that a bundling strategy can successfully address the farm operator's value chain. First, the distinctive competencies required at various points are very different. Achieving a distinctive competency in any one area requires a certain scale and depth of experience. There's a reason that businesses specialize in serving different parts of the customer's value chain: As Adam Smith pointed out more than 200 years ago, the degree of specialization is determined by the size of the market: The larger the market, the more likely it is that firms will specialize in developing a particular competency to serve a part of the market's needs.

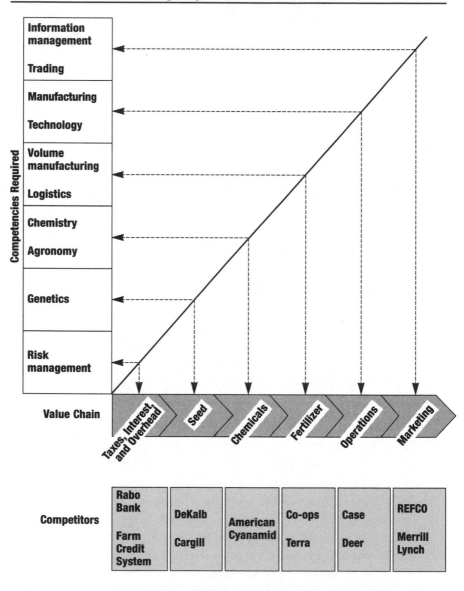

Figure 6-5

Second, the established specialized players are not without defenses. Attempting to consolidate the market for farm inputs is akin to starting a four- or five-front war with the other players and distribution channels.

The ability to bundle products successfully across the customer's value chain depends also on the importance of the core product, the ease of acquiring the additional competencies, and the ability to capture a sufficient portion of the added value. Thus far, no one has found a way to create these favorable conditions in the market for farm inputs.

The Informationalization Route

Pioneer's third possible route for increasing the value of its relationships is through informationalization. Using information technology, Pioneer believed it could extend its presence on the farm operator's value chain without diversifying into other tangible products. In fact, Pioneer's credibility regarding other elements of the farmer's value chain is aided by not being a supplier of those products.

Pioneer saw the evolution of precision farming as an important trend that influenced its customer relationships. The company knew that today's precision farmer isn't buying seed just on the basis of per-acre yield; rather, today's farmer is evaluating an ingredient in a complex recipe. Seed performance depends not only on local growing conditions but also on the type and amount of fertilizer and crop chemicals used. Increasingly, farm operators want information on the total package and will buy from suppliers who can deliver the highest economic yield.

Recognizing that the seed itself embodied only a part of the knowledge it possessed about genetics and agronomy, Pioneer decided to invest heavily in equipping its sales representatives with customer connecting technologies. These customer connecting technologies enabled reps to access detailed profiles of Pioneer's own and competing seeds and to create on-the-spot comparative crop-plan analyses for the grower that incorporated recommendations about other inputs, such as fertilizer. Pioneer, in cooperation with Farmland Industries and the Illinois Farm Bureau, even went so far as to develop a satellite-based farm management information system called *Farmdayta* (since sold) that delivers real-time information on weather patterns and commodity markets directly to growers' terminals.

Future Trends

Pioneer is studying the trend of end users, such as food producers, to participate more actively in the growing process as a possible avenue for enhancing its core value proposition and leveraging its knowledge. Whereas in the past they generally were content to buy the types of corn offered on the market, end users have begun moving upstream in the process to assure themselves that producers are using the appropriate raw materials. For example, in some cases, a food processor would contract with a farm operator to produce a particular type and quality of corn. Although contract farming is not new, it is spreading into more types of food products.

End users are interested also in developing strains of corn tailored to their specific needs. A starch manufacturer, for example, could reduce its costs substantially if it could secure a corn with a particular chemical makeup. Recognizing this, Pioneer resolved, as a next step, to develop an understanding of end-users' value chains and to think about how to "design" corn that would solve these users' business problems.

EXTENDED-VALUE PROPOSITIONS

The American Skiing Company
Moving the Mountain

The experience of the American Skiing Company (ASC), which operates Sunday River ski resort, illustrates the evolution of an extended-value proposition from a core product by building on and leveraging its competencies and developing new capabilities as required.[4] ASC concentrated first on perfecting its core product— the mountain terrain, snow conditions, and lift operations at the resort. Only when this part of the value proposition was perceived widely by skiers as superior did ASC undertake to offer its customers extended services. Throughout its evolution, ASC has focused on the customers it knows best—skiers.

The more extensive the value proposition, the more intensive is the customer knowledge requirement. The seller needs not only to understand the buyer's criteria for the original component of the value chain or experience; the seller needs also to appreciate the customer's value criteria and decision-making process for the other elements in her value chain or total experience. Before ASC could move into lodging and other services, it had to expand its knowledge beyond the buyers' preferences for snow conditions and lift configurations to encompass preferences for food, lodging, and shopping values.

Similarly, the buyer of any extended-value proposition needs more information about the seller, particularly the seller's ability to deliver beyond the original value proposition. The buyer may extend to the seller some degree of trust based on previous experience or reputation, but this will be limited to new areas that are related in some way to the seller's acknowledged competency. Ski-trip buyers probably are more likely to believe that a former ski-lift operator, such as ASC, can deliver high-quality ski lessons and equipment sales because these activities are related to and benefit from experience operating ski lifts. However, ski-trip buyers are less likely to trust a ski-lift operator's ability to provide outstanding food and accommodations. In any event, buyers are not likely to extend trust or grant credibility to a broader value proposition if the seller does not perform well in providing the basics.

Because it is difficult to establish credibility across a large number of areas, many firms extend the range of their value proposition in conjunction with allies or partners with special competencies. The decision of whether to partner or to self-produce depends on which element in the total value proposition is the dominant source of value, the difficulty of acquiring the needed competencies, and the share of the added value that would be captured. ASC could have contracted with a recognized restaurant or hotel chain to provide those parts of the package in which its credibility was lowest. This approach might have increased the probability that buyers would purchase the expanded product, but it would have reduced the share of the total value captured by ASC.

In some cases, sellers extend the range of their value proposition to capture externalities created by their core product. Disney leveraged its Disney World theme park with hotels and other services after watching with dismay how others captured some of the value created by the original Disneyland. In some cases in which the original or core product is the dominant factor in buyers' decision making about other purchases, the seller might be able to offer only reasonable quality or value on the extended part of the value proposition. Nonetheless, the seller still might succeed with its extended-value offering if the extended part of the value proposition always is bundled with the core product. Such bundling works best when the core of the proposition is unique, proprietary, or difficult to replicate. ASC was able to bundle skiing and lodging at Sunday River because the core product was a decisive factor, the competencies necessary to operate a hotel can be acquired fairly easily, and ASC's control of the acreage around its remote mountain diminished the ability of rivals to capture the externality created by the resort.

Most businesses begin in the core product position. Over time, competitive forces, technological changes, or an accumulation of knowledge about customers prompts many, but not all, firms to seek ways to extend their value proposition. Any move to extend the range of the value proposition must be grounded in an understanding of both the potential gains and the reasons for leaving the existing position. A poor core product cannot be saved by integrating it into a broader offer.

Many firms misjudge the strength of their relationships and attempt to exploit them by charging high prices for related or aftermarket purchases. Automobile manufacturers and dealers are notorious for charging premium prices for replacement parts and service. As a result, they see a precipitous drop in their share of repair expenditures after their warranties expire. This breaks the chain of customer interactions during the period buyers are most likely to consider repurchase. In contrast, John Deere prices its aftermarket services competitively and captures a large share of customer expenditures through both additional service revenues and higher repurchase rates.

TOTAL SOLUTION STRATEGIES

The total solution position on the value proposition dimension represents the most extensive coverage of the buyers' value chain or experience. USAA frequently is cited as an example of a firm that offers a broad set of insurance and financial products to address its customers' total risk management experience.

The total solution position offers the highest potential to create and capture value. However, as we noted earlier, many attempts to provide one-stop shopping, integrated solutions, and the like have failed. Too often, efforts to build customer value by *cross-selling* related products degenerate into an attempt to be all things to all customers. It appears that just possessing a distinctive and leverageable competency and reputation or brand is not sufficient; the business must identify strongly with its customer base. Although nothing in principle precludes a business from identifying strongly with many customer groups, in practice such identification is very difficult.

Inc. is an example of a business that brings together the three components of a total solution strategy: leverageable competencies, reputation, and identification with its customer base. In building its core product, *Inc.* developed a set of competencies that was based on understanding the needs both of growing businesses and of advertisers who wanted to reach those businesses. Building on its understanding of growing firms' needs for business knowledge and its reputation for delivering useful knowledge, *Inc.* created a set of related products to address its customers' need for management knowledge. Building on its understanding of advertisers' needs, *Inc.* extended the range of its offer to include direct-marketing support, consulting, and customized publishing.

Inc. Magazine
Reading the Customers' Needs

In many ways, Bernie Goldhirsh, founder of *Inc.* magazine, acts as a role model for his entrepreneurial, iconoclastic readers.[5] After graduating from MIT in 1961, Goldhirsh first went to work teaching at a private school in Cambridge, Massachusetts. After a few months he proposed that the century-old school completely restructure its curriculum. Out of a job soon after, he launched a shipboard school by placing a small newspaper ad. The response surprised him: "Here I was with no experience, offering to take these people's children out on the ocean for several months." The school ship was a pedagogical success, but Goldhirsh returned to land with approximately $65.00. Naturally, he launched a new business.

While outfitting and preparing the school ship, Goldhirsh had been frustrated by the lack of hands-on, how-to information for the average sailor. The introduction of fiberglass was bringing the cost of sailing within reach of more middle-income people, but established sailing magazines of the day, such as *Yachting,* were aimed at blue-blooded readers who either had grown up with and understood boats or hired someone else to do the work. From his own experience, Goldhirsh knew that there was a growing, largely neglected group of people who were hungry for useful information about sailing.

Sail started as a sort of samizdat of the boat world. Using discounted downtime from a printer, Goldhirsh began with an annual that was sold at newsstands to the underground of do-it-yourself sailors. The publication attracted attention from advertisers eager to reach this growing market and, with this support, *Sail* was born. Nicholas Negroponte, a "cyberguru" who, according to Goldhirsh, still "believed in atoms," designed *Sail*'s logo. After *Sail* became the largest magazine in its category, Goldhirsh sold the magazine to Meredith Corporation for almost $12.5 million but insisted that the new publisher stay in Boston and keep the staff. Then he started another business.

While growing *Sail,* Goldhirsh had noticed that there was no ready source of practical, hands-on information about building a small business. The reigning business magazines—*Fortune, Business Week,* and so on—like the blue-blood

yachting magazines, catered to managers and followers of large, established
corporations and paid little attention to emerging entrepreneurial businesses.
Goldhirsh also sensed the boom in small-company start-ups and identified
closely with these entrepreneurs whose interests and needs were not always
the same as those of the big corporations. His passionate commitment to the
people whom he believes are driving the economy's growth and expanding
opportunity has provided *Inc.*'s focus. It also has guided *Inc.*'s evolution from
simply a magazine to a provider of a wide range of products for growing businesses and of services for the advertisers who want to reach those businesses.
At the same time, *Inc.* has become an advocate and champion of the entrepreneurial sector of our economy.

From its first issue in 1979, which featured a couple of guys named Wozniak
and Jobs who were working out of their garage, *Inc.* has grown to serve nearly
660,000 paid subscribers and to generate approximately $70 million in annual
revenues, almost three-fourths of which are derived from the magazine, the rest
coming from extended services.

The Early Days

In its early days, *Inc.* defined its target customer bases fairly broadly as small,
growing businesses and the advertisers who wanted to reach them. Its core
product in the small-business market was the magazine, which provided readers
with management information relevant to growing a small business. For advertisers, *Inc.* offered access to a group of valuable readers who were otherwise difficult to reach in a concentrated way. *Inc.*'s role with both customer groups was
that of a typical product manager providing a well-defined service with relatively
modest interaction or direct collaboration.

The economics of the magazine business once were fairly straightforward: Build
circulation and the advertisers would come. Subscription revenues for a magazine such as *Inc.* were typically a relatively insignificant source of profits. Even
using fairly optimistic assumptions about the cost of acquiring additional readers
through various sources, the net present value of a 5-year subscription has
remained between $10 and $15.

Most of a magazine's profits are generated by selling access to the magazine's
readers. The magazine's access charges are expressed as its cost per thousand (CPM) for a standard black-and-white page. *Inc.*'s latest black-and-white
ad page cost $48,265.00 to reach nearly 650,000 readers, for a CPM of
$67.50. Because *Inc.*'s readers are concentrated among a highly desirable

group of owners and managers of small, growing companies, *Inc.*'s CPM is a little higher than that of other business magazines.

If advertisers are willing to pay $67.50 per thousand, the equivalent access charge per reader is $.0675. Therefore, *Inc.*'s 12 issues, with approximately 60 pages of ads per issue, generate almost $48.60 per reader per year. Looked at this way, a 5-year reader produces more than 10 times as much value in ad revenues (approximately $163.00 at a 15-percent discount rate) than in subscription revenues. Therefore, attracting an additional 5-year reader and holding the number of advertisers constant increases the present value of revenues by $175.00 or so. Similarly, holding the number of readers constant while attracting an additional advertiser who would pay 6.75¢ per reader and who would place an ad in each issue for 5 years would produce a revenue stream with a present value of approximately $1.55 million. Under these conditions, *Inc.*, like other magazines, concentrated on building circulation of the core product and attracting as many advertisers as possible.

Exploring Growth Options

Inc.'s original value propositions resulted in extraordinary early growth. From 1981 through 1985, *Inc.*'s circulation increased from approximately 230,000 to more than 605,000, a 5-year growth rate exceeding 164 percent. By the mid-1980s, however, circulation growth rates dropped to single digits. The cost of acquiring additional customers approached or exceeded the subscription revenue. In addition, advertisers began cutting back on print ads and negotiating concessions on the ads they did place. *Inc.* was faced with the same dilemma many of its entrepreneurial readers faced: How do you maintain growth when the momentum of the original value proposition levels off due to changes in market conditions?

Inc.'s growth options included staying with the successful core product and continuing to build its reader and advertiser bases or leveraging its competencies to deliver value-added products deeper into the value chains of its customers. These strategies were not, of course, mutually exclusive, and *Inc.* has, in fact, pursued both courses. However, our primary interest here will be to explore the development and execution of the extended services built on the competencies gained in creating the core product.

Inc.'s editorial content efforts put it in constant touch with its customer community and the people serving that community. This gave rise to a set of specialized competencies related to providing information and knowledge-based services to both readers and advertisers. *Inc.* increased the yield on its two customer asset bases by leveraging these competencies to create a set of differentiated or customized products, which we've labeled *extended reader services* and *marketing and sales support*, respectively. Extended reader services comprised conferences, videotapes, books, and the like. For advertisers, the range of extended-value propositions included direct mail; event, electronic, and database marketing; and customized newsletters. Each of these additional points of interaction with *Inc.*'s customers involved more exchanges of information and strengthened the connections between *Inc.* and its customer bases.

Value was created for and captured from these assets in both undifferentiated and differentiated forms. At the core product level, readers bought undifferentiated content (the magazine) and advertisers bought undifferentiated access to readers (ads in the magazine). Still, in the course of providing its core product, *Inc.* received a great deal of both explicit and implicit information from its customers (both readers and advertisers) that enabled it to direct its editorial efforts more precisely to their needs. Explicit information was gathered through surveys, discussion groups, customer letters, and such devices as reader response cards. From its earliest days, *Inc.* gathered summary-level information on its readership and periodically surveyed readers on topics of interest. This information was shared with advertisers, who also received information from reader response cards and circulation audits. Implicit information was received through such indicators as customers' actions, the sales levels of particular issues, and requests for reprints.

Inc.'s extension of its value proposition was motivated by its mission to serve growing companies, stimulated in part by the slowing growth of its core product and enabled by its special competency-knowledge about the needs of growing businesses and advertisers that targeted them. As Bob LaPointe, president of *Inc.* Business Resources, has pointed out, companies that fail to take full advantage of their competencies by leveraging them into related areas are overlooking one of the most effective forms of growth.

Many magazines have extended their value proposition to include books and videotapes (e.g., *Sports Illustrated*), but very few cover their customers' total experience as comprehensively as does *Inc.* (Figure 6-6). In addition to books, videos, and conferences, *Inc.* also offers consulting: Through *Inc.* Eagles, the company is actively engaged in assisting CEOs to work through strategic issues.

Although the magazine remains *Inc.*'s core product, the firm's expansion into conferences, seminars, on-line services, books, videos, custom publishing, electronic publishing, and consulting are not truly extensions of the magazine

Simplified Value Flow Diagram for *Inc.*

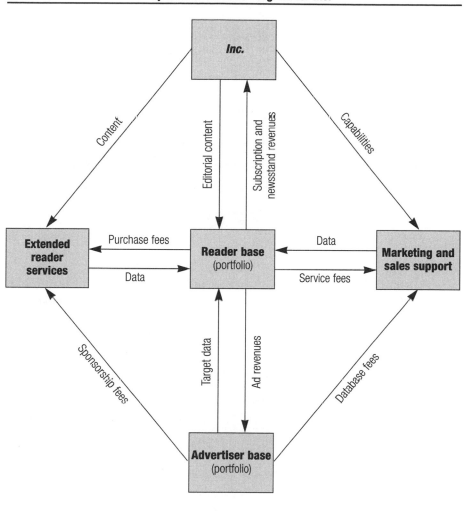

Figure 6-6

but are extensions of its competencies. The extended services provide additional points of contact with *Inc.*'s target market—managers and executives of growing businesses who are not necessarily limited to readers of the magazine. In fact, the majority of conference attendees are not current *Inc.* readers. *Inc.*'s extension of its value proposition has allowed it to reach new customers and to offer differentiated products that are more closely tailored to the specific needs of groups within the firm's overall market.

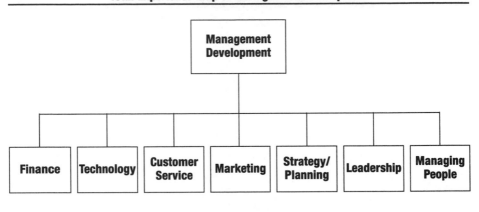

Figure 6-7

Inc.'s extended-value proposition now covers most of the management development experience illustrated in Figure 6-7 with a range of media. Based on its research into customer needs, *Inc.* focuses on seven topics: finance, technology, customer service, marketing, strategy and planning, leadership, and people management.

Inc. delivers information on these seven topics through the magazine, books, videos, and conferences. Conferences are tailored to reach companies of varying sizes and different levels within the organization. For example, *Inc.* World is geared to a general audience, primarily in New England, whereas the CEO symposium reaches senior executives at larger companies. Unlike most companies that offer business conferences, *Inc.* has moved to make its conferences regular features on the management calendar and essentially to brand them. The Customer Service Conference, for example, is now in its seventh year and attracts a sizable repeat business from firms and individuals.

Inc.'s newest vehicles for delivering knowledge, *Inc.* Online and *Inc.* Eagles, represent both an extension of the basic product and a change in the company's role and means of interacting with customers. *Inc.* Online offers access to archived material and also offers a "virtual consultant," allowing users to communicate with their peers on management topics, to complete interactive worksheets, and to link to selected legal and business databases.

Inc.'s consulting group provides growth strategy consulting to companies in the $1 million to $100 million range, a market that most major consulting firms find unprofitable to serve. *Inc.* Eagles, a part of the consulting group, also provides a unique service, bringing CEOs together with their regional peers to wrestle with shared issues. With these ventures, *Inc.* is moving beyond its initial product manager role and has introduced elements of network management.

The Growth Bonus

The economic payoff from extended products comes from increased customer relationship value. *Inc.*'s early growth was fueled by customer acquisition—increasing the number of readers and advertisers. As the growth rate of the magazine slowed, *Inc.* shifted its emphasis toward a developmental strategy of increasing the value of customer relationships.

As a result, approximately one-fourth of *Inc.*'s total revenues now is generated by sources other than the magazine. This growth results from both increasing the value of existing customers and attracting new, higher-valued customers.

The increase in value of existing customers can be illustrated by the effect of offering conferences. As noted earlier, a magazine-only customer represents an incremental value of nearly $175.00 (including both subscription and advertising revenues). In contrast, a 5-year customer who has only a 10-percent probability of attending a conference in any given year has an expected value of more than twice that of a magazine-only customer. The potential economic value of *Inc.*'s customers (the intrinsic value discussed in Chapter 4) is the weighted sum of their probabilities of purchasing each of the products offered, where the weights are the net cash flows or margins for each product. For simplicity, using only the magazine and conferences, Figure 6-8 shows the expected value of customers with conference participation probabilities of 10 to 50 percent.

The increase in *Inc.*'s customer portfolio value attributable to the extended products depends on the proportion of customers who participate in the extended offers. Figure 6-9 indicates the substantial leverage in customer portfolio value possible from even moderate levels of customer participation rates. A customer portfolio made up entirely of 5-year magazine subscribers has a value of approximately $171.6 million ($2.60 times 660,000). As shown, if the average conference participation rate is only 0.01 (1 customer in 100), the average relationship value increases by 7 percent. This average participation rate could be achieved with any number of combinations of customers with high and low probabilities of participating. If the average participation rate were as high as 0.1 (1 in 10), the customer portfolio value would rise by 71 percent even if no new customers were attracted.

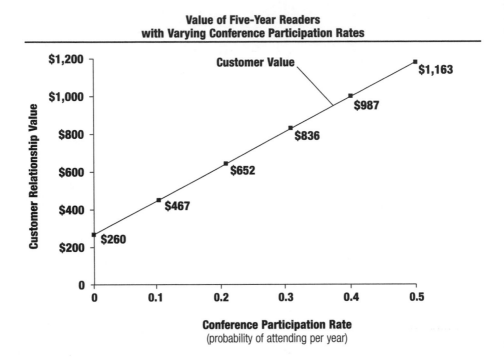

**Value of Five-Year Readers
with Varying Conference Participation Rates**

Figure 6-8

Customer Portfolio Value

	Reader Only	0.01% Conference Profitability	0.1% Conference Profitability
Magazine subscription income/customer	$16.00	$16.00	$16.00
Advertising income/reader	$244.00	$244.00	$244.00
Conference participation rate	0%	0.01%	0.1%
Conference income value/customer	0	$18.40	$184.00
Customers	660,000	660,000	660,000
Value/customer	$260.00	$278.40	$444.00
Portfolio value	$171,600,000	$183,900,000	$293,000,000
Increase in value	—	7%	71%

Figure 6-9

Inc.'s experience shows how maintaining focus and identification with the targeted customer base and leveraging competencies and reputation (brand) across
the customer value chain or total experience can result in increased customer
value and growth.

....

In this chapter, we have illustrated how successful product or value proposition development is related to the knowledge of your customers. Development
of a firm's value proposition should be firmly rooted in an appreciation of the
customers' final objective and their means of achieving that objective as portrayed by the customer value chain or total experience map. Movement deeper
into the customer value chain or across their total experience depends on the
competencies required to deliver the broader range of value proposition, the
trust or confidence customers have in your ability to extend your presence, and
the competitive advantages and reactions of rivals serving the same customer
value chain or experience.

Increasing your presence on the customer value chain does not necessarily
involve providing additional or extended products, as Pioneer Hi-Bred illustrates. A core product can be enhanced to reduce costs upstream or downstream in the value chain. The firm that does capture additional space on the
customer value chain usually does so on the basis of the leverage of its core
product, either due to an appropriable externality or because the core product
is the key ingredient in the customer's process for achieving his objective.
Moving deeper into its customers' value chain often involves a shift in a business's view of itself from selling product to helping the customer succeed.
Extensions work best when supported by a common basis or platform of capabilities. One of the most important of these capabilities may be a close identification with and deep understanding of a particular group of customers, as
illustrated by Pioneer, ASC, and *Inc.*

Producing and delivering value

PLAYING THE RIGHT VALUE-ADDED ROLE

In most of our discussions so far, we have observed how the interaction of buyers and sellers played out on the field of the buyer's value chain or total experience. Therefore, we have been concerned with *added value*—the difference between the price or revenues received and the costs of serving the customer. Now we step back to consider the position taken by sellers in the overall *value-added chain*—the sequence of steps from primary inputs to final output. Each step might be performed by separate firms, or two or more steps might be conducted by a single firm, in which case the firm is said to be *vertically integrated*. A value-added chain for automobiles might look like that shown in Figure 7-1.

Between each step, a transaction takes place, in many cases involving a fair amount of interaction between the parties. Traditionally, these transactions have been treated as "arm's length" in nature and as occasions to gain advantage. More recently, a growing emphasis has been placed on establishing partnerships across steps in the value-added chain and on leveraging information to facilitate and increase the value of those transactions. The use of information to make the value-added chain flow more efficiently is exemplified by just-in-time delivery, whereby the supplier aligns its delivery schedule closely with a customer's production schedule and reduces inventory-related costs. More elaborate information exchanges might lead to shifting activities from one party's

Value-Added Chain

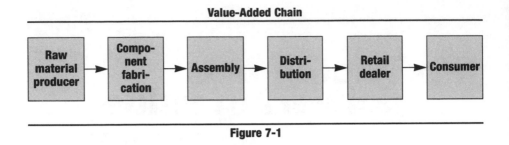

Figure 7-1

value chain forward or backward in the value-added chain (e.g., when a supplier undertakes to perform design or testing functions for a customer).

A rich and growing literature highlights the increasing application of information and technology to alter the nature of the value-added chain and to forge new relationships, partnerships, and "virtual" corporations. The basic forces determining the role played by firms within an industry's value-added chain were laid out by Adam Smith more than 200 years ago in his famous theorem, "The division of labor is limited by the extent of the market." In general, as the market increases in size, it pays people to specialize in particular functions and to adopt production techniques suited to the larger scale of operation. In determining its role or the division of labor most advantageous to it, a firm must identify those functions in which it has a comparative advantage. In some cases, this role will involve performing a number of functions, in others only a few and, in some cases, firms might perform only the role of bringing together customers and suppliers.

In this chapter, we are interested primarily in the way in which the interactions among buyers and sellers are affected by the nature of the value proposition and the search and transaction costs incurred across steps in the value-added chain. The different roles played by sellers and their position relative to their customers' and their industry's value chains depend on a number of factors:

- The basis on which the seller creates added value.

- The means by which that value is delivered to the buyer.

- The structure of the market and the nature of demand.

As there are uncountable variations and combinations of these factors, it is easiest to illustrate the range of roles by describing three representative roles—product manager, process manager, and network manager—with increasing proportions of information or intangible content in the relationship. The gener-

General Characteristics of Representative Roles

	Product Manager	Process Manager	Network Manager
Primary focus of value creation	Supply chain	Customer value chain	Bridge supplier and customer value chains
Growth factor	Volume: market share	Share of customer expenditure	Share of traffic
Approach to market	One to many	One to one	Many to many
Buyer/seller search and transaction costs	Low	Moderate	High
Tangible to intangible ratio	High	Balanced	Low

Figure 7-2

al characteristics of these roles, which are illustrative rather than prescriptive or universal, are shown in Figure 7-2.

In the following sections, we'll discuss each role in more detail, outline the conditions under which each is most appropriate, and illustrate each with cases involving Tyson Foods, United Parcel Service (UPS), and Delta Dental Plan of Massachusetts.

PRODUCT MANAGER ROLE

The product manager delivers value by exchanging a well-defined and "finished" product in a series of relatively discrete transactions with buyers. The seller's contribution to value creation is embodied largely in the product, and his responsibility generally is confined to meeting the quality and functionality claimed. The seller's involvement or degree of interdependence with buyers usually is limited.

The product manager is focused on supply-chain management both to control costs and, just as important, to control product consistency and availability. In most cases, the product manager pursues a volume- or share-based strategy, and marketing efforts are directed broadly to all potential product users.

Tyson Foods exemplifies the product manager role. Operating primarily in the intensely competitive chicken market, Tyson achieved exceptional growth by establishing a powerful brand identity, continually enhancing its product to align with changing customer and consumer needs, and achieving the lowest-cost position within the industry.

Tyson Foods
First in the Pecking Order

Tyson Foods has excelled in the product manager role by its continual search for new ways to add value to its core product, by establishing and building its brand equity, and by achieving the industry's lowest-cost position based on scale, vertical integration, and investments in technology.[1]

From 1935 to 1995, advances in genetics, nutrition, and disease control produced remarkable gains in chicken production. In 1935, the average marketed broiler was a 16-week-old bird weighing some 2.8 pounds. For each of those pounds, the bird consumed 4.4 pounds of feed. By 1995, the typical broiler was a mere 6.5 weeks old, it weighed more than 4.5 pounds, and each of those pounds required only 1.9 pounds of feed. This dramatic increase in productivity, even with increased costs for some inputs, has enabled the chicken industry to maintain constant real prices for the past 35 years and to achieve a relative price advantage over such other protein sources as beef and pork, the prices of which have risen during the same time.

In part stimulated by chicken's growing price advantage and in part due to changing dietary and health concerns, chicken rapidly has gained "share of stomach" from 1960 to the present. From 1960 to 1990, the U.S. per-capita consumption of chicken more than doubled, from 30 to more than 70 pounds per year, while beef and pork consumption declined by 3 and 8 percent, respectively.

Until the 1960s, chicken's tremendous cost reductions were shared throughout the industry and did not provide a competitive advantage to any firm. Although all of this was good for chicken consumers, the industry itself was marked by relatively modest returns and volatile earnings. Historically, the industry was fragmented along the six functional steps necessary to move chickens to market (Figure 7-3).

Chicken producers seemed doomed to pecking out a precarious existence in the agricultural commodity sector until 1969, when a remarkable thing happened. Frank Perdue, president of the eponymous company, began to brand

The Chicken-to-Market Value-Added Chain

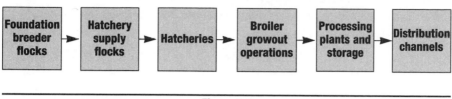

Figure 7-3

his chickens and to differentiate them by developing a feed mix that gave Perdue chickens their distinctive yellow color. Until Perdue, it was agreed generally that "parts is parts." Beginning in 1971, Perdue supported his strategy with extensive advertising. The results were dramatic: Perdue sales increased 25-fold from $60 million in 1971 to $1.5 billion in 1994.

In response to Perdue's success, a number of other firms, including Holly Farms (now part of Tyson), began aggressively marketing and developing their own brands. Branding and differentiation with extensive promotional support began to do what economies of scale and efficiency had not—consolidate the industry. Competitive advantage that couldn't be achieved in the chicken coop was found on the air waves and in the distribution network. Thirty-eight percent of domestic broiler production in 1983 was concentrated in the top five companies; by 1995, the five largest companies accounted for better than 50 percent of total sales. Today, Tyson accounts for one in three chickens grown in the United States.

Tyson's vertical integration through the processing-plant stage was the foundation for its product management strategy. Vertical integration provided the quality control necessary to offer a differentiable product. Like most large poultry operations, Tyson even produced its own scientifically designed feed to ensure a consistent product. Control over its supply chain also enabled Tyson to manage costs better and to take an integrated view across the entire poultry value-added chain.

Tyson manages its product through four major divisions, each of which serves a particular customer group with a differentiated value proposition. The Foodservice Division markets to commercial, industrial, and institutional customers, serving 94 of the top 100 restaurant chains and all 50 of the top food service distributors. The Wholesale Club Division serves the fast-growing wholesale membership clubs. Tyson won the bulk of this market on the basis of low-cost production and distribution and the ability to offer product tailored to the consumer's willingness to buy larger quantities for a lower price. The Retail Division's customers—largely grocery chains and grocery wholesalers—sell a wide range of fresh or further-processed products for at-home consumption. Tyson also earned the number-one position in the $5 billion fresh-chicken category. The International Division, begun in the mid-1980s, is expected to grow rapidly as global markets open, incomes rise, and consumer demand for poultry increases around the world.

Tyson also benefited from the increase in households' "outsourcing" of meal preparation; households were spending a larger and larger proportion of their food budgets in restaurants, which resulted in rapid growth of the food service industry. Americans spent almost 50 percent of their food budget in the food service sector in the mid-1990s. This produced a number of large, sophisticated buyers who have formidable bargaining power and are not likely to pay a premium for the carefully cultivated brand names of the leading producers; they want value. In the food service sector, Tyson added value to its core product by configuring its look and taste to fit the requirements of its customers.

During the 1980s, the retail grocery business also consolidated, increasing the bargaining power of the larger chains. Reacting to the same structural shifts that were putting a greater share of the consumers' food money into restaurants, retail grocers increased their pressure on vendors and invested in information technologies that provided them with even more leverage over producers. Grocers started to charge shelf-stocking fees, demanded more favorable terms and, in many cases, extended house brands.

Tyson calibrates its value proposition to align closely with the requirements of each major customer group. In the food service sector, Tyson provides everything from fresh chickens to highly processed products configured to a particular customer's needs. In the wholesale club market, the emphasis is on product development and packaging for consumers who buy in bulk to achieve cost savings. In the retail grocery sector, Tyson often has a comparative advantage because of its knowledge of the consumer; therefore, Tyson is able to provide marketing support and advice in addition to a full suite of products from fresh to further-processed meals.

PROCESS MANAGER ROLE

The process manager role involves an ongoing interaction between buyer and seller, in which the seller assumes responsibility for some portion of the buyer's production function or value chain. In this role, the seller's contribution to value creation occurs through leveraging a skill or competency to achieve the customer's objective. The added value *per customer* for the process manager potentially is much greater than for the product manager, because the created value reflects a larger scope of activities and the management of more input variables. For example, when UPS acts as a product manager (providing package delivery service), its added value comes from the difference between the competitively determined price it receives and the costs under its control. When UPS acts instead as a process manager and assumes responsibility for a retailer's logistics, its ability to create value for the buyer extends to changing the way material is handled, prepared for shipment, and the like. This extended scope allows for creating and capturing more value. The process manager pursues a strategy of capturing the share of the buyer's expenditures compatible with the company's competencies. Outsourcing may lead to a process manager role, but many instances of outsourcing do not involve significant levels of ongoing interaction or collaboration and are simply a matter of buying an intermediate product formerly produced in-house.

The process manager role has grown as advances in information technology have made it easier to coordinate activities among different firms, and intense competition penalizes firms that produce in-house what they could procure more efficiently outside. Although many people equate outsourcing with cost reduction and nonstrategic or support activities, research by Clifford Moore at the Customer Outsourcing Performance Center indicates that firms increasingly are relying on suppliers to provide critical customer-related services, including fulfillment and aftermarket service and support. Accustomed as we are to thinking about customer relationships as a firm's most valuable assets, we were surprised at the degree to which many firms put these assets into the custody of third-party providers.

In the process manager role, marketing and relationship management is conducted one-to-one, often with dedicated teams serving particular buyers. In many cases, rewards sharing is based on the joint contribution to added value and the attainment of the customer objective. UPS is an example of a firm that has extended its role with large customers by leveraging its competencies and increasing its degree of interdependency.

United Parcel Service
Moving Beyond Pick-Up and Delivery

Founded in 1907 by Jim Casey and Claude Ryan, the American Messenger Company began operations in the basement of a Seattle saloon.[2] Casey and

Ryan delivered messages and telegrams, ran errands, delivered groceries, and even provided baby-sitting services—just about anything their customers wanted.[3] The American Messenger Company eventually grew to become United Parcel Service, the world's largest package delivery company.

Until fairly recently, the UPS relationship model was typical of most product-driven firms. UPS focused on a basic, no-frills core product—package delivery. Its market was defined very broadly, with relatively few distinctions among shippers. Sharing of risks and rewards with customers was essentially neutral, with pricing based on UPS's market position as a superior alternative to U.S. postal services. Prices reflected very broad measures of average costs and often concealed the relative profitability of customers and products. In its role as a product manager, UPS focused largely on sales volume and production efficiency. Its slogan, "The tightest ship in the shipping business," pretty accurately portrayed what UPS did and how they did it. The ubiquitous dark-brown trucks provided a low-cost, reliable product. Of course, customers were expected to do their part (i.e., to have the package ready on time and to ensure that it was the correct weight and size).

UPS's obsession with industrial engineering and cost management is legendary. Sometimes its emphasis on measuring and reducing costs inhibited its ability to innovate. Although it was the first package company to enter the air business and although it pioneered the now common hub-and-spoke system, it allowed others to pioneer next-day delivery. UPS tracked costs religiously, but it was slow to go to the next level with IT, particularly IT that served customer needs.

Under Kent "Oz" Nelson, one of those rare CEOs who truly deserves the title of visionary, UPS began a remarkable transition toward a more customer-based strategy. Asked why he undertook the change, Nelson responded, "The impetus? In a word, Roadway. In two words, Federal Express."[4] UPS's shift from a one-size-fits-all strategy to that of a firm eager to partner with its customers and develop customized solutions is one of the most remarkable and underreported transformations in U.S. history.

Though packages still accounted for the bulk of UPS's revenues, by the mid-1990s, UPS was beginning to resemble the American Messenger Company in many respects. In its new form, UPS delivers letters, manages customer warehouses, performs order fulfillment services, deals with customs requirements, sells logistics consulting—in other words, offers just about anything a customer wants, except baby-sitting.

UPS manages its largest, most valuable customers on an individual account basis. With many of these customers, UPS no longer just provides a product

UPS Transformation

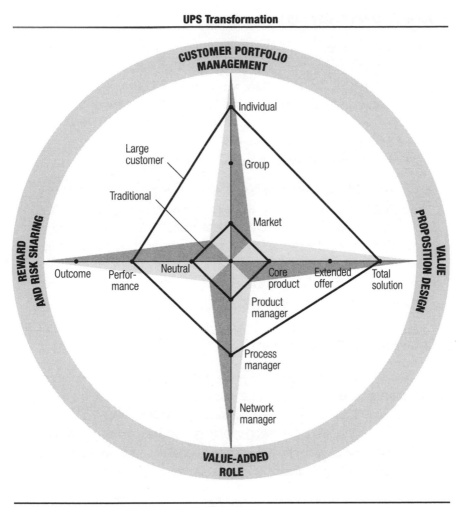

Figure 7-4

but actively manages or assumes responsibility for all or part of the customer process. Rewards no longer are based solely on volume but, in some cases, on a sharing of the gains from the relationship. The evolution of UPS's relationship strategy is illustrated in Figure 7-4.

Although in Chapter 2 we discussed UPS's extensive investments in IT and its application to its core package business, our emphasis here is on UPS's evolution from the role of a product manager providing package delivery services to that of a process manager taking responsibility for the full spectrum of customers' logistics and distribution.

Value Proposition Development

In the face of increasing competition, UPS focused initially on making its core product competitive by extending the range of its package delivery services. Historically, UPS had offered regular ground service and express service, each with fairly rigidly defined pick-up times and delivery terms. Today, UPS offers a wide variety of delivery options, from same-day service to next-day, second-day, third-day, and the like. Customers don't have to wonder whether their packages arrive; they can track them in real time and even verify the signature of the recipient.

According to Ed Brockwell, vice president of strategic accounts, to remain competitive and to respond to customers who were looking for ways to cut costs and focus on their own core competencies (which rarely include logistics and distribution), UPS had to adopt a customer relationship strategy based on offering total solutions. The skills and competencies developed in creating the extended-value propositions provided the basis for moving from a product manager to a process manager role.

Customer Portfolio Management

Although UPS provides services to anyone in its operating territories, its core customers are the 1.5 million shippers who require daily pick-up service. Approximately 5 percent of these customers generate or have the potential to generate more than $1 million each in annual revenues. These customers, UPS's strategic accounts, were assigned national account representatives responsible for enhancing customer relationships.

One of the most important indicators of the move from a product manager role to a process manager role is the assumption of responsibility for part or all of the customer's objective, not just the part that a given firm typically provided. UPS's large-customer relationship program superbly illustrates effective ways to assume responsibility for the customer's objective.

Like many other firms in the intensely competitive printing business, Curtis 1000, a medium-sized national printing company, had been scrambling to cut costs. Printing is a very time-sensitive business; customers expect fast turnaround. Curtis's main competition came from smaller, local shops which competed by offering fast response. To offer comparable turnaround, Curtis had built a network of 19 distribution centers scattered around the country. Although the centers allowed Curtis to stay close to its customers, the centers were too small to achieve the economies of modern printing or distribution technology.

Recognizing that it had too many centers, Curtis approached UPS for help in redesigning its distribution network. Jim McKinley, UPS's national account manager for Curtis, brought in UPS logistics experts who worked with Curtis to devise a plan to move from 19 to five centers. When one of the new centers experienced growing pains, McKinley reached into the UPS engineering support group for an engineer to help with racking problems.

In the territories formerly served by the 14 closed centers, consolidation meant that Curtis sales personnel could no longer drop off customers' orders at a local center. As they often contained fragile artwork and paste-ups, the orders couldn't be faxed or e-mailed. UPS's solution was to substitute its network for Curtis's, developing a special next-day air program that allowed the sales force to operate with the same turnaround time.

Is this just another story of exceptional customer service? We don't think so. What UPS does for customers such as Curtis allows UPS to preempt low-cost rivals. UPS has taken responsibility for more of the customers' value chain and can charge more for doing so. As Jim McKinley says, UPS is not a cheap operation—but you get what you pay for.

At Gateway 2000, UPS took on even greater responsibility for its customer's success. Gateway had enjoyed phenomenal growth rates of 30 to 35 percent per year in the mail-order computer business by offering customers tailored personal computer configurations with exceptionally fast order fulfillment. Gateway's added value to customers was the assembly of just the right components into the package desired by the customer. To accomplish this, Gateway acted as a network manager, orchestrating the flow of material from a multitude of vendors and shipping assembled machines to customers. To make this process work without maintaining large inventories, all the components (e.g., a CPU from Sioux City, a printer from Epson, and a monitor from the West Coast) had to arrive simultaneously at the customer's location.

Traditionally, these components went first to Gateway, which bundled them and reshipped them to the customer. Gateway believed that this involved unnecessary steps and costs and, in 1994, challenged its transportation suppliers to develop a solution. In what turned out to be the account-winning move, UPS agreed to solve the problem, although it had no off-the-shelf solution. Collaborating, Gateway and UPS developed DockMerge, a sophisticated system to coordinate shipments from multiple locations and merge them for final delivery to the customer. With DockMerge, Gateway never touches the components. The components move from the various manufacturers directly to UPS facilities, where they are combined and delivered to the customer. DockMerge now serves as an evolving platform for continued collaboration and innovation between Gateway and UPS.

As Gateway began running into constraints at its South Dakota location, UPS also helped it locate and plan a new facility in Hampton, Virginia. The new facility promised substantial savings by allowing more direct shipments of East Coast products to East Coast customers. At Hampton, UPS developed a 2-day inter-modal product tailored to the facility's needs.

UPS not only moves things for Gateway. It also provides warehousing services that include inventory management, pick-and-pack services, and quality-assurance testing of monitors and printers by UPS Worldwide Logistics personnel. The interdependence of the two firms extends even to facility locations; Gateway locates new sites strategically to optimize its access to the UPS ground network.

Maintaining and extending a close, collaborative relationship of this sort required a substantial commitment of personnel from UPS and a broader, more multidisciplinary approach. A global account manager, three full-time people, and a cross-functional team from the customer resource group coordinate the relationship throughout all levels of Gateway. Seven on-site customer support people and 20 on-site operations people were dedicated solely to Gateway. Gregg Mau, the UPS global account manager, pointed out that this type of relationship cannot be developed by dealing only with a traffic manager. Mau met regularly with Gateway's most senior executives to develop an understanding of their strategic and operational needs. Mau saw his role as evolving from that of reducing transportation costs to that of maximizing logistics value. Mau neatly describes the UPS search for value-added opportunities as "looking for things that Gateway does that do *not* add value." Talking to the CFO, for example, involved integrating concerns about inventory turns with possible transportation solutions, concerns that might never have been discussed when UPS saw itself solely as providing a package delivery product. The UPS-Gateway customer connection became so close that UPS representatives frequently were invited to attend Gateway strategy meetings, and joint design teams frequently developed new systems.

In 1994, Gateway solicited bids for a winner-take-all contract, which was won by UPS. Why would one of the nation's largest shippers single-source one of its most critical business activities to anyone, no matter how committed they were to the relationship? Also, how can Gateway protect against the possibility that UPS could extract additional returns from its sole-source position? UPS saw the contract as a validation of its efforts to date and of the trust it had built with Gateway. By investing in the Gateway relationship and collaborating to develop DockMerge, UPS increased the range of its services and went from serving less than half of the Gateway account to becoming its sole provider. In addition, Gateway and UPS both were stimulated to collaborate by an unusual profit-sharing provision in the contract—unusual in that it applies symmetrically to cost reductions for either party. In other words, it provides for sharing the savings from actions that either company takes to reduce costs for the other. For example, as parts of tailored loads, Gateway's shipments can bypass the first UPS hub. This allows UPS to deliver more efficiently and to share those savings with Gateway.

NETWORK MANAGER ROLE

Network manager strategies are attractive when a market is characterized by relatively large numbers of buyers and sellers who individually face significant information, search, or transaction costs. These buyers and sellers would gain by connecting to one another, but a number of factors make it difficult or costly for them to establish one-to-one connections. The network manager occupies a central location between at least two groups of buyers and sellers. We use *network* to describe relationships that traditionally have been called *intermediaries*, because we believe that the former term better captures the dynamic, interactive role played by such managers and is more evocative of the "many-to-many" web of buyers and sellers connected through a central point. Examples of network managers include health maintenance organizations (HMOs) and on-line computer services. HMOs act as intermediaries or points of connection between a large population of medical providers and an even larger population of medical consumers. On-line computer services connect content providers with computer users.

The relationship with a network manager adds value for both buyers and sellers by providing a form of connection more efficient than either could achieve by operating independently. In this role, the network manager expands the market by making it more economical for buyers and sellers to connect with one another. Whatever you may feel about HMOs, for example, they certainly expand the number of people who have access to health insurance.

A firm playing the network manager role captures value in two ways. First, it captures a part of the value it creates for buyers and sellers by reducing their information, search, and transaction costs (and charging them for the service). Usually, this is accomplished by establishing and controlling a gap between the price paid by the buyer and the price received by the seller—in effect, charging a toll or access fee for connecting buyers and sellers. Second, under the right circumstances, the network manager can leverage its control of access to buyers and sellers and extract part of their consumers' or producers' surplus.

The network manager can increase its total added value by expanding the amount of traffic over the network, by increasing the gap between the price paid by the buyer and the price received by the seller, by leveraging control of buyer or seller bases to extract consumer or producer surplus, and by extending the range of the value proposition for buyers and sellers. Expanding network traffic depends largely on giving both buyers and sellers a compelling reason to use the network. Many networks exhibit positive feedback characteristics. The more buyers attracted by the network, the more sellers become interested, and vice versa. The value of access for buyers and sellers is mutual. No subscriber is interested in an on-line service that doesn't provide access to valuable content. No content provider will use an on-line service that doesn't deliver valuable users. Network builders may leverage the buyer base by attracting subscribers with free or low-cost enrollments so as to attract and charge more providers for access to them, or vice versa. America Online, for example, has been pursuing a strategy of building a dominant buyer base through low entry pricing, extensive promotion, and relatively user-friendly interfaces. Prodigy, in contrast, has emphasized content to attract buyers.

The ability to extract the full value of network access depends on the ease with which buyers or sellers can bypass the network. The greatest threat to the major on-line services well may be the direct access to the Internet provided by such companies as Netscape and the likelihood that access will become a built-in utility on future computers. Similarly, many health care providers, physician groups, and hospitals are searching actively for ways to offset or sidestep the power of the HMOs.

The ability of a network manager to extract a portion of the buyer's consumer surplus or the seller's producers' surplus depends on its ability to control each party's access to the other. Indemnity-fee medical insurance programs have far less leverage over physicians than do managed care plans that direct patients to member physicians and monitor the doctors' use of procedures and fees as a condition of membership. This form of leverage is particularly potent when excess capacity exists in the sellers' industry or when the seller previously enjoyed a knowledge-based advantage over the buyer, conditions that existed in the medical industry.

Delta Dental of Massachusetts
Capping the Pain

"This will only hurt for a second" is part of an experience many of us consider only slightly less frightening than dealing with our insurance company afterward. For this reason, Delta Dental of Massachusetts is exceptional: providing preferred provider organization (PPO) dental services to more than 500,000 primary subscribers, enjoying a 96-percent renewal rate among its employer accounts, and achieving a 55-percent growth in revenues over the last 3 years on the basis of guaranteed savings and no-hassle service.[5] Companies such as Delta are using network manager strategies to transform the dental industry through acute understanding of customer economics, deep functional knowledge, and the leverage provided by its patient base.

With its high information, search, and transactions costs for both patients and dentists, dentistry practically cries out for a network manager strategy. Most of us haven't a clue as to how to pick a dentist or evaluate a dental procedure. We rely on secondary factors, such as the dentist's chairside manner, recommendations from friends who are as orthodontically challenged as we are, and the hope that the dentist's education and professional standards will prevent us from suffering any great harm to our mouths or our wallets. Aware of our ignorance and our overriding desire to end the pain of toothache, some dentists became as adept at gauging the size of the patient's checking account as the depth of a cavity. There is even an industry term for this: *PID*, or professionally induced demand. To be sure, dentists are no more or less unscrupulous than the rest of us but, in the game between buyer and seller, they held a commanding lead in knowledge and knew that the pressures to conclude an agreement were literally felt by the buyer. Dentists were in a good position to extract not only teeth but a large share of consumers' surplus as well. As a result, "usual and customary" fees—the benchmark used by dentists to calibrate their charges—typically increased by 5 to 7 percent per year.

Competition among dentists was inhibited by a number of professional factors, such as prohibitions on advertising, the use of community pricing guidelines, and the importance of cross-referrals as a source of patients. However, compared to physicians, dentists were a fragmented group of sole practitioners with very little collective or organized market power. Even if desirous of pursuing a competitive, price-based strategy, a dentist would have faced enormous information, search, and transactions costs to locate and win customers. Consumption of dental services is unpredictable; patients have little expertise to evaluate competitors and, if they are insured, have very low price sensitivity.

Traditionally, indemnity or fee-for-service plans that base their premiums on average patient costs and the actuarial experience of the employer's or group's population effectively acted as a pass-through mechanism and were relatively uninterested in controlling costs or the use of procedures. Practicing dentists often played prominent roles in dental insurance companies, serving on their boards or professional committees so as to design standards. Indemnity plans usually featured first-dollar coverage and put no restrictions on a patient's choice of provider, conditions guaranteed to maintain the dentists' advantage in their customer relationships.

By the 1980s, structural forces began changing the economics of dental practice and the dental insurance business. Rising premiums caught the attention of employee benefits managers who were under enormous pressure to reduce costs. Many employers viewed dental coverage, which accounts for only some 10 percent of total medical benefits, as a frill that could be eliminated or scaled back. Fewer than half of U.S. workers have dental coverage, compared to 80 percent with medical benefits.[6] At the same time, success in preventive dental programs (e.g., fluoridation), reduced birth rates (adolescents and teenagers account for a substantial share of total dental spending), and an increasing dentist population combined to create excess dental service capacity in many areas. Many dental plans were operated as sidelines by medical insurance corporations more focused on dealing with the changes taking place in the medical sector.

In 1986, Delta Dental Plan of Massachusetts was extracted from its parent, Blue Cross–Blue Shield of Massachusetts. In a relatively short period, it had to assume responsibility for more than 200,000 subscribers, develop an identity, and establish a business strategy. Delta knew that it could not prosper by continuing traditional insurance business practices. Therefore, with the opportunity to design an operating company from scratch, Delta set out to reinvent dental insurance.[7]

Delta's Economic Model

Delta's business is built around flows of information and value among three groups: patients, employers, and dentists (illustrated in Figure 7-5). Delta adds value to employers primarily in two ways. First, it acts as a risk manager by bringing superior knowledge and actuarial skills to assessing the probable level of claims and their costs. This allows Delta to offer the employer a predictable cost stream. Delta also wholesales dental services to employers and their workers at a cost lower than they could achieve on their own. If Delta cannot do these things, employers have the option of self-insuring (and, in fact, some large employers do take this route). For some employers, Delta offers administrative services only (ASO).

Delta Dental's Network of Information and Value Flows

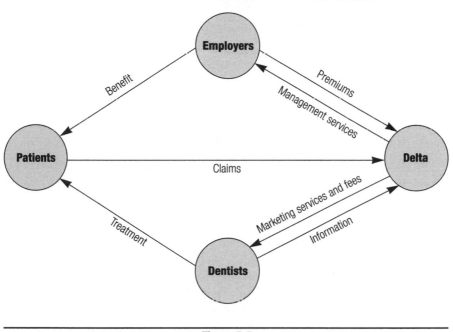

Figure 7-5

Delta also adds value to dentists in two ways. First, it provides a marketing service. Membership in Delta's network provides dentists with preferential access to a source of high-value customers. These customers are high-value because they have indicated an expected need by subscribing and they are insured, so that payment is virtually certain. Although only approximately 50 percent of the population is covered by dental insurance, 70 to 80 percent of a dentist's customers have dental insurance. Second, Delta reduces dentists' operating costs by assuming responsibility for a large part of the customer service function. (An emerging, third value-added function—improving the efficiency of the dentists' operation—will be discussed later.) Delta adds value for patients by providing a list of dentists, which reduces patients' search costs and, like any insurance product, allows the patient to convert a highly uncertain liability into a more certain but moderate cost stream made up of their share of the premium and any copayments.

Customer Portfolio Management

Customer selection in the insurance business is a little more complex than in most other markets. Obviously, the insurer cannot select only individuals who are unlikely to need treatment. Though undoubtedly there are a few very risk-averse people with little expectation of needing service but willing to subscribe anyway, the patient base will be made up largely of people who have a reasonable expectation of future dental work. Though the expected dental needs of an individual are almost impossible to predict, the patterns for groups are relatively predictable. Different groups exhibit different mean expected rates of use, and different variances around that mean. The art of actuaries is to set a premium sufficiently higher than the expected (mean) cost so as to capture the risk-bearing premium of the group, but not so high as to invite competitors or discourage subscribers.

Delta manages its exposure in a number of ways. It guards against adverse selection—the danger that a plan will attract only the "toothless Charleys"—by requiring that an employer plan enroll at least 75 percent of the eligible population. Delta also continuously reviews the total margins on accounts and, if it cannot adjust prices sufficiently to produce a reasonable margin at contract renewal time, it declines the account. Perhaps 4 percent of Delta's accounts are not renewed.

Over time, Delta has learned to target those employers with the most attractive patient bases. Perhaps counterintuitively, given that this is a margin business, the highest-volume (biggest) employers are not the most profitable accounts. As Figure 7-6 indicates, the margin per subscriber (a proxy for intrinsic customer value) is almost perfectly correlated inversely with the size of employer. Delta's margin is the difference between the premium level and the claims level actually experienced.

Why are the large-volume accounts the least profitable on a per-subscriber basis? Recall that the premium level is partly a function of the employer's ability to self-insure and the adverse employee-relations consequences of not providing dental coverage. Therefore, all other things being equal, smaller employers with employees who value dental coverage highly will be willing to pay somewhat more per subscriber than will a larger employer (and one more able to self-insure) whose employees don't value coverage as highly. Highly educated people tend to have a higher demand for dental insurance than do the typically less-well-educated employees found at large manufacturing or processing facilities. On the cost side, once the initial acquisition costs are digested, it doesn't cost Delta much, if anything, more to service a subscriber at a small firm than to service one at a large firm. In addition, highly educated people tend to be better informed about preventive practices and seek care at earlier, less expensive points in the course of dental problems. Therefore, over time, they may actually cost less to cover.

When operating and administrative costs are allocated against the margin on employer accounts, Delta finds that more than half its accounts are unprofitable

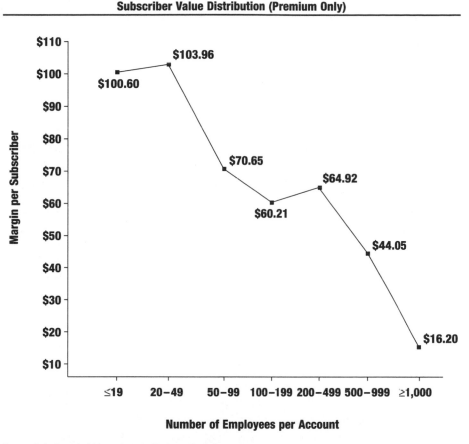

Subscriber Value Distribution (Premium Only)

Source: Delta Dental of Massachusetts Business Analysis

Figure 7-6

from an accounting perspective. Delta continues to acquire and service large accounts because some of them are judged *strategic* and because the volume of patients provides leverage with the providers.

Range of Value Proposition

Delta's entire value proposition is built on information and knowledge. Delta does not provide dental services directly; it acts almost entirely as what Stan Davis calls an "infomediary." However, these skills alone are not enough to explain Delta's exceptional performance. After all, there are plenty of actuaries in the world, knowledge of dental technology is readily accessible, and a directory of Massachusetts employers is available free from the state.

As an intermediary, Delta has to defend its central position not only from the threat of rivals and self-insurers but from the possibility that its providers will be motivated to create their own vehicle for reaching customers efficiently. This reality places a limit on the amount of producers' surplus they can extract from dentists by controlling access to the patient base.

Delta's product development must be calibrated to meet the interrelated needs of the three primary groups in its network: employers, patients, and dentists. Delta's initial innovations were directed largely at employers and, coupled with its guarantees, provided an improved benefit management experience. In the future, Delta expects that products will have to be designed for and appeal directly to subscribers (patients), who will have greater choice and who may be self-allocating benefit dollars across a wide menu of choices. On the dentists' side, Delta is considering a number of ways of providing extended office management services or even of employing dentists directly.

Delta's success can be explained in large part by the way it changed the rules of the game: offering a unique value proposition and risk- and reward-sharing arrangement with its customers. Its first major innovation, and one that drove many others, was to provide one-stop shopping: a single toll-free number that anyone (dentists, benefits managers, or patients) could call (without being transferred) for an answer to any question related to Delta Dental. This simple idea had enormous implications for staffing, training, and information systems, but paid enormous dividends. At the time, one-stop shopping was a unique concept in the insurance business and one that can be appreciated by anyone who has spent an hour on hold waiting for a claims representative. Having opened this connection to its customers and suppliers, Delta focused its operational efforts on increasing responsiveness and reducing costs. Delta's second major innovation was offering the first service performance guarantee in the dental insurance business. This concept is discussed in detail in Chapter 8.

Delta's product management is similar in many respects to that of an airline: balancing the subscribers' value and willingness to pay with the available capacity. With respect to subscribers, Delta is offering two managed-care options: a PPO and a capitation plan (a dental HMO). Both plans offer deep discounts off the standard plan in exchange for limiting access to a smaller number of dentists. Participating dentists bid lower fees in exchange for the

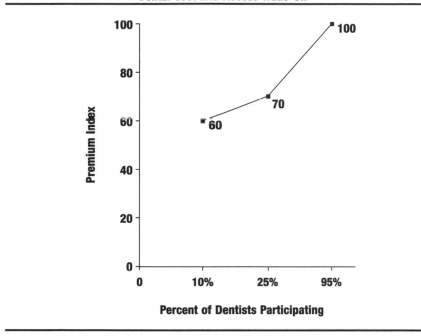

Dental Cost and Access Trade-Off

Figure 7-7

patient flow and volume that fills otherwise empty chairs. Figure 7-7 illustrates the trade-off between discount and access.

The obvious alternative to relying solely on control of patient flow is to create additional value for the dentists. Here, Delta is looking at ways of using information to help dentists operate more efficiently, adding back, in some sense, new value to replace the value surrendered in the contracted discount. Two avenues are open here: improving operating efficiency and expanding professional capacity.

In this chapter, we've shown how the role a firm plays in its relationship with customers and the overall industry value-added chain depends on the nature of its value proposition, on its ability to leverage its competencies, and on the information, search, and transaction costs encountered by buyers and sellers. Tyson, which provides a fairly specific and tangible product, has developed a supply-side advantage and strong brand equity to achieve scale and share. UPS has leveraged its logistics and information management competencies to assume greater responsibility for its large customers' needs and thus to distinguish itself from low-cost commodity providers. Delta Dental operates on both sides of the market to align customer needs and provider capacity more efficiently than either one could by undertaking its own search and transaction efforts.

c h a p t e r **8**

Creating value together

REWARD AND RISK SHARING

Consider two scoundrels—call them Bonnie and Clyde—who are arrested by a sheriff who suspects them of robbery but has only enough evidence to charge them with the lesser crime of possessing stolen property. The sheriff locks them in separate cells and attempts to plea-bargain. To each he says, "If you confess and your partner doesn't, I'll let you go and use your statement to convict your partner of robbery, which carries a 5-year jail sentence. If you both confess, I'll reduce the charges, and you'll both spend 2 years in jail." Unstated is a third option: If both remain silent, they would go free. The *prisoners' dilemma* is the classic introduction to game theory and an excellent primer in interdependent decision making: The optimal decision for each party depends on the decision of the other.

The dilemma faced by Bonnie and Clyde is illustrated in the payoff matrix in Figure 8-1, with the consequences for Bonnie shown in the upper triangle of each cell and those for Clyde in the lower. Clyde may reason that if Bonnie confesses and he doesn't, he'll spend 5 years in jail while she goes free; if they both confess, he'll spend only 2 years in jail. Therefore, if Clyde believes Bonnie will confess, his best option is to confess. If he believes Bonnie will not confess, he goes free if he confesses. Again, the best option is to confess. Bonnie goes through the same thought process, with the result

Prisoners' Payoff Matrix

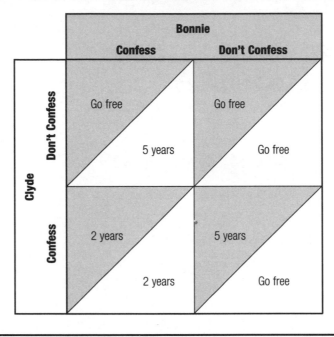

Figure 8-1

that both confess and receive 2-year sentences. Although both would be better off if they did not confess, the lack of communication and trust leads them to a suboptimal position.

The central lesson of the prisoners' dilemma game is that only by considering the consequences of your decision for both you and your "opponent"—and vice versa—can you make rational decisions. Not all trades or relationships produce optimum outcomes, as the prisoners' dilemma proves. Rational individuals acting competitively on the information available to them can, as the unfortunate prisoners learn, produce a result that is individually rational but collectively suboptimal. However, if the parties collaborate, they can produce a better outcome—at least for them. Each still is pursuing personal interests but, by recognizing their interdependence, both do better.

Many buyer-seller relationships, like the one between the prisoners, create some value but could create more if an effective means to collaborate were available. Many relationships are like non–zero-sum games, in which both parties can do better by collaborating.

Extensive analyses of prisoners' dilemma games has shown that if the game is played many times, the most successful strategy is "tit for tat." Gaining experience with the other player's moves and behaviors can result in greater value for both players. However, unless there is an incentive to collaborate, repeated plays of a game can result in reducing the value of the relationship.

RELATIONSHIPS *as* GAMES

The game metaphor is a useful way to examine the interactions between buyers and sellers and to explore their incentives to collaborate.[1] The cost-plus contract often is played as a zero-sum game, wherein what one party gains, the other loses. The buyer realizes that the supplier likely will learn over time and be able to operate more efficiently. The seller would like to retain the gains from learning. The buyer wants the supplier to reveal its excess profits (confess) so that it can reduce its payments, but it knows this action is unlikely, so it engages in extensive investigations to determine the supplier's real costs. The supplier knows its costs much better than does the buyer, can estimate the probability that the buyer will find excess costs, and can take steps to conceal its costs.

For example, if the supplier improves its productivity by $5 million and it believes the buyer has only a 25-percent probability of finding this savings, the game can be illustrated by the payoff matrix in Figure 8-2. The $5 million benefit to either the seller or the buyer is expressed relative to the situation *before* the productivity improvement.

If the supplier reveals its productivity gain to the buyer (upper half of the figure), the buyer benefits by the entire $5 million, and the supplier's position is unchanged relative to the situation before the productivity improvement (net gain, $0). If the supplier conceals the improvement, it gains an expected value of $3.75 million, on the basis of the 75-percent probability that the buyer will not find the improvement $[(0.25)(\$0) + (0.75)(\$5) = \$3.75]$. The buyer's expected gain is the remainder of the $5 million, or $1.25 million. Because the supplier expects to gain $3.75 million by concealing the productivity improvement and is certain to have no gain if it is revealed, the supplier will not reveal the improvement.

Suppose the buyer announces a $2 million auditing program to discover suspected productivity improvements. The supplier estimates the effect of this program as changing to 75 percent the probability of the buyer's finding the concealed savings. The supplier still has no incentive to reveal its productivity improvement, because it stands to lose the entire $5 million by doing so.

Initial Condition in Cost-Plus Game

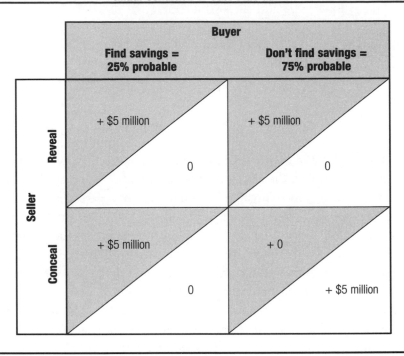

Figure 8-2

However, the expected value of its concealed improvement has decreased to $1.25 million [(0.75)(0) + (0.25) ($5) = $1.25].

The buyer's expected share of the benefit increases but not by the $2.5 million that the supplier has lost relative to the first case. The buyer must pay $2 million for the auditing program, so the buyer's *net* expected share is only $1.75 million [(0.75)(3) + (0.25)(–2) = $1.75]. Why would the buyer spend $2 million for so little gain? In practice, the buyer likely would ascribe to the auditing program the full amount realized, as it has no easy way of estimating what would have occurred without the program.

After assessing the likely consequences, the supplier might respond to the buyer's announcement by concealing its costs further. If the supplier could spend $1 million to shift down to 50 percent the probability of the buyer's finding the performance improvement, the supplier would increase its expected share of concealed savings to $1.5 million [(0.5)($-1) + (0.5)($4) = $1.5]. The buyer's expected gain is reduced to $0.5 million [(0.5)($3) + (0.5)($–2) = $0.5].

Results of the Cost-Plus Game

	Initial Position	Final Outcome	50-50 Sharing Agreement	Benefit from Sharing vs. Final
Buyer-expected benefit	1.25	$0.5	$2.5	$2.0
Seller-expected benefit	3.75	$1.5	$2.5	$1.0
Total benefit retained	5.0	$2.0	$5.0	$3.0

Figure 8-3

Note that now *both* parties are worse off than they were initially. Both have taken rational actions based on their adversarial relationship but have ended up spending $3 million to influence their shares of a $5 million benefit. Both would have been better off had they developed and abided by an agreement to share in any revealed productivity improvements and excess costs, as shown in Figure 8-3.

However, showing that it would have been better to share doesn't solve the problem of actually getting the parties to do so. In our hypothetical example, the seller would be worse off under a sharing arrangement than it was when the buyer's monitoring efforts were only 25-percent effective, which may tempt the seller to cheat and set in motion the same series of measures and countermeasures. The solution is to change the rules of the game so that it is in the interest of both to be honest. One change would be to impose such a high penalty for cheating that even with a modest possibility of discovery, the expected value from cheating would be a huge loss. However, though the penalty might eliminate cheating or concealment, it does nothing to encourage the seller to search for savings.

The problem is: How can the buyer structure the rules of the relationship so that the supplier has an incentive both to work hard at achieving benefits and to share them? One way is for the buyer to invert the rules so that instead of having to monitor and catch the supplier, its actions reveal its assessment of potential gains. This strategy works best when the actions of the supplier are visible to the buyer, such as in the case of a distributor whose extra effort would produce more sales. Suppose the buyer suspects that the potential for additional sales ranges from 20 to 10 percent above some base level, say $100.00. At a 20-

percent commission rate, the buyer expects to pay the distributor $20.00. In this case, the buyer initially could offer the distributor a choice of two contracts. One might have a fixed payment equal to 90 percent of the base level commissions ($18.00) but would allow the supplier to keep 40 percent of the additional revenues in excess of $100.00. The second contract might offer 95 percent of the base ($19.00) and 30 percent of the additional revenues.

As a general rule, the variable (or incentive) component of the reward- and risk-sharing structure should be related inversely to the parties' relative risk aversion and related positively to the expected yield on their effort. If results are sensitive to the amount of effort put forth by the supplier, the incentive component should be higher, and the fixed component should be lower. In addition, the return to the supplier has to be highest when it achieves the highest level of performance and takes the greatest risk. In our example, if the distributor believes that through extra effort it can achieve the 20-percent gain in sales, it is more likely to accept the $18.00 fixed payment and capture 40 percent of the additional sales, for a total of $26.00. On the other hand, if the supplier believes it can achieve only 10 percent in additional sales, it is more likely to take the $19.00 (95-percent) fixed payment and the 30-percent commission and receive a total of $22.00. Alert readers will have noticed that the supplier would also receive $22.00 if he took the $18.00 fixed payment and 40 percent commission on $10.00 in additional sales but, because he is risk-averse, the higher fixed payment is more attractive.

Parties can change the rules of the game along these lines in a number of ways that involve shifting responsibility or altering the timing of rewards to lock in or guarantee one party's rewards while allowing the other to reap the benefits of future savings. For example, a number of sophisticated buyers, such as Wal-Mart, are using performance-based systems to stimulate their suppliers. Under its vendor-managed inventory (VMI) program, a major supplier such as Tyson Foods is required to provide complete inventory, restocking, and reordering services without an increase in price per unit. It can, however, keep any savings. Tyson has been able to find cost savings that Wal-Mart, for all its sophistication, has not. By assuming responsibility for the entire order-inventory process, Tyson can execute its marketing plan much more precisely, resulting in fewer lost sales. This change in the reward- and risk-sharing structure provides Wal-Mart with immediate savings in inventory and administrative costs and motivates Tyson to look for and capture additional cost savings, some of which may flow to Wal-Mart later when unit prices are reset.

A strong understanding of the buyer's value and costs can enable a seller to "time-shift" the rewards of an extended relationship. The innovative MCI fund, discussed briefly in Chapter 1, is a mechanism to provide the buyer with immediate confirmation of the savings from the relationship and a source of cash to buy equipment or software related to its communications needs. In this case, the buyer locks in a known savings, and MCI enjoys any subsequent savings (as well as bearing the risk that costs would go higher than anticipated).

FINDING OPPORTUNITIES *to* COLLABORATE

Despite the difficulties of working together illustrated in the foregoing games, buyers and sellers often find it mutually beneficial to move beyond simple exchanges of product for payment and to enter into extended relationships in which they act jointly to create additional value and share risk. Extended relationships involve some degree of interdependency or collaboration and more closely resemble an ongoing process rather than a series of events or exchanges. The joint development of knowledge and the application of connecting technologies are increasingly prominent factors in creating and maintaining extended relationships.

Our aim is to explore the ways in which buyers and sellers interact to create and share value and to distribute the risks of their relationships. The topics of reward and risk usually are treated as pricing and contracting issues that involve consideration of costs and uncertainty and demand elasticity. Although pricing and contracting are very important in distributing the rewards and risks of an exchange, they are well-covered elsewhere and are not our central concern here.

We are interested primarily in two considerations: the conditions and structures under which buyers and sellers choose to engage in extended relationships and the implications for strategy. To put matters in perspective, we begin by asking why and under what conditions people choose extensive *private* exchanges of information and knowledge rather than relying on *public* or *market* mechanisms. The answer is not as obvious as it may first appear; markets usually are extraordinarily efficient processors of information and, in fact, the vast majority of exchanges (by volume) are conducted on terms defined by the market. Entering into an extended relationship with one party or only a few parties is not costless or riskless. Choosing a partner usually means limiting access to many others and often has resulted in the unintended creation of a new rival.

Buyers and sellers engage in extended relationships because they expect that the gains from greater interdependency or collaboration outweigh the benefits of relying on market mechanisms. For example, a manufacturer might pare its bidders' list to a few favored suppliers (thus foregoing the benefits of open competition among all potential suppliers) but might hope to offset this loss by more intense support from the selected group. We will show that extended relationships are not a panacea but can be a powerful strategy when the right conditions exist. Among the most important conditions are bargaining power, appropriability, relationship management costs, and complementarity.

Bargaining power reflects the structure of the market. The incentive to collaborate depends on the size of the potential gains relative to whatever market power each party enjoys. In a perfectly competitive market, neither buyer nor seller has much incentive to invest in an extended relationship with the other. In imperfect markets, if either has a very strong market position relative to the other, the dominant party might not gain through collaboration more than it already enjoys. Therefore, most opportunities for extended relationships occur in those intermediate circumstances wherein markets are imperfect but parties have a reasonable range of options.

Appropriability refers to the likelihood of making a return on the investment in the relationship.[3] It is one thing to create value for buyers, another to capture a share of that value large enough to increase shareholder wealth. The amount of economic value created in a particular relationship increases with the level of interdependency or collaboration between the parties. The more accurately the seller understands the buyer's needs, the more precisely it can match its product to that buyer's needs. The more the buyer understands the seller's capabilities, the more effectively it can express its requirements. Collaboration can result in an increase in both total value and the amount received by each party. When United Parcel Service (UPS) consolidates component shipments to a Gateway 2000 customer by creating a virtual pallet, Gateway's material handling and inventory costs are reduced and UPS shares part of that gain. However, a components maker who invests in specialized equipment to meet a particular customer's needs may find itself squeezed by the buyer who knows that the equipment has no other application.

Relationship management costs include search, surveillance or monitoring costs, and ownership costs. We introduce the concept of *supplier value*, which is analogous to customer equity as a framework for examining strategies based on optimizing the total cost of relationships. In many cases, an extended relationship can be based on increasing supplier value, by reducing either the buyers' overall ownership costs or the costs of acquiring and maintaining relationships with suppliers.

Complementarity refers to the different competencies, resources, or knowledge brought by each party to the relationship. To create more value jointly than singly, each party must provide the other with something that the recipient could not reproduce or acquire at a lower cost. Complementarity is an important consideration when parties agree to share risks and rewards on the basis of the outcome of their collaboration.

··

MARKET-BASED *or* NEUTRAL REWARD *and* RISK SHARING

Market-based reward sharing is neutral in the sense that the initial rules that govern sharing rewards and risks are determined by the structure of the market and the parties' relative bargaining positions. Neutral does not mean equal shares or even that the resulting distribution of value is "fair," as many people would define fairness.

It is important to define clearly what is meant by the value created in a relationship, what constitutes the shares of that value received by buyer and seller, and how those shares can change. To do this and provide a point of departure for the later discussion, we need to revisit the notions of economic value, consumers' surplus, and producers' surplus.

Economic Value

Before discussing how specific relationships are structured, it is useful to revisit the shares of value captured by buyers and sellers through the workings of the market. The shares of the value that are created in a market and are received by the buyer and seller are called *consumers' surplus* and *producers' surplus*, respectively. These typically elegant economic terms refer simply to the value received by the buyer beyond the price paid and the value received by the seller above the cost of production. The total value (or utility) received by the buyer is the sum of the values of all the units purchased. As the marginal value of successive units diminishes, the buyer's demand curve—which indicates the number of units purchased at different prices—slopes downward. The buyer's volume of purchases is the point at which the value of the last unit equals the price to acquire it. Consumers' surplus equals the difference between the aggregate value of all units and the total cost of acquiring them.

The seller's situation is the reverse of the buyer's. If the seller's production function is subject to diminishing returns, over some range the cost of each successive unit produced will increase, leading to an upward-sloping supply curve. The seller will produce up to the point at which the cost of the last unit just equals the price received. The difference between the total revenue received and total costs incurred is the producers' surplus. Economists refer to producers' surplus greater than the cost of capital as *rents* or *excess returns*. In a truly competitive situation, the producers' surplus just equals its capital costs, and no excess returns or additional shareholder value are created.

In a perfectly competitive market or in one that approaches that condition, both buyer and seller maximize their shares of the total value created by trading at the market-clearing price, and neither has any incentive to change the rules of their relationship. Therefore, extended relationships will occur only when the market is less than perfectly competitive, which is the condition in the overwhelming share of cases. However, the degree and nature of market imperfections vary greatly, and the forms of extended relationships can take many shapes, depending on the nature of the market structure.

Market Structure and the Sharing of Rewards and Risks

The form of reward and risk sharing in a relationship follows from the market structure. Trying to adopt a sharing arrangement that works in one industry can lead to disappointing results in a market with different levels of buyer and seller bargaining power or different relationship management costs. The amount of the total value that is created in an exchange and is captured by the buyer or seller depends on both parties' relative bargaining power. For our purposes here, the relative power can be approximated by the number of competing buyers and sellers. Obviously, numbers alone are not indicative of power if the distribution of purchasing or production capacity is concentrated. Figure 8-4 illustrates nine market structures defined by the relative number of buyers and sellers and the resulting balance of bargaining power. The relative bargaining power indicates roughly how the added value created by the exchange will be shared.

The competitive market represented by many buyers and sellers results in one price for all or only a narrow price dispersion, due to local market imperfections, modest differentiation, or residual information costs. By and large, sellers are unable to extract any consumers' surplus from buyers, because the buyers simply can turn to another seller. Similarly, buyers cannot extract any producers' surplus from sellers who can find another buyer at the market clearing price. No basis for extended relationships exists, as each party can wait until the next period and secure the market price.

For our purposes, the more interesting cases are the imperfect markets characterized by some degree of buyer or seller scarcity. In these cases, some form of negotiation or extended search will take place, and the gains from trade will be captured or appropriated by the parties in proportion to their bargaining power. It is in these situations where the most opportunities for various forms of extended relationships exist.

In a situation in which only a few buyers but many sellers are found, prices tend to be administered by the buyer. Extended relationships may form but

Market-Based Forms of Reward Sharing

		Number of Buyers		
		Very Few	**Moderate**	**Many**
Number of Sellers	**Many**	**Administered** Very strong buyer power	**Negotiated bid** Modest buyer power	**One price** Narrow range
	Moderate	**Negotiated** Strong buyer power	**Negotiated** Balanced	**Negotiated** Modest seller power
	Very Few	**Negotiated** Offsetting power	**Auction** Moderate seller power	**Administered** Strong seller power

Figure 8-4

largely on the buyer's terms. The buyer will seek to force the seller's share of added value as close to zero as possible. Because a simple cost-plus arrangement provides the seller with no incentive to achieve productivity gains, often it is augmented with a range of performance-based bonuses or penalties that involve sharing with the buyer the added value from the seller's productivity gains. This arrangement inevitably leads to a significant degree of interdependency and interaction between buyer and seller, because it is necessary to exchange information and to monitor performance.

At the other corner of the matrix, markets characterized by the existence of a few sellers but many buyers, such as patented pharmaceuticals, proprietary operating systems, and some computer components, also operate under administered prices but on the seller's terms. In the case of finished goods sold to the final customer, the seller operates as a classic monopolist, setting its price to maximize its producers' surplus and, if practical, discriminating among buyers on the basis of their price elasticity.[4]

The case of components sellers or of goods sold through intermediaries is a little more complicated because both the components maker and the intermediary are competing for shares of the final buyer's consumers' surplus, and their bargaining positions will reflect their relative contribution to the value created. A branded component, such as Nutrasweet or Pentium, captures part of its added value by commanding a premium price in the eyes of the final consumer as well as through its patent-based position with the intermediary. A proprietary seller of components for which there is no good substitute will attempt to set prices that result in the level of final product output that maximizes profits to the component seller—which is unlikely to be the level that maximizes the profit to the manufacturer. The components manufacturer with sufficient bargaining power might capture a portion of the value created by the manufacturer. The relationship between the manufacturer and the components market might include joint marketing and promotion (e.g., "Intel Inside") that reinforces the component's brand image but may do little to distinguish the final product manufacturer. Examples of effective use of seller bargaining power are found in the relative profitability of Intel (a proprietary component) and Microsoft (a proprietary operating system) versus other firms in the computer industry.

When very few buyers square off against very few sellers, both parties feel a strong need to cooperate and to execute the trade, as they have limited options. The potential range of sharing the added value is fairly broad—anywhere between the seller's cost of production and the buyer's full valuation of the product. Where they wind up is indeterminate and depends on their relative negotiating skills but, in practice, usually they wind up somewhere in the middle because of their offsetting bargaining power.

When a relatively small number of buyers faces a moderate number of sellers (e.g., in the case of manufacturers selling into concentrated retail channels), the prices will be negotiated but usually to the advantage of the buyer. The concentration of grocery chains, do-it-yourself outlets, and discount retailers has shifted the balance of bargaining power away from many branded goods and toward the retailer. For some branded products, a single chain may account for 20 to 25 percent of total sales. The effect of retail concentration is to make shelf space a scarce resource for sellers and to compel them to purchase it directly (paying stocking fees) or to make other concessions. This power might enable the buyer to extract a portion of the seller's brand equity and thereby capture part of the seller's producers' surplus. The sellers may find themselves in an extended relationship, with the buyer increasingly dominating decisions as to order quantities, packaging, inventory management services, and the like.

The situation involving a moderate number of sellers but many buyers, found in air travel, package delivery, and many other markets, is marked by negotiated prices. Buyers may not literally negotiate with the seller but, by investing in search costs, they effectively achieve the same result. Sellers in these markets are somewhat interdependent because the joint profit-maximizing price and output levels depend on the actions of their rivals. Their situation is similar to a cartel; collaboration would result in a price and a shared output level that would be more profitable than those resulting from competition. However, the costs of collaboration (not to mention the antitrust laws) make it difficult to achieve and maintain a mutually satisfactory set of prices. When total capacity exceeds demand at existing prices, periodic price wars may break out, primarily to the benefit of the buyer. In 1996, Airborne Express attempted to increase its market share by lowering its prices below those of Federal Express (FedEx) and UPS, apparently in the belief that its lower costs would enable it to outlast its rivals. Both FedEx and UPS, however, were committed to the market and matched or exceeded each reduction, resulting in what one observer characterized as "trading customers among ourselves at increasingly lower prices."[5]

To avoid ruinous price wars, sellers in these markets often attempt to offer selective discounts that are as nondestabilizing as possible. Customer information and knowledge can be important strategic assets in these cases, because they allow sellers to target their offers very precisely. The business with the better understanding of the distribution of customer relationship values will be able to deploy its resources more effectively. Other strategies are designed to discourage buyers from searching (negotiating) for the lowest price by rewarding them for repeat purchases. The airlines' use of frequent-flyer programs is the most prominent example of this technique.

When a moderate number of buyers confronts many potential sellers, which is the case for many business-to-business purchases of specialized goods and services, negotiated bidding processes are used frequently. Competition among the sellers may drive prices reasonably close to a competitive level. Beyond that point, the buyers and sellers may create elaborate performance- or outcomes-sharing arrangements to share the benefits of the relationship.

When one seller faces only a moderate number of buyers, as in the case of rare works of art, offshore oil tracts, and the radio spectrum, the seller may economize on search and negotiation costs by conducting an auction. Auctions are a form of one-time game and not, therefore, an extended relationship as we are using the term. In an open auction, the seller's ability to extract consumers' surplus from the buyer depends on the value placed on the good by the last unsuccessful bidder, as the successful bidder need offer only $1 more than the highest bid.

Supplier Value

For buyers or sellers to forgo all or part of the advantage granted them by market structure, they must see some benefit to collaboration. Clearly, sellers subject to buyer power want the buyer to relax the rate at which it is extracting the added value created in the relationship. Conversely, buyers subject to seller power want to convince those sellers that it is in their mutual interest to collaborate. What can these parties offer or trade to achieve a better situation?

In focusing on the value of customer relationships, it's easy to overlook the fact that suppliers' relationships have value to their customers. The adage "Good help is hard to find" applies to many markets. With the increasing use of outsourcing, the careful selection and management of suppliers is critical.

To get a better picture of the potential for extended reward and risk sharing, it is helpful to introduce the concept of supplier relationship value, the buyer's analog to customer equity. The calculation of supplier value to the buyer is analogous to the estimation of customer equity discussed earlier but with some important differences in terminology and estimating procedures. Figure 8-5 illustrates the calculation of supplier relationship value. Supplier value has both product and relationship management components. The product component depends on the total utility derived by the buyer, the price paid, and the ownership or operating costs incurred. The relationship management component includes the buyer's expenses necessary to maintain the relationship and the foregone expenses of searching for another seller (which would be a "negative cost" and, therefore, would offset the maintenance cost). Any switching costs would be included in search costs, as they are incurred in the move to a new supplier.

REDUCING THE BUYER'S OWNERSHIP AND OPERATING COSTS. By itself, the seller's relative price is not a factor in the buyer's decision to enter into an extended relationship. Unless the seller can make access to the low price conditional on a buyer commitment, the buyer can always simply buy from the low-price vendor the next time. The low-price seller will enjoy a higher repeat purchase rate, particularly if the buyer's experience leads it to conclude that the relative price positions among sellers is constant. Buyers will reduce their search efforts if they lead repeatedly to the same result. For this reason, everyday low pricing is an effective strategy if well-executed. If the buyer engages in relatively extensive searches for a few periods and finds that Wal-Mart always offers the lowest price and acceptable quality, a reputation or brand identity is created. The buyer will economize by cutting back on search costs and become loyal to Wal-Mart. Stores using sales promotions will have to cut even deeper to overcome buyers' inertia and prompt them to reengage in searching.

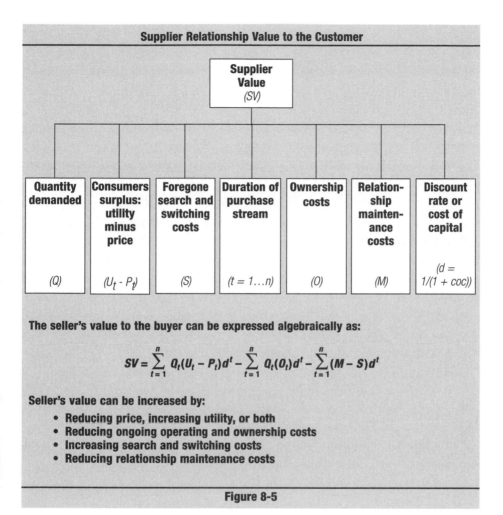

Supplier Relationship Value to the Customer

Supplier Value (SV)

Quantity demanded	Consumers surplus: utility minus price	Foregone search and switching costs	Duration of purchase stream	Ownership costs	Relation- ship mainten- ance costs	Discount rate or cost of capital
(Q)	$(U_t - P_t)$	(S)	$(t = 1...n)$	(O)	(M)	$(d = 1/(1 + coc))$

The seller's value to the buyer can be expressed algebraically as:

$$SV = \sum_{t=1}^{n} Q_t(U_t - P_t)d^t - \sum_{t=1}^{n} Q_t(O_t)d^t - \sum_{t=1}^{n}(M - S)d^t$$

Seller's value can be increased by:
- Reducing price, increasing utility, or both
- Reducing ongoing operating and ownership costs
- Increasing search and switching costs
- Reducing relationship maintenance costs

Figure 8-5

The buyer's ownership and operating costs—which might include such things as installation, maintenance, fuel costs, and the like—usually are not entered directly into the calculation of consumers' surplus or added value for the product. These factors may influence the price the buyer is willing to pay (e.g., a more efficient air conditioner commanding a higher price owing to its lower operating costs). Ownership and operating costs across the set of products consumed in the buyer's value chain are an important consideration in outsourcing, which was addressed in Chapter 7.

Reducing the buyer's ownership and operating costs is one avenue for establishing an extended relationship. In many cases, the costs of using the product are a significant portion of the buyer's total costs. Earlier, we discussed the implications of this fact in automobile and aircraft design. SKF Bearings increases its value to customers by relieving them of the difficult chore of replacing and repacking bearings. When the reduction in ownership costs occurs in this way, it is an extension of the value proposition.

REDUCING THE RELATIONSHIP MANAGEMENT COMPONENT. Search and relationship maintenance costs reduce the buyer's consumers' surplus but in different ways. If search costs are incurred on a per-unit basis (as is the case with most recurring purchases), they are, like a sales tax, an increase in the per-unit cost of acquisition. Thus, search costs reduce consumers' surplus from an exchange in the same way as does a price increase. Relationship maintenance costs, however, usually are not incurred on a per-unit basis. For example, membership fees in a wholesale club are assessed independent of volume purchased. Even in more complex business relationships, the buyer's costs of interacting with the seller are relatively fixed. For purposes of illustrating the buyer's net consumers' surplus, we can think of relationship costs as a premium on the price of the first unit purchased. Fixed relationship maintenance costs reduce the total value of the exchange but do not affect decisions at the margin.

Seeking to establish anything but an arms-length position, the seller must convince buyers that they will be better off limiting their search efforts. At first glance, this might suggest that sellers direct their efforts toward buyers with high search costs, but this is often unproductive. Buyers will resist extended relationships as long as they believe that the yield on their search efforts exceeds the benefits of closer ties to suppliers.

The level of search undertaken by a buyer depends on the incremental cost of searching (e.g., evaluating one more bid, visiting one more store, etc.) and on the expected gain. The basic economics of information and search costs were set out by George Stigler in a seminal 1961 article that forms the basis of much of what follows.[6]

The expected gain from search increases with the value of the purchase and with the buyer's perception of expected price dispersion (range of asking prices from suppliers) in the market. A buyer will contact more sellers when it believes that prices are widely dispersed, because it increases the chance of finding a low price. To confirm this, consider a case in which asked prices from $10 to $20 are normally distributed among many sellers. If the buyer contacts only one seller, the buyer might receive any price between $10 and $20, but its expected price would be $15. The more sellers it contacts, the greater the probability it will encounter one at the low end of the price range. The buyer will continue seeking sellers until the expected gain just equals the cost of the search. As long as buyers perceive a wide price dispersion, they will resist constraining relationships unless the seller can assure them convincingly that they will not forgo the future benefits of search.

Buyers are more likely to enter into extended relationships when they believe that the gains from search will be low or when they believe that the costs of monitoring the seller's price performance will be relatively low. Therefore, extended relationships will be less common during the early stages in a market cycle when vigorous competition and new entrants provide more opportunity to search for savings. Significant rates of technological change also will inhibit formal relationships, because buyers will be reluctant to limit their options while future opportunities are uncertain.

Extended relationships will tend to emerge in relatively mature, stable markets. In these cases, prices tend to be dispersed in a narrower range, diminishing the buyer's incentive to search. The narrow price range also reduces the buyer's relationship maintenance costs because monitoring and surveillance of the seller's price performance is less expensive. As the price dispersion narrows, the buyer's return on searching for lower prices is reduced. Among other reasons, this advantage accounts for why large firms in relatively stable markets can trim their list of subcontractors without sacrificing much in price savings.

PERFORMANCE-BASED REWARD *and* RISK SHARING

Risk bearing and uncertainty are special and often expensive forms of ownership and operating costs. The buyer may not be able to judge the likely performance of the product, may be concerned about future access to the product, or may be apprehensive about the future price. Although third-party insurance and derivatives are available to manage these risks in some markets, often the buyer will enter into extended relationships with sellers on the basis of sharing or managing these risks.

In many cases, sellers can increase their value to buyers by offering to assume part of the buyer's risk associated with the use of the product. The common warranty or guarantee is the most basic form of performance-based risk sharing. In most cases, these guarantees are signals of quality and differentiation by which the seller signals to the buyer a commitment to the relationship and a willingness to insure the buyer form unanticipated operating and other ownership costs associated with the product.

Guarantees are especially effective in markets in which they are not offered routinely. ScrubaDub Car Wash, introduced earlier, employs a 3-day ("pigeon proof") warranty on its deluxe car wash and will give buyers another wash for free if anything, including bad weather, spoils the car's appearance. Customers who might have hesitated for fear of bad weather thus are encouraged to have their car washed. Buyers also are allowed to go through the wash as many times as is necessary to satisfy them. In a similar vein, Sunday River ski resort offers a "free look" guarantee to skiers: The customer can take the lift, check conditions, and decide whether conditions are adequate. This feature entices many skiers to try the mountain on questionable days and results in very few redemptions.

In some cases, monetizing a guarantee with a set of penalties can make it an integral part of a business strategy that drives behaviors and resource allocation. As a new and untested firm, Delta Dental Plan of Massachusetts felt it needed to make a dramatic statement of its commitment to its customers and distinguish itself from established rivals. Inspired in part by Christopher Hart's writings on the value of guarantees,[7] Delta's guarantee of service excellence (GOSE) was the first service guarantee offered in the dental insurance industry.

How much would you be willing to pay someone to tell you that you've screwed up? Well, if Delta doesn't send you an accurate ID card within 15 days of your signing on, it pays $25.00 to your group. If Delta employees don't resolve your question immediately, the company promises to give you an update within one business day or it pays your group $50.00. If a participating dentist charges you for the difference between Delta's negotiated discounted fee and his usual fee (a practice called *balance billing*), Delta pays your group $50.00. If 90 percent of claims aren't paid within 15 days, the group's monthly administrative fee is refunded. From our perspective (and we suspect most employers' as well), GOSE's most important feature is its guarantee of a minimum 10-percent savings over each policy year on the program's administration costs. Delta makes up the difference between the 10-percent guarantee and any lesser amount saved.

In effect, Delta burned its boats at the water's edge and imposed on itself a form of performance-based reward and risk sharing with its customers. By doing this, the company signaled to employees, accounts (employers), and dentists alike its commitment to play the game seriously. Once the plan was announced, the firm had no choice but to figure out how to manage the business to achieve sustained cost reductions. Despite some initial trepidation, the program has been successful; only $36,000 of the $150,000 budgeted for first year refunds was paid out. Since then, refunds have run nearly $220,000 (approximately one-tenth of 1 percent of annual revenues), an amount Bob Hunter, president, believes is a bargain in terms of the service-failure information and customer goodwill it produces.

OUTCOMES-BASED REWARD SHARING

Outcomes-based reward sharing involves a mutual investment by both the buyer and seller in anticipation of a future payoff, in which that payoff is determined in large part by the actions of others. For example, a large electric power company needed to refurbish several of its older fossil-fueled plants neglected during the construction of nuclear units. Unable to finance the refurbishment at reasonable costs, it offered several manufacturing and engineering firms the opportunity to share in the revenue flows from the plants when they were again operating. As a result, the power company reduced its cash outflows, and the engineering firm that won the job actively searched for ways to bring the plants back on line sooner and to operate better because it was compensated from the profits on sales from the plant, rather than engineering hours.

Some consulting firms have moved away from fees based on hours spent on the engagement and toward a sharing of documented results. An even more radical example in the services industry is the practice of Ramsey/Beirne, an executive search firm that has recruited a number of prominent corporate executives to lead small start-up firms. Ramsey/Beirne extends its value proposition by offering advice on the type of executive to hire and links its own future to that of its clients by taking an equity position in addition to customary fees.[8] The practice of taking equity positions in customers, though fairly uncommon, has a long history. The Dodge brothers acquired 50 shares of Henry Ford's Model A venture by contributing $7,000 worth of materials and $3,000 in cash.[9]

Another way by which companies link their future to their customers is through joint product development. The buyer's incentive to collaborate is the prospect of getting a new product that will better serve its needs or enable it to change the way it conducts business. The seller's incentive is to gain insight into as yet unmet or undiscovered needs and to be better able to pioneer innovative new products or value propositions. One of the best examples of this collaboration is Silicon Graphics's use of "lighthouse" customers—companies such as Industrial Light and Magic, which are on the cutting edge of applications and from whom Silicon Graphics can learn what is being done with their machines and what more they would like to do. By investing in solutions to the problems of lighthouse customers, Silicon Graphics gets ahead of the rest of the market.[10]

The ability of technology to pinpoint the source of transactions is leading some major advertisers to consider outcomes-based rewards for ads on the Internet. As discussed in the *Inc.* case in Chapter 6, ad rates traditionally have been based on cost per thousand readers or, in the case of Web sites, cost per view. Proctor & Gamble has proposed paying for Internet ads on the basis of hits or number of people who actually click on the ad. Going further, Nabisco has negotiated a set of deals with Web sites in which it will pay a share of the revenues (estimated between 5 and 20 percent of sales) that result from the ad.[11]

In this chapter, we introduced the metaphor of relationships as games to illustrate the concept of interdependent decision making and the role of rules in stimulating effort and distributing rewards in a relationship. We showed how the type of game played and the initial positions of the players depend in part on the structure of the market that determines bargaining power and appropriability. The notion of supplier value—the complement of customer equity—was used to suggest avenues for fruitful collaboration or bases for extended relationships. These concepts were illustrated by examples of progressively more interdependent reward- and risk-sharing arrangements: neutral, performance-based, and outcomes-based.

chapter 9

Putting it together

CREATING A CUSTOMER-BASED STRATEGY

The art of strategy is, in many ways, a matter of pattern recognition. The successful strategist sees before others do the forces that will disrupt the existing balances and provide a basis for creating an advantage over rivals. He somehow recognizes anomalies or conditions in one system that seem out of line with another, very similar system, and wonders why this is so. Such recognition requires a grasp of the dynamics of a system, which is very different from spotting trends. The world is adequately supplied with bankrupt visionaries whose vision of the inevitable never materialized. The trend spotter sees a single force moving in one direction. The successful strategist realizes that there are always opposing forces that, even if unequal, will push back and determine when an idea really is an opportunity.

If you really want to understand why a particular strategy worked, look at the conditions that existed before, not after, the strategy was executed. What did the office supply business look like before Tom Stemberg created Staples? Why did the superstore concept work there and then? How did entrepreneurs get practical, how-to management advice before Bernie Goldhirsh launched *Inc.*? Why did the magazine work for that group at that time?

We selected these two cases because they illustrate some very important points about recognizing patterns. Stemberg's background was in the grocery business, a high-volume, low-margin business that equipped him to understand efficient distribution and retailing. A personal experience with a stationery store convinced him that he could apply this competency to the office supply business. Bernie Goldhirsh had started and run a successful small business (*Sail* magazine) and knew firsthand that there were few reliable sources of quality management advice for entrepreneurs; everyone was focused on the *Fortune 500*. Goldhirsh's publishing experience provided the know-how to launch a magazine, but his knowledge of the market told him which one to start up.

Standing back, before Staples and *Inc.* were a reality, we could have discerned the trends toward home offices and increasing rates of small-business formation that fueled both companies. In fact, this trend was fairly well reported before both firms were founded. Still, what exactly would we have done with this information? Perhaps starting an office superstore or a magazine would have occurred to us, but we doubt it; we have no publishing or retail experience or competency and have never owned a small business. More to the point, why didn't people already in those businesses who did have the competencies see the opportunity? Undoubtedly some did and simply didn't act. A few may have tried and failed but, by and large, two fairly sizable business communities missed two great opportunities on which a couple of outsiders capitalized.

We believe it was the combination of insight into customer needs and a relevant competency that enabled both Stemberg and Goldhirsh to recognize a pattern where others had not. Goldhirsh was up against business magazines that, while not hostile to small businesses, didn't take an active interest in them. Goldhirsh saw a poorly served group within a relatively concentrated industry, just as he'd earlier discovered the middle-class sailing enthusiast among the blue bloods. On the other hand, Stemberg could see that the stationery or office supply business was a fragmented industry made up of many local operations with local market power, which, in too many cases, resulted in the type of customer service and pricing policies that such power entails. In short, the office supply business looked a lot like the old grocery business before modern distribution methods reshaped it.

Of course, the rise of home offices and small businesses aided the growth of both companies. Likewise, the previous experience and competency of both men equipped them to succeed. Finally, their insight into customer needs most certainly sparked the creation of their firms. Our point is that all three factors must be present to some degree for a pattern to be recognized and for a strategy to succeed.

We cannot teach strategic pattern recognition or instill competencies relevant to a variety of markets and industries. However, we can suggest some signs regarding customers for which you should be alert and some patterns for which you should watch that might signal opportunities to increase the value of your customer portfolio.

CREATING *a* CUSTOMER-CONNECTED STRATEGY

Although we are reluctant to espouse a one-size-fits-all approach to strategy development, this section outlines a plan of attack for bringing to the surface and evaluating alternative configurations using the value compass framework. We have found that moving around the four axes on the compass, keeping in mind the conditional nature of positions on the axes, is a useful way to organize and consider demand-side strategies. In general, it is best to start by considering the right customer portfolio and to move in turn through the range-of-value proposition, role, and reward- and risk-sharing dimensions. Such a process means identifying those customers with whom you want to do business, defining the value proposition you will offer to them, determining the position on the value-added chain that best leverages your capabilities, and finding the level of collaboration and interdependency that best stimulates value creation and capture within relationships. This general approach is depicted graphically in Figure 9-1.

We have shown the process as continuous but, in practice, companies often deal with each element separately. There is nothing inherently wrong with working on one dimension at a time, but you should be ever mindful of the need for overall alignment across the axes. In the following sections, we outline the steps in the process of building a customer-connected strategy, highlight some of the major points to bear in mind in searching for patterns, and relate them to the models and cases of the preceding chapters.

Identifying the Right Customer Portfolio

What indicators exist for assessing the health of your customer portfolio and for suggesting ways of increasing its value? Because building a customer portfolio is similar to managing a financial portfolio, you might approach this by thinking of yourself as performing a customer-relationship value audit. The purpose of this audit is to identify the current value of your business in terms of your existing customer relationships, to estimate the potential value, and to uncover gaps or unexploited opportunities. To perform this audit, you need to recognize and understand the patterns of customer value in your existing portfolio, the market portfolio, and the portfolios of your competitors. Thus, some of the major considerations in evaluating your performance as a customer portfolio manager are (1) the value of your existing customer portfolio, (2) the composition of your portfolio compared to those of the market and of your competitors, and (3) the

General Approach to Customer Connection Strategy

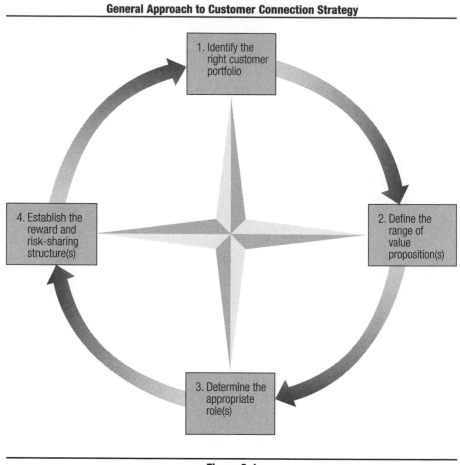

Figure 9-1

alignment of resource deployment and customer relationship value. With this insight, you can begin to identify gaps and opportunities.

UNDERSTAND THE VALUE OF YOUR EXISTING CUSTOMER PORTFOLIO. Unless you understand the value and recent performance of your portfolio, you cannot make rational decisions about how to deploy your customer acquisition, development, and retention efforts. To determine the value and performance of your portfolio, you need to appreciate the dynamics of individual customer value, total portfolio value, and customer-based growth. In Chapter 4, we outlined the tools for accomplishing this. As you begin, you might not have all the information you need to develop precise estimates, but with a little common sense and judgment, you can begin by making your best estimates. As we pointed out in

Chapter 2, a knowledge book is often a useful way to collate the knowledge resident in an organization and to identify gaps.

Once you've pulled together such material, you can focus your analysis and discussion by asking some of the following questions:

- What does the distribution of customer relationship value look like? Is it fairly compact, with most customers falling pretty close to the mean; is it very broad, having a great deal of variance; or is it somewhere in between?

- How concentrated is the total value, say, among the top 15 to 20 percent of your customers? (ScrubaDub, UPS, Wachovia, and Pioneer Hi-Bred all face highly concentrated distributions of relationship value. In contrast, Harley-Davidson customers, with their extraordinary repurchase rate and shared identity, represent a more homogeneous value distribution.)

- If the value is fairly concentrated, are there any clear differences between these customers and others? Do they buy more, buy more frequently, buy higher-margin products, stay with you longer, and so on? (In the ScrubaDub case, it was frequency of purchases that made a difference. In Pioneer's case, all farmers buy with roughly equal frequency but some buy a much greater volume. In insurance, it may be duration that determines the most valuable relationship.)

- If there is a significant number of unprofitable relationships, are there any common characteristics of these customers in terms of volume purchased, product mix, duration, and the like?

- Can you assess probability of purchase or share of customer across different value levels? Are they uniform, or do they vary systematically?

- Can you plot your acquisition costs against the customer value distribution and determine how long customers with various relationship values must stay with you so that you break even? Does it make sense to stratify your acquisition strategies and business models (as Staples did) for different groups?

- Can you determine how much of your total growth in the past 3 to 5 years came from acquiring new customers compared to developing or increasing the value of existing customers? Do you expect this trend to continue?

- What part of the customer distribution is accounting for the growth? Is it coming at the high end or at the middle? Do you have a good idea of why you're more successful in attracting and keeping these customers than others?

- Where is your customer turnover occurring? Can you estimate the turnover rates for the top 20 percent, the next 20 percent, and so forth? Do you have a good idea as to why customers of different relationship values are leaving?

After you've gone through these questions, you'll have a pretty good idea of the quality of your existing portfolio and you'll be able to understand its performance over the past few years. Next, you'll need to develop a sense of your relative success at managing your customer portfolio.

COMPARE THE COMPOSITION OF YOUR PORTFOLIO TO THOSE OF THE MARKET AS A WHOLE AND OF YOUR COMPETITORS. You cannot gauge the potential for improvement or anticipate the barriers to building a better portfolio without understanding the market portfolio (the distribution of intrinsic customer values), evaluating the relative weightings of customers in your competitor's portfolios, and being able to explain the differences between your portfolio and your competitors' or the market's. Consider the following questions:

- How does your customer portfolio compare with that of the overall market? Is the distribution of customer value about the same, or are you overrepresented or underrepresented at certain value levels? If you are over- or underrepresented at different value levels, can you explain why this is so?

- Can you estimate your major competitors' portfolio of customers? If so, are there any significant or systematic differences? For example, do customers with particular value structures tend to favor one or more competitors (e.g., are high-duration customers heavily represented in one competitor's portfolio)?

- Can you assess the concentration of value in competitors' portfolios? Are they more or less concentrated than your own?

- Are your competitors' probability-of-purchase rates or share of customer significantly different from yours? Is this difference uniform across relationship value levels?

- What factors have contributed most to competitors' growth—new customers, increased sales to existing customers, retention rates?

- Are you able to discern a pattern among competitors in terms of their emphasis on particular levels or structures of customer relationship value? Are they focusing primarily on high volume, frequency, or duration?

ALIGN RESOURCE DEPLOYMENTS AND CUSTOMER VALUE. Unless you have an idea about the potential payoffs from focusing or refocusing your portfolio-building efforts, you cannot deploy resources for their highest expected return. Such effective deployment involves knowledge of customer responsiveness, which is the propensity of customers to form a relationship with your business. In addition, you should have a grasp of the costs of acquiring, developing, and retaining economic value in the form of more or better customer relationships. To assess the alignment of your portfolio-building efforts with the potential payoff, consider these questions:

- Is your allocation of resources against customer relationship value and responsiveness aligned? Could you get a better yield by shifting resources from one value level to another?

- Are you spending about the same amount as, more than, or less than your rivals on acquiring and developing customers with high intrinsic value? Would a substantial shift in resources yield a worthwhile increase in the number of these customers?

- Are there groups of customers for whom your relationship model seems ill-suited, as evidenced by low representation, high turnover, or concentration in the portfolio of a rival with a different business model?

- How many of your low- to moderate-value customers would be profitable if you could substantially reduce the nonproduct costs of serving them? Are there connecting technologies that would reduce significantly the search, information, and transaction costs? Is there an alternative business model that might offer better economics?

After you've identified your target customer portfolio and have a reasonable understanding of how much investment is warranted, it's time to consider the value proposition that you can offer these customers.

Defining the Range of Your Value Proposition

How well can you assess the potential range of your value proposition? Many businesses have a fairly good notion of how customers feel about their products, but relatively few have a good understanding of the total context within which their products are used. In Chapter 2, we outlined a number of knowledge types, such as observational or conversational knowledge, that can stimulate insight into the context of customer decisions. In Chapter 6, we discussed the application of the customer value chain or total experience map as an aid to assessing the potential range of your value proposition.

In assessing the range of your existing and potential value proposition, you might want to consider (1) your current customer–value proposition matrix, (2) your customers' total expenditures across their value chain or total experience, and (3) the potential profitability of extended-value propositions.

UNDERSTAND THE CUSTOMER–VALUE PROPOSITION MATRIX. One of the first things you need to know is who is buying what from you. A matrix that relates your customer portfolio to your current product portfolio will give you an idea of how well you've aligned your offer with your target customers. Some of the questions you should consider are as follows:

- What parts of your product line are purchased by your target customers? Do your target customers account for a substantial proportion of those products' sales?

- Are there products that are purchased only occasionally by your target customers? Are these products predominantly bought by nontarget customers? What would be the implications of trimming these products from the line?

- Can you determine the share of high-value target-customer purchases that you are achieving? How does this compare with the lower-value, non–target-customer purchase behavior?

- Are there evident groups or clusters of products that are purchased by target customers? How much of the total value of those customers is derived from purchases of these products?

- Are there clear differences in the channels favored by target versus nontarget customers?

- How much of your product development and support efforts are directed toward the products favored by your target customers?

- What is the information content of your value proposition? How much of the knowledge you possess is conveyed to your customers?

ESTIMATE YOUR CUSTOMERS' TOTAL EXPENDITURES ACROSS THEIR VALUE CHAIN. Without understanding the context of customer expenditures, you cannot effectively target extensions or contractions in the range of your offer or calibrate potential gains. To understand the context of customer expenditures, you must map one of two expenditure patterns—the customer's value chain or the customer's total experience—depending on how your customers use your product. Use the *customer's value chain* when buyers combine or assemble a set of inputs to achieve their objective (e.g., a component or process in a larger final product). Use the *customer's total experience* when a customer's objective is met by a series of discrete (uncombined) products or events (e.g., different types of insurance or educational subjects). Once you've developed these maps, you are in a position to evaluate the potential economic gain from extending the range of your value proposition.

- How long and complex are your customer value chains? Are they similar for customers at different levels in the relationship value distribution? Is there a reasonably typical chain (or experience) for your target customers?

- How much of the customer's total expenditures on her value chain do you capture? How significant is your contribution to the customer's objective?

- What other parts of the customer's value chain (or experience) would benefit from your skills or knowledge?

- Are there opportunities to redesign your product to capture value from another part of the chain?

- What parts of the value chain now performed by the customer could be performed more effectively on a scale larger than the individual customer's operation?

- Would your customers benefit if you were to perform part of their assembly process, either for components joined with yours or for a common activity such as stocking?

- Could the customer's value chain be reconfigured substantially to achieve the objective more economically or faster? What role could you play in the redesign?

ASSESS POTENTIAL PROFITABILITY OF EXTENDED-VALUE PROPOSITION(S). Without reasonable knowledge of the gap between current and potential added value, you can neither justify the development of nor assess the relative yield of an extended offer versus other value-building efforts. Such justification and assessment will depend on customer responsiveness (the degree to which customers will react positively to the extended offer *and* their confidence that you can deliver it) as well as on direct development and infrastructure costs (total costs of being in a position credibly to deliver the extended offer). If promising opportunities are seen to exist after you have addressed the questions regarding a customer's total expenditures across his value chain or total experience, consider the following questions:

- What are the potential revenues of the new value proposition? How many target customers appear responsive to it? What is the probable change in target-customer relationship value?

- What are the costs of developing and supporting the new proposition?

- What will be the likely reaction of other firms serving the customer value chain? Is your proposed extension readily duplicated? Are there potential allies or partners to market or support the new proposition?

- Does the new proposition raise customer concerns about excessive dependency on you? What uncertainties will customers have about performance? What implications do these have for introduction and pricing?

- Will the new proposition have to be marketed and sold to a different buyer or buying unit than is your current product?

EVALUATE REQUIRED COMPETENCIES VIS-A-VIS COMPETITORS, PARTNERS, AND INTERNAL LEVERAGE. The battle for a greater share of the customers' total expenditures will depend not only on the initial positions but also on the relative capabilities of the rivals. Assessing your position to extend your offer involves adding three things to your map of the customers' value chain or total experience: (1) the competencies required to execute the extended proposition, (2) the competitors occupying space on the customers' value chain or total experience, and (3) the buyers' perceptions of your and your rivals' capabilities to deliver at each point on the chain or experience. We discussed these factors in Chapter 6, with respect to Pioneer Hi-Bred's strategy of enhancing its core product with information rather than with an offer of chemicals or fertilizer. The American Skiing Company expanded its value proposition substantially because of the strength of its core product and its ability to bundle several elements of the skiing experience. *Inc.* has moved toward offering a total solution by leveraging its competencies and the confidence it enjoys with its customers.

- What competencies necessary to perform your part on the customers' value chain are applicable to other parts?

- Taking into account your existing skills and competencies, how much of the total value chain could you deliver? Could the necessary skills and competencies be reasonably acquired (as in the American Skiing Company's case), or would they require a substantially different business model (as in the Pioneer Hi-Bred example)?

- How do your customers evaluate your competency: narrowly, with respect to your product, or more broadly, across the activities on their value chain?

- How strong is your brand identity outside of the current product?

- How do the competencies of your direct competitors and firms serving other parts of the value chain compare to your own competencies?

- Would it be feasible to develop a partnership or alliance with another firm serving the value chain? Would the combination be attractive to customers?

Determining the Appropriate Role(s)

How can you tell whether you are playing the right role in the total value-added chain? Are you performing relatively low added-value functions that would be better done by businesses up- or downstream from your position? Are you overlooking opportunities to relieve your customers or other people of activities that you could perform more profitably and effectively than they can? In short, are you maximizing the leverage from your existing competencies and investing in the appropriate new competencies that you'll need for growth?

Determining the appropriate role(s) hinges on understanding the market's value-added chain (as we described in Chapter 7), on being able to identify places where your own competencies provide you a competitive advantage, and on assessing opportunities to reconfigure the chain to achieve a more advantageous and profitable position. In assessing your current and potential role, you should (1) map the value-added chain for your market and your current position, (2) identify where added value currently is created, and (3) examine the potential of connecting technologies to reconfigure the value-added chain.

MAP THE VALUE-ADDED CHAIN FOR THE MARKET AND YOUR CURRENT POSITION. Mapping the entire value-added chain is an opportunity to view your market from a high-altitude perspective and to see patterns and relationships that are not always evident when you concentrate on your own link in the chain. We described the value-added chain in Chapter 7 and illustrated how Tyson Foods developed a vertically integrated production capability that enables it to manage costs and quality effectively and consistently in its product manager role. UPS, which already covered the upstream portion of its value-added chain, looked downstream to performing logistics and materials-handling functions for its large customers, such as Curtis 1000 and Gateway 2000, by taking responsibility for customer functions and assuming a process manager role. Delta Dental focuses on the connections among providers, employers, and dental patients, and adds value to all three by operating an efficient network that reduces search, information, and transactions costs for all involved.

As you are looking at the value-added chain and its various links, here are some of the factors that you should consider:

- How long and complicated is the chain? How many handoffs are there that involve search, information, and transaction costs? Is there an opportunity (as in Delta's case) to establish a network that brings together customers and providers?

- Looking upstream at the supplier portion of your chain, are there opportunities to reconfigure, shorten, or consolidate upstream components?

- Looking downstream at your customers and, if appropriate, beyond to their customers, is there an opportunity to reconfigure, shorten, or consolidate links? Can you, like UPS, move downstream and operate in parallel with your customers' operations?

- Are there pressures from your customers to manage their supply chains and shift activities upstream? Can you anticipate your vulnerability or preempt it by assuming a different role?

IDENTIFY WHERE ADDED VALUE CURRENTLY IS CREATED. Once you've diagnosed the market value-added chain, look at the magnitude of added value within the specific links.

- Are there particular links that represent a very high proportion of the total added value?

- Are there players on particular links who are exceptionally profitable relative to others?

- What factors seem to account for the relative profitability of players at different points in the value-added chain?

- What types of knowledge and competencies are required to operate at different points?

EXAMINE THE POTENTIAL OF CONNECTING TECHNOLOGIES TO RECONFIGURE THE VALUE-ADDED CHAIN. Taking over another activity in the value-added chain, whether that activity will become embodied in a product (as in the case of Tyson controlling its supply chain) or will be performed in concert with a customer's operation (as was done by UPS), usually involves reconfiguring the flow of information. Just-in-time inventory management requires direct, real-time (or nearly so) communication between buyer and seller, for example. The techniques for reconfiguring value-added chains often depend on the application of information technology and, in many respects, are similar to those of process reengineering. The major techniques are parallel processing, one-time collection of data at the point where it originates, and management of variances at the source. In your evaluation of the potential of connecting technologies to reconfigure the value-added chain, consider the following questions:

- Could activities that are undertaken serially within the chain be performed in parallel? (UPS and Gateway 2000 took a serial process of component shipment and bundling and transformed it into a parallel process, with UPS moving the parts directly from vendor to final customer.)

- Is information that is needed at various links in the chain developed and processed at multiple points, or is it passed down through the chain? (Custom Foot develops extensive point-of-sale information, which is transmitted directly to its manufacturers and is used for follow-up sales efforts.)

Establishing the Reward- and Risk-Sharing Structure(s)

How effective are your current relationships at creating mutual value? Would alternative structures stimulate more mutual value creation? Can you move past knowing about your customers to working together and even learning together?

Some factors to consider when you are evaluating a change in the way that you and your customers create and share value are (1) the market structure and levels of bargaining power and appropriability; (2) the customer's total costs, supplier value, and incentives to collaborate (game structure); (3) the degree of customer complementarity and responsiveness to collaboration; and (4) the relative risk-bearing capability of customers.

UNDERSTAND MARKET STRUCTURE AND LEVELS OF BARGAINING POWER AND APPROPRIABILITY. As outlined in Chapter 8, the initial positions of buyer and seller are determined by the competitive structure of the market. To the extent that markets are very competitive and efficient, the room for special relationships or collaboration is reduced. At the other extreme, highly concentrated markets may provide so much advantage to one party as to diminish the motivation for greater collaboration or for changing the terms of interdependency. Gauging the potential for moving beyond neutral or market-based reward and risk sharing involves a number of issues.

- How concentrated is the buying power of your customer base?

- How is this power, if any, exploited (e.g., in low margins, demands for additional services, etc.)?

- How concentrated is production capability among your rivals?
  How is the seller's power, if any, exploited?

- Do your margins vary significantly across customers or groups (as
  was seen in the Delta Dental case)? To what extent does this
  reflect the customers' or groups' bargaining power?

**ESTIMATE TOTAL CUSTOMER COSTS, SUPPLIER VALUE, AND CURRENT INCENTIVES
TO COLLABORATE (GAME STRUCTURE).** In many cases, the costs of searching,
evaluating, using the product, and dealing with the supplier are as significant as the purchase price. Therefore, sellers often can increase their share
of the rewards in a relationship by reducing the buyer's cost of doing business with them.

- What are the major determinants of supplier value to your customers? Are they the same across all customers?

- What incentives do you have to collaborate with your customers
  and they with you? Do you approach the relationship as though
  it were a zero-sum game?

- Does the existing basis of interaction with your customers inhibit
  your incentive to collaborate? Which factors could be modified
  to promote mutually beneficial behaviors?

EVALUATE CUSTOMER COMPLEMENTARITY AND RESPONSIVENESS TO COLLABORATION.
Creating and capturing additional value in a relationship depends in part
on whether the buyer and seller each bring something that the other lacks
but that is essential to achieving some shared purpose. Hence, creating and
capturing additional value in a relationship might hinge on something as
simple as the buyer's ability to communicate her needs or as complex as
joint research and development on a new product. The UPS–Gateway 2000
collaboration on DockMerge is a case in point. In evaluating your customers' complementarity and responsiveness to collaboration, consider the
following questions:

- Are particular customers pushing the envelope of your product's capabilities, or are they especially demanding with respect
  to performance?

- Are there particular customers who, by their position in the market, tend to set performance standards?

- Which, if any, customers would you invite to participate actively in your product development efforts?

- Which points of connection between you and your customers would be more efficient if there were more open or timely sharing of information?

ASSESS THE RELATIVE RISK-BEARING CAPABILITY OF THE PARTIES. Many firms have created more valuable relationships by changing the share of total risk borne by each party. Delta Dental put real teeth (sorry) into its guarantees by coupling them with a schedule of payments for every service failure instead of a simple refund or promise to make it right. ScrubaDub promises its club members a minimum of three clean-car days, come rain or shine. Some of the questions that may stimulate thoughts about alternative positions include the following:

- To what extent does your customers' aversion to risk or uncertainty inhibit a more collaborative relationship? To what extent can you allay these concerns by changing the rules of the relationship?

- How committed are you to your customers' success? Are you prepared to make that commitment tangible in the terms of your transactions?

- What are the sources of risk faced jointly by you and your customer? Are each of you addressing those aspects over which you have the most control?

RECOGNIZING *the* CONNECTED BUSINESSES

As we've stressed throughout this book, there are no one-size-fits-all configurations across the value compass framework. Too many times, the characteristics of a leading firm have been extrapolated from anecdotal evidence to form a universal recipe—often with disastrous results. Each business must determine the combination of positions that makes the most sense for it.

Even within industries, a mix of successful models usually exists. In the financial services sector, for example, you have Olde, a broker that manages its relationships uniformly, provides a very basic core product (inexpensive security transactions), operates in a product manager role based on tight supply-chain management, and offers neutral, market-based prices. In contrast, Merrill Lynch manages relationships on an individualized basis, offers a near-total solution, operates a network of service and product providers (including the ability to underwrite issues), and prices at least some of its services on a performance basis. Pioneer Hi-Bred's strategy of managing individual relationships, offering an enhanced core product through a product manager role, and using neutral pricing is competitive with the genetic engineering subsidiaries of chemical companies that, while they manage their customer portfolios less intensively, provide extended offers of seed, crop protection, and fertilizer.

Hence, we cannot offer prescriptions, but we *can* share our observations about commonly observed characteristics or traits of companies that we believe are effectively pursuing customer-connected strategies. Such companies (1) have a clear idea of who their customers, especially their best customers, are and what the company is trying to do for them; (2) have moved beyond collecting and analyzing information toward seeking and using customer knowledge; (3) have sought to engage customers at many points and in many venues, not constrained by traditional channels or boundaries; and (4) are disciplined and focused in deploying resources both to create customer value and to capture a share of that value for shareholders.

Knowledge of Who the Firm's Customers Are

At their highest level, customer-connected strategies often are based on a close identification with and respect for customers. This goes beyond the usual platitudes about service levels or quality.

When you ask people at *Inc.* who their customers are, as we did, you do not hear a broad demographic description of readers (although the company has these data); rather, you hear an empathetic tale of an entrepreneur or small-business owner working hard to create value and jobs. An *Inc.* employee who recently left the company sent e-mail to all of his former coworkers explaining that his greatest regret was no longer being part of an enterprise that was helping in some small way to create new jobs and opportunities. The aspirations, in terms of lifestyle and excitement, of Harley-Davidson's customers are known exactly by the firm's managers. Pioneer Hi-Bred employees often think of themselves as "just farmers," although it's pretty clear that they don't think being just farmers is a bad thing.

Movement Beyond Information to Knowledge

Many companies study their customers; some of the best truly try to get to know them. This often involves moving beyond a quantitative to a qualitative perspective.

The American Skiing Company just kept digging until it discovered what people really meant by "good snow," and then the company set out to manufacture it. The firm enlisted its customers as quality-control experts by offering them a guaranteed skiing experience. Harley-Davidson went so far as to engage ethnographers to gain insight that couldn't be revealed by data alone. Wachovia Bank has studied carefully the pattern of financial needs over the life cycle of its customers, so that it can engage customers in a conversation about their needs rather than a description of the product line.

Engagement of Customers at Many Points and Venues

Customer-connected companies overflow their traditional channels. Many of our examples highlight companies that see the whole customer and appreciate the customer's total experience. UPS worked with Gateway 2000 to create the DockMerge solution and with Curtis 1000 to consolidate operations while maintaining local presence. In both instances, these solutions might never have arisen if UPS workers had talked only to the shipping manager, and UPS couldn't have delivered them without involving many parts of its organization.

Silicon Graphics sends teams of engineers to work with and learn from its lighthouse customers, in effect shifting its product development process downstream coincident with its customers' planning processes. Harley-Davidson sponsors and its managers attend more than 50 events annually. *Inc.* delivers its value through the mail, in person, on videotape, and over the Internet.

Disciplined and Focused Deployment of Resources

Customer-connected companies appreciate the linkage between the amount of value they create for customers and that available for shareholders. They understand the economics of their customer portfolios and direct investment in relationships accordingly.

Staples calibrates its business design and offers carefully among different groups of customers, providing exceptionally low prices to those customers to whom that is most important and higher service levels to those who need and can afford them. Delta Dental carefully tracks the relative contribution of employer accounts and, if warranted, does not renew uneconomical relationships.

ScrubaDub transformed its value proposition to attract and retain the most frequent car washers and carefully nurtures relationships with its club members. MCI focuses on the most profitable prospects and sets aggressive acquisition and development targets to support its investment in relationship management and expertise.

....

Escaping the grasp of the Red Queen involves a lot of hard work. Sometimes it's difficult not only to make progress but even to know in what direction to head. We have tried to provide you with a compass to guide you in your search for customer and shareholder value, but we recognize that all the answers cannot be found in this or any other book. In the end, you must set your own course, make difficult choices, and continue to learn. In closing, we remind you that Alice, finally exasperated with the Red Queen, whom she considered to be the cause of all the mischief she endured, reached over, shook the Queen violently, and awoke from her dream, ready to take on the challenges she faced.

Appendix

This appendix contains background and highlights of a research study jointly funded by Ernst & Young's Center for Business Innovation and Marketing and Planning Systems (MaPS), a marketing consulting and research firm. We participated in the survey design and analysis process. The study was designed to gather data about the application of customer knowledge management, customer economics, and connecting technologies at large firms.

In June 1996, MaPS conducted a telephone survey of 200 senior executives from Fortune 500 companies. The survey consisted of 56 questions and usually lasted 25 minutes. A series of follow-up, in-depth interviews was conducted to probe the basis of initial responses. Executives were drawn from general management, marketing, MIS/IT, and operations. We interviewed a mix of general managers, CEOs, directors, and senior vice presidents—each of whom had P&L responsibility.

The following sections describe in detail findings from the research organized around the following areas:

- *Customer knowledge management*: The sources and uses of customer information and applications of information technology to build more valuable relationships.

- *Customer economics*: Understanding the absolute and relative value of customer relationships and deploying resources accordingly.

- *High- vs. low-growth companies*: Differences between companies in terms of customer knowledge, technology, and economics.

- *Future needs*: The major barriers to increased performance identified by the executives.

CUSTOMER KNOWLEDGE MANAGEMENT

Nearly all Fortune 500 companies (90 percent) are, in one way or another, gathering and disseminating customer information collected through customer service interactions such as customer call centers, informal customer complaints, hot lines, and sales force contacts. Although a number of companies (67 percent) are using direct mail to capture customer information, only half of the companies are actively using techniques such as inbound and outbound telemarketing to collect customer information. (See Figure 2-2 in Chapter 2 for a complete tabulation.)

Although most companies rely on several methods for keeping in touch with customers (e.g., market research, sales force data bases, customer care centers), many companies have begun efforts to collect customer information at all points-of-contact. However, only one-third (31 percent) capture information at all of their points-of-contact with the customer. About one in six (16 percent) are using only three or fewer channels for collecting customer information.

Once they have collected the data, many companies struggle to synthesize, integrate, and build a complete view of their customers. Most companies report that their current customer information systems are inadequate for developing a comprehensive view of customers. To develop comprehensive customer profiles on wants, needs, values, and behaviors, most companies (85 percent) have to rely on multiple internal and external data bases. Only 19 percent have successfully built a single system that provides a complete view of the customer. The data in marketing data bases most often includes:

- Current customers (97 percent)

- Former customers (76 percent)

- Prospective customers (53 percent)—as high as 70 percent among companies that define "customers" as intermediaries or channel partners

- Links to external data sources such as census, subscription lists, proprietary data bases (67 percent)

We asked executives to describe how they used the customer information knowledge developed. Today, most Fortune 500 companies are using customer information technology to:

- Focus customer retention efforts (78 percent)

- Identify prospects for acquisition (76 percent)

- Identify customers for cross-selling efforts (66 percent)

- Test marketing and product launches (58 percent)

CUSTOMER ECONOMICS

Most companies we surveyed realize that not all customers are created equal and that understanding customer relationship value is a critical building block in developing customer-based growth strategies. We found that two-thirds (66 percent) of Fortune 500 companies have a financial measure of customer relationship value. However, it is most often based on revenue or usage, rather than profit. Four out of five (79 percent) of those with a financial measure of customer value calculate and track value at the individual customer level. We also found that fewer companies know their customer acquisition costs (43 percent) than know customer retention costs (68 percent).

A significant number of companies are aware of the concentration of relationship value in their customer portfolios. Forty percent of the companies know the amount of revenue or profit their top 10 percent of accounts or customers represent. On average, these customers represent 46 percent of total revenues and 44 percent of profits.

Companies recognize that the value of customer relationships can change significantly year-to-year and 72 percent track changes in customer relationship value over time. Eighty percent reported that they track customer retention rates at the individual customer level and, interestingly, few companies (8 percent) believe their retention rates are better than competitors in their industries.

High- *vs.* Low-Growth Companies

For this analysis, we defined high-growth companies as those with annual rates of revenue and profit growth of 10 percent or more from 1993 to 1995; moderate-growth as six to 10 percent; and low-growth as five percent or less. The sample population contained 32 percent high-growth, 47 percent moderate-growth, and 21 percent low-growth companies defined in this way. For convenience and clarity, we will illustrate the differences between high- and low-growth companies. The moderate-growth cases fell between these extremes. The major results are shown in Figure A-1.

A distinct pattern of differences among high- and low-growth companies emerged in terms of their levels of customer knowledge management (as measured by our proxies), successful use of customer-related technologies, and understanding of customer economics. The correlation between customer-related competencies does not, of course, prove causation. The results for high-growth companies may simply be one of many aspects of well-managed firms; the high-growth firms may be better able to afford the investment, for example. Nevertheless, the results highly suggest the pay-off in better customer connections.

Customer Knowledge

While more than two-thirds (71 percent) of companies have formal schemes for segmenting customers, many high-growth companies are pushing beyond segments to determine value at the individual customer relationship level. For many high-growth companies, knowing individual customer relationship value is the basis for targeting customers and matching offers to individual customer needs. However, some leading companies have realized that managing the customer at the individual level is cost prohibitive. An office supply company executive reported:

> As we grew, we realized that we wanted to keep assigning value to each customer, but we had to begin to manage customers at a higher level. We look to see who is most valuable, we group them together to develop products. We then develop segment level marketing programs, which we review and update as customer relationship values change.

High-growth companies report substantially higher customer satisfaction levels than do the low-growth companies, as shown in Figure A-2. The data suggest

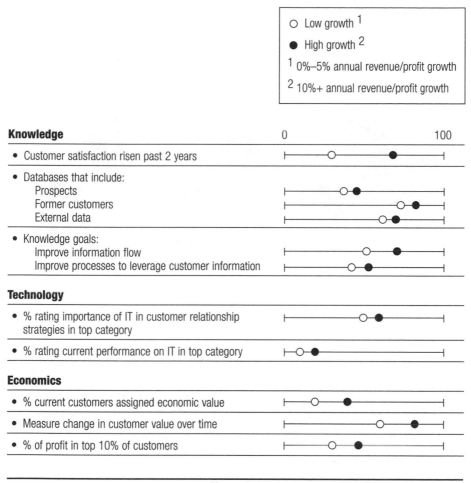

Figure A-1

that the superior level of customer knowledge developed by high-growth companies contributes to higher levels of customer satisfaction.

Information Technology

High-growth companies have also recognized that creating strong customer connections takes more than just lots of information about customers. Companies are increasingly concerned with closing the loop(s) of information flowing from

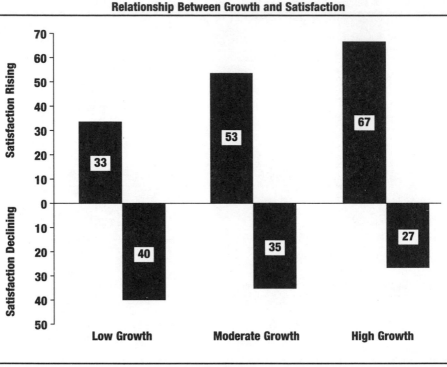

Figure A-2

customers to company points-of-contact and through to functions such as product development.

While nearly two-thirds (60 percent) of high-growth companies believe information systems are critical in customer relationship strategies, only 22 percent believe they are currently performing at a level that provides competitive advantage. High-growth companies believe they perform well on the "people" dimension but recognize that competitive advantage will come in better integrating customer processes and information technology. In contrast, only six percent of low-growth companies believe their customer information systems provide them with competitive advantages.

Customer Economics

The high-growth companies appear to have a much stronger grasp of the economics of their customer relationships. Twice as many high-growth companies calculate an economic value for their customer relationships as do low-growth companies. Furthermore, 84 percent of high-growth companies recognize the importance of measuring change in customer value over time compared to 62 percent of low-growth companies.

In addition, 30 percent of all Fortune 500 executives believe that they have an "extremely clear view" of their most valuable customers: They know that, on average, 44 percent of their profit comes from the top 10 percent of their customers; they have a financial measure of customer value; and they know and actively track the acquisition costs of new customers.

FUTURE NEEDS

In thinking about future customer information management priorities, companies view customer information technology and systems as increasingly important elements of customer relationship strategies. Executives see customer information systems contributing relatively uniformly across several activities:

- Drive customer acquisition strategies (68 percent)

- Identify ways to develop, test, and track new products and cross-sell to existing customers (61 percent)

- Identify vulnerable customers and configure customer retention strategies (66 percent)

The two customer relationship strategy issues Fortune 500 executives are most concerned about are:

- Where will the growth in customer value come from?

- How can we improve the flow of information across the organization?

Where will the growth in customer value come from? To address the first issue, we asked executives where they saw future growth coming from in terms of rating the relative importance of customer acquisition, development, and retention. Figure A-3 underscores the importance of customer acquisition and development efforts as sources of future growth. We asked companies to distribute the expected shares of future growth from customer acquisition, development, and retention with the results shown in Figure A-3. The major source of customer value will come from developing the profitability of existing customers (52 percent). Most companies report that future growth will more likely come from customer acquisition activities (35 percent) than initiatives aimed to reduce customer defection (13 percent). With the exception of the financial

Sources of Future Customer Value Growth (Greatest Contribution)

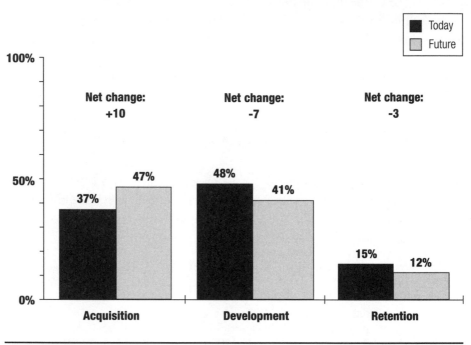

Figure A-3

services industry, most companies see a relatively small proportion of growth coming through customer retention efforts.

How can we improve the flow of information across the organization? We found that 62 percent of Fortune 500 executives think that "improving the flow of information across the organization" is nearly twice as important as "capturing more valuable customer feedback" in implementing a successful customer relationship strategy. The challenge executives face in integrating different types and sources of customer knowledge that already exist within organizations was expressed by a respondent:

> It's no longer adequate to survey customers periodically to determine their wants and needs. What's important in the future is integrating all of the information we have about a customer from all points-of-contact. For example, we can learn about a consumer's past and current spending, what they buy, and usage behavior from our credit data base and call center. We can combine this with predictive models of behavior developed from external research. Link this to census data

at the block level and we can develop very strong customer targeting efforts. However, while research data plays an important role, it is also key to think about unsolicited data from customers. This must be included in the total marketing equation.

A close second in importance was "ensuring there are processes in place to leverage customer information." What do executives mean by leveraging customer knowledge? Nearly one-fourth (23 percent) believe redesigning business processes around customers is the highest priority in achieving a successful customer relationship strategy. The priority customer process improvements are in the areas of:

- Integrating internal infrastructures (21 percent). A health care company executive observed, "Improving the flow of information between people is the biggest problem. We need to break down the barriers between internal groups and divisions."

- Integrating customer feedback into the product development process (19 percent). A defense manufacturer believes, "Improving our time-to-market with new products is essential. At the same time, we need to build the customer into the process. There is an enormous opportunity to improve in this area."

- Developing systems to collect and integrate all types of customer information (14 percent). A tool manufacturer stated, "We need a system which can collect information, all different types of information, about customers at each point of contact—integrating information into one system linking data bases."

Notes

....

INTRODUCTION

1. Frederick E. Webster, *Market-Driven Management* (New York: Wiley, 1994). The first chapter, "Putting the Customer First—Always!" contains an excellent survey of the development of marketing strategy. Chapter 6, "Strategic Alliances and Network Organizations," introduces the concept of partnering across the marketing value chain.
2. Theodore Levitt, *The Marketing Imagination* (New York: Free Press, 1983), 5–7.
3. Frederick F. Reichheld, *The Loyalty Effect* (Boston: Harvard Business School Press, 1996), 5.
4. Michael E. Porter, *Competitive Strategy* (New York: Free Press, 1988). The first chapter, "Competitive Strategy: The Core Concepts," recaps the five forces and generic strategies introduced in his earlier book, *Competitive Strategy: Techniques for Analyzing Industries and Competitors* (New York: Free Press, 1980). The second chapter, "The Value Chain and Competitive Advantage," introduces the value chain model, a greatly simplified version of which we use throughout this book. Our framework addresses what Porter called positioning (competitive posture within an industry) and scope (breadth of a firm's targets and activities).
5. See, for example, Gary Hamel and C.K. Prahalad, *Competing for the Future* (Boston: Harvard Business School Press, 1994), especially pp. 22–25; and George Stalk, Jr., and Thomas M. Hout, *Competing Against Time* (New York: The Free Press, 1990) for discussions of leveraging resources and competencies. See Robert G. Eccles and Nitin Nohria, *Beyond the Hype* (Boston: Harvard Business School Press, 1992), especially Chapter 5, for comparisons of strategic schools of thought.
6. John Kay, *Why Firms Succeed* (London: Oxford University Press, 1995), 25.
7. This view of strategic positioning is similar to the new concept of marketing expressed by Webster as managing strategic partnerships and positioning

the firm in relation to customers and vendors in the marketing value chain to provide superior value (Webster, *Market-Driven Management*). The notion that businesses are essentially a collection of relationships can be traced back to ideas advanced by Alchian and Demsetz that portrayed firms as collections of contracts with customers and suppliers (Armen Alchian and Harold Demsetz, "Production, Information Costs and Economic Organization," *American Economic Review,* December 1972, 777–795).

8. Although the notions of firm value and shareholder wealth have long been known to finance and economics, interest in shareholder value as a metric for business success was stimulated by the work of Alfred Rappaport in *Creating Shareholder Values: The New Standard for Corporate Performance* (New York: Free Press, 1986) and by Stewart's concepts of economic value added (EVA) and market value added (MVA), in G. Bennet Stewart III, *The Quest for Value* (New York: Harper Business, 1991).

9. Levitt, *The Marketing Imagination.* See especially Chapter 6, "Relationship Management" (pp. 111–126), which anticipates much of the current customer literature. Although Levitt felt that the economic theory of supply and demand cannot deal with time or exchanges that take place over time, we show that this theory can be useful in managing customer relationships.

10. Robert C. Blattberg and John Deighton, "Manage Marketing by the Customer Equity Test," *Harvard Business Review,* July–August 1996.

11. Richard P. Rumelt, "How Much Does Industry Matter?" *Strategic Management Journal* 12 (1991): 167–185.

12. Dwight L. Gertz and João P. A. Baptista, *Grow to Be Great* (New York: Free Press, 1995).

....

CHAPTER 1

1. Lewis Carroll, *Through the Looking Glass* (St. Martin's Press, 1977), 43.

2. Data on primary market research is from the 1995 Council of American Survey Research Organizations (CASRO) survey.

3. Dartnell's Sales Force Compensation Survey, 1995, Dartnell Corporation, Chicago, Illinois.

4. New product failure rate is from the Product Development and Management Association, PDMA Research on New Product Development

Practices: Updating Trends and Benchmarking Results, and discussions with Professor Abbie Griffin, University of Chicago.

5. Ted Williams, *The Science of Hitting* (New York: Simon and Schuster, 1970, 1971), 24.

6. Jeff Cole and Charles Goldsmith, "Rivalry Between Boeing, Airbus Takes New Direction," *Wall Street Journal*, 30 April 1997, B4.

7. Eric von Hippel, *The Sources of Innovation* (London: Oxford University Press, 1988), 5, 43–75.

8. See Karl Sabbagh, *Twenty-First Century Jet: The Making and Marketing of the Boeing 777* (New York: Scribners, 1996) for a fascinating discussion of the interactions among Boeing and its customers throughout the conceptualization to production process. Pages 53–54 and 191 outline the various contract provisions.

9. The MCI case is based in part on materials provided by the company and on discussions with Marc Schaub, vice president of business marketing; Brian Brewer, senior vice president of business marketing; Lon Cunninghis, executive director of midmarkets, channel marketing; and Matt Sines, executive manager of technical services.

10. Philip Cantelon, *The History of MCI: The Early Years* (Baltimore: Heritage Press, 1993).

11. MCI Corporate Business Analysis provided to authors.

....

CHAPTER 2

1. Ikujiro Nonaka and Hirotoka Takeuchi, *The Knowledge Creating Company* (London: Oxford University Press, 1995), 8, 58.

2. Henry Mintzberg, *The Rise and Fall of Strategic Planning* (New York: Free Press, 1994). Also, Henry Mintzberg, "The Fall and Rise of Strategic Planning," *Harvard Business Review*, January–February 1994.

3. The GE Answer Center case was based in part on materials provided by the company and on discussions with Merrill Grant, manager of the GE Answer Center; Jim Cabral, manager of market growth; and Mark Larson, manager of engineering support.

4. Sir Francis might be pleased to know that today his words can be verified (as we did) on the Internet at America Online's electronic *Bartlett's Quotations*.

5. The Pioneer Hi-Bred case is based in part on material provided by the company and on discussion with Dennis Gaukel, database marketing manager; Jerry Armstrong, director of North American sales operations; Will Raiser, sales communication manager; and John Ferin, director of customer relations information management.

6. The Staples case is based in part on materials provided by and on discussions with Jim Forbush, senior vice president of marketing; Donna Rosenberg, vice president of marketing strategy; and Barbara Socha, vice president of marketing strategy.

7. The Tyson Foods case is based in part on material provided by the company and on discussions with John Lea, vice president of retail sales and marketing, and Bob Howard, director of retail marketing.

8. Ronald B. Lieber, "Storytelling: A New Way to Get Close to Your Customer," *Fortune*, 3 February 1997, 102–108.

9. The Sunday River/American Skiing Company case is based in part on discussions with Jim Rundle, director of advertising and direct marketing, and Chris Brink, vice president of marketing.

10. Johny K. Johansson and Ikujiro Nonaka, "Market Research the Japanese Way," *Harvard Business Review*, May–June 1987, 16.

11. The Harley-Davidson case is based in part on material provided by and on discussions with Frank Cimermancic, director of business planning.

12. Eric Von Hipple, *The Sources of Innovation* (London: Oxford University Press, 1995).

13. See John W. Schouten and James H. McAlexander, "Subcultures of Consumption: An Ethnography of the New Bikers," *Journal of Consumer Research* 22 (June 1995): 43–61, for a detailed ethnographic analysis of Harley-Davidson customers.

14. The AT&T case is based on materials provided by the company and discussions with Virginia Smith, MSO Strategy and Planning.

15. James Heskett, "The Profitable Art of Service Recovery," *Harvard Business Review*, July–August 1990, 148.

16. Our results were similar to those reported in the 1996 American consumer satisfaction index, jointly compiled by the University of Michigan business school and the American Society for Quality Control, as reported in *Fortune*, 3 February 1997, 108–110. In their study, only 71 of 206 companies were judged by customers to have improved their service quality.

17. The Delta Dental Plan of Massachusetts case is based on material provided by the company and on discussions with Bob Hunter, president and CEO, and Scott O'Gorman, senior vice president.

CHAPTER 3

1. Ernst & Young, *1996 Technology in Banking Study*.
2. Jeffrey F. Rayport and John J. Sviokla, "Managing in the Marketspace," *Harvard Business Review*, November–December 1994, 141–150.
3. Regis McKenna, "Real-Time Marketing," *Harvard Business Review*, July–August 1995.
4. The Lexus case was developed using material provided by the company and obtained through conversations with Lisa White, customer satisfaction administrator.
5. The IBM case was developed using material provided by the company and obtained through conversations with Nancy Roath, director of client/server, and Ray Oram, marketing programs manager, network computing solutions.
6. The Pioneer Hi-Bred case is based in part on material provided by the company and on discussions with Dennis Gaukel, database marketing manager; Jerry Armstrong, director of North American sales operations; Will Raiser, sales communications manager; and John Ferin, director of customer relations information management.
7. The Custom Foot case was developed through conversations with Laureen Kirsch, director of marketing.
8. John Holusha, "Making the Shoe Fit, Perfectly," *New York Times*, 20 March 1996.
9. The Plymouth Place case is based on discussions with Steve Bruyn, national marketing plan manager, and Jim Holden, executive vice president of sales and marketing for Chrysler. Plymouth Place is a trademark of the Chrysler Corporation.
10. In addition to those of American Airlines, electronic travel initiatives in this increasingly crowded business include TravelWeb, Internet Travel Network, and Travelocity. Official Airline Guides, a division of Reed Travel Group, also has a new electronic edition for booking reservations.
11. The Virtual Vineyards case is based on discussions with Peter Granoff, vice president and general manager of Virtual Vineyards, Palo Alto, California, and Carl Petrich of the Ernst & Young Center for Business Innovation.
12. Jared Sandberg, "Entrepreneur Brings Auctions On-Line in New Bid at Success," *The Wall Street Journal*, 19 July 1996.

13. The Cisco case was developed in part with materials provided by and discussions with Helen Kampion, account representative; Chris Sinton, director of Cisco Connection; Peter Corless, content manager of Cisco Systems (Online); Andrew Kelly, systems engineer; and Hoover's Company Profiles.

CHAPTER 4

1. Willie Sutton, with Edward Linn, *Where the Money Was* (New York: Viking Press, 1976). See pages 119–121 for Sutton's attribution of the famous phrase to an enterprising reporter.

2. Garth Hallberg, *All Consumers Are Not Created Equal* (New York: Wiley, 1995). This book contains many fascinating facts about the fallacies of treating all customers the same. Folgers and Maxwell House data are on page 89.

3. The ScrubaDub case is based in part on material provided by and interviews with Marshall Paisner, Bob Paisner, and Dan Paisner.

4. Kevin J. Clancy and Robert S. Shulman, *Marketing Myths That Are Killing Business* (New York: McGraw-Hill, 1994), 106. Clancy and Shulman also discuss the reasons that profitability of relationships is often overlooked and the consequences on pages 116–118.

CHAPTER 5

1. The Harley-Davidson case is based in part on material provided by and on discussions with Frank Cimermancic, director of business planning.

2. "Ad Age 300 Special Report," *Advertising Age*, 20 June 1994, 24

3. An overview of Capitol One's information-based strategy and its consideration of risk and profitability is in Gary H. Anthes, "Customer 'Data Mining' Pays Off," *Computerworld*, 15 May 1995.

4. The Staples case is based on discussions with Jim Forbush, senior vice president of marketing; Donna Rosenberg, vice president of marketing strategy; and Barbara Socha, vice president of marketing strategy.

5. The Wachovia case is based on materials provided by the bank and on discussions with David Pope, senior vice president of consumer strategy development, and Lawrence Baxter, senior vice president of insurance services and emerging businesses.

CHAPTER 6

1. See Stanley M. Davis, and Bill Davidson, *2020 Vision* (New York: Simon and Schuster, 1991) for instances of incorporating information into value propositions.
2. David H. Freeman, "Top Seed," *Forbes ASAP,* 29 March 1993, 43–46.
3. The Pioneer Hi-Bred International case is based in part on material provided by the company and on discussions with Dennis Gaukel, database marketing manager; Jerry Armstrong, director of North American sales operations; Will Raiser, sales communication manager; and John Ferin, director of customer information management.
4. The Sunday River/American Skiing Company case study contains information provided by Jim Rundle, director of advertising and direct marketing, and Chris Brink, vice president of marketing.
5. The *Inc.* magazine case is based in part on material provided by and conversations with Bernard Goldhirsh, chairman and CEO, Robert LaPointe, president of *Inc.* Business Resources; Deborah Gallagher, director of circulation and database development; Linda Gitlin, director of conferences and seminars; and Erica Caplan, director of operations for *Inc.* Online.

CHAPTER 7

1. The Tyson Foods case is based in part on materials supplied by the company and in part on conversations with John Lea, vice president of retail sales and marketing, and Bob Howard, director of retail marketing.
2. The United Parcel Service case is based in part on materials supplied by the company and in part on interviews with Ed Brockwell, vice president of strategic accounts; Dale Greene of strategic accounts; Jim McKinley, national account manager; Jennifer Jiles, corporate public relations; and Gregg Mau, global account manager.
3. Mark Dickens, "UPS, Past and Future," *GSE Today*, 8 August 1995, 26–30.
4. Charles R. Day, Jr., "Shape Up and Ship Out," *Industry Week*, 6 February 1995, 14–20.
5. The Delta Dental Plan of Massachusetts case is based in part on materials supplied by the company and in part on interviews with Bob Hunter, CEO, and Scott O'Gorman, senior vice president.
6. Carolyn Stevenson, "Dental Vendors Develop Programs Focusing on Cost and Quality," *Employee Benefit Plan Review*, January 1996.

7. Thomas Raffio, "Quality Award Winner: Quality and Delta Dental Plan of Massachusetts," *Sloan Management Review*, Fall 1992, provides an excellent overview of Delta's early history and strategy.

....

CHAPTER 8

1. Game theory increasingly is prominent in business analysis. A number of books go far beyond our limited purpose of introducing game theory as a way to assess relationship structures. See John McMillan, *Games, Strategies and Managers* (London: Oxford University Press, 1992), for an exceptional overview of business-related applications. J.D. Williams, *The Compleat Strategyst* (New York: Dover, 1986) provides an accessible introduction to computational methods. John Kay, *Why Firms Succeed* (London: Oxford University Press, 1995) applies game theory to a number of business issues including relationships, reputation, and innovation.
2. For a thorough treatment of pricing, see Thomas T. Nagel, *The Strategy and Tactics of Pricing* (Englewood Cliffs, NJ: Prentice-Hall, 1987).
3. See John Kay, "Appropriability," in *Why Firms Succeed* (London: Oxford University Press, 1995), 174–189, for a thorough discussion of appropriability and the distribution of added value to other stakeholders.
4. Even monopoly sellers will, on occasion, share with buyers a portion of their added value, albeit indirectly, by licensing other sellers. This procedure assures buyers of alternative sources, usually under contracts that strictly limit the licensee's output and pricing discretion.
5. Fred R. Bleakley, "Going for Growth," *The Wall Street Journal*, 7 May 1996, p 1.
6. George J. Stigler, "The Economics of Information," *Journal of Political Economy*, June 1961. Reprinted in George J. Stigler, *The Organization of Industry* (Homewood, IL: Richard D. Irwin, Inc., 1968), 171–190.
7. Christopher Hart, "The Power of Unconditional Service Guarantees," *Harvard Business Review*, July–August 1988.
8. Bart Ziegler, "The Brash, Young Headhunter Who Lured Mandl from AT&T," *The Wall Street Journal*, 20 August 1996.
9. Robert Lacy, *Ford: The Man and the Machine* (New York: Ballantine, 1987), 75.
10. See Steven E. Prokesch, "Mastering Chaos at the High-Tech Frontier: An Interview with Silicon Graphics' Ed McCracken," *Harvard Business Review*, November–December 1993.
11. Chuck Ross, "Nabisco Linking Web Ad Rates to Sales Results," *Advertising Age* 67 (1996): 48.

Index

About the Authors

Robert E. Wayland is president of Robert E. Wayland & Associates, a firm specializing in corporate and marketing strategy. Previously, he was a vice president of Mercer Management Consulting and of its predecessor firm, Temple, Barker & Sloane, and chief economist of the Public Utilities Commission of Ohio. He is a frequent speaker to major business groups and senior executive forums.

He welcomes your examples of customer-connected strategies or comments on the book and can be reached at rew@rewayland.com

Paul M. Cole is the national director of Ernst & Young's Customer Connections Solutions practice within the firm's management consulting organization. He is also a trustee of the Marketing Science Institute. Before joining Ernst & Young, he was a vice president of Mercer Management Consulting.

He invites you to share your ideas or thoughts on customer-based strategy. His e-mail address is paul.cole@ey.com